WHERE FILM MEETS PHILOSOPHY

FILM AND CULTURE

JOHN BELTON, EDITOR

FILM AND CULTURE

A series of Columbia University Press

EDITED BY JOHN BELTON

For the list of titles in this series, see page 245.

HUNTER VAUGHAN

WHERE FILM MEETS PHILOSOPHY
GODARD, RESNAIS, AND EXPERIMENTS
IN CINEMATIC THINKING

COLUMBIA UNIVERSITY PRESS   NEW YORK

COLUMBIA UNIVERSITY PRESS

Publishers Since 1893

NEW YORK   CHICHESTER, WEST SUSSEX

cup.columbia.edu

Library of Congress Cataloging-in-Publication Data

Vaughan, Hunter.

  Where film meets philosophy : Godard, Resnais, and experiments in cinematic thinking / Hunter Vaughan.

      pages cm. — (Film and culture)

  Includes bibliographical references and index.

  ISBN 978-0-231-16132-9 (cloth : alk. paper) — ISBN 978-0-231-16133-6 (pbk. : alk. paper) — ISBN 978-0-231-53082-8 (ebook)

  1. Motion pictures—Philosophy.   2. Godard, Jean-Luc, 1930—Criticism and interpretation.   3. Resnais, Alain, 1922—Criticism and interpretation.   I. Title.

  PN1995.V375 2013

  791.4301—dc23

2012039151

The world of French cinema and philosophy is a magnificent one; this book is dedicated to the memory of Jean-Louis Leutrat, who so passionately brought that world to life for me and so many others.

CONTENTS

LIST OF ILLUSTRATIONS

ACKNOWLEDGMENTS

I WOULD LIKE TO THANK THE FOLLOWING FOR THEIR SUPPORT and help with this project since its beginnings at Christ Church, University of Oxford: Reidar Due, Jean-Louis Leutrat and Suzanne Liandrat-Guigues, Adam Marlowe, Michael Sheringham, Will Brown, and David Martin-Jones; the people of Christ Church College, the Maison Française d'Oxford, and the Cinémathèque française. In turning it into the book as it appears today, I acknowledge the important support from Columbia University Press and the invaluable input from its reviewers, and in particular thank Jennifer Crewe and John Belton, along with the continued efforts of Asya Graf, Kathryn Schell, and Joe Abbott. I would like to express special thanks to Dustin Iler, whose diligent reading of the book helped it into its final form. I would also like to thank the lovely and loving Michal McConville and her family for their continued support and encouragement, and my wonderful parents for raising me to pursue a balance between the life of the mind and the world at large.

WHERE FILM MEETS PHILOSOPHY

Where Film Meets Philosophy

Creating new circuits in art means creating them in the brain too.
—Gilles Deleuze, *Negotiations*

Contemporary philosophy consists not of linking concepts,
but of describing the mixing of consciousness and the world, its
involvement in a body, its coexistence with others, and . . . this is
a cinematic subject *par excellence.*
—Maurice Merleau-Ponty, "Cinema and the New Psychology"

THE PAST THREE DECADES HAVE WITNESSED A BURGEONING
interest in the intersection between philosophy and cinema studies. From
Stanley Cavell's Wittgensteinian forays into American cultural morality to
Fredric Jameson's explorations of the filmic postmodern, to the Deleuzean movement toward cinema as a medium of particular philosophical
interest, this interdisciplinary intersection continues to foster debate and
new theoretical developments, generating self-applied methodological
terms that range from the positivist ("cognitive") to the methodologically
experimental ("filmosophy").[1] Despite its often rigorous juggling act that
keeps afloat so many concepts, texts, and intellectual histories, however,
the field that has popularly come to be called "film-philosophy" seems to
have moved past—without ever clearly addressing—fundamental questions concerning what film and philosophy share. That is to say, is—and, if
so, *how* is—the medium of film philosophical? How might the moving
image help us to understand our mental and perceptual processes, our internal structures and our interaction with the world external to our bodies,
and even offer us new organizations of these relationships?

Mine is certainly not the first attempt to engage this disciplinary intersection, but I hope it will serve a useful role in the skeletal basis for

what has proven and promises further to be a realm of productive and progressive scholarly work. Gilles Deleuze's *Cinema* project provoked an entire genre of metaphysical approaches to cinema;[2] more recently, Nöel Carroll and Berys Gaut have surveyed different vistas for the terrain of film-philosophy in, respectively, cognitive and more generalist fashions;[3] and John Mullarkey has greatly cultivated our knowledge of how philosophers have approached or been applied to cinema and media studies.[4] Engaging with these and other theorists, and placing the field of film-philosophy within the wider history of film theory and criticism, I aim in this book to ground film-philosophy in a central foundation: what about film form aligns it with philosophical thinking, especially the modern philosophy of the twentieth—or "cinematic"—century? And, how can cinema help us to challenge, transform, or expand our way of perceiving, understanding, and engaging with the world?

I argue that the experimental cinematic practices of Jean-Luc Godard and Alain Resnais, taken together, offer unique insight into these questions, and this study will provide referential consistency and clarity to the foundation of film-philosophy by systematizing its theoretical content within a comparative and close reading of a handful of texts by these two directors. While Resnais and Godard are often considered philosophical directors who explore issues of great historical and existential depth, the actual connection between their work and philosophy has not been thoroughly explored; *Where Film Meets Philosophy* conceptualizes their philosophical importance according to how the audiovisual construction and deconstructions of subjectivity (Resnais) and objectivity (Godard), thematic across their respective work, provide experiments in understanding memory, reflection, and expectation—in short, experiments in cinematic thinking. It is important to clarify here what this phrase from my title means, given that much of this book struggles against what I view as oft-cited facile claims to cinema as thinking or perceiving: the cinema does neither of these, of course, as it is a formal medium. However, there are ways through which cinema's configurations can offer us new ways to think—not because film itself thinks but because it offers us alternative relational organizations or distributions that might, in fact, challenge the way that *we* think. As such, "experiments in cinematic thinking" refers not to cinema in the process of thinking but to how the use of cinematic form—as Deleuze might put it—carves new paths for our own modes of thought. The questions posed above must be asked in order for us to understand the relevance of moving-image analysis to the evolution of human self-understanding and our relation to the world around us, which should always remain an important goal of academic inquiry. I will illustrate that this topic can be distilled to the fundamental question of what I call *subject-object relations*, a conceptual focus central to philosophy from Descartes to Hegel to Deleuze, and of special interest to much film theory from the formalism of Hugo Münsterberg to the semiotics of Kaja Silverman.

Film has a unique ability to transform and shift its sensory focus between the auditory and visual, a flexible malleability that can be reduced to shifting dynamics in subject-object relations. Where is the origin of meaning? How are we positioned in relation to this meaning? How fixed is this meaning? *Where Film Meets Philosophy* situates film form's ability to challenge traditional subject-object hierarchies and configurations within a larger conceptual philosophical framework, one that reconciles the two seemingly unbridgeable methodologies that have been most influential to the field of film-philosophy: Maurice Merleau-Ponty's phenomenology of perception and Deleuze's image-philosophy—two philosophies that have been so fruitful for moving-image studies precisely because of their shared central goal of challenging conventional theories of the relationship between subject and object, interior and exterior, real and imaginary. While most studies of postwar philosophy and twentieth-century French intellectual history convey the importance of these two thinkers, they are rarely attributed common ground. Yet Merleau-Ponty and Deleuze often inform works on film-philosophy for the very same reason they meet in this book; as Elena del Rio has written, in a rare consideration of the pair: "The drive to determine a clear dividing line between subject and world, perceiver and perceived, objective reality and subjective experiences, is equally suspected and accordingly undermined by both thinkers."[5] That Del Rio incites these authors in a study of Godard's later films is not anomalous to the frequent use of philosophy in studies of art cinema; however, like many similar works, hers goes both beyond the image (including Godard's extrafilmic presence, as is inevitable in his work from the 1980s) and also not far enough, as it does not ground the two philosophical influences in respective methodologies, nor does it acknowledge that these philosophers themselves have historical ties to writing about cinema.

My task is to systematize the relationship between film and philosophy through a framework that renders it possible to situate such opposing poles as phenomenology and semiotics within an overarching set of terms. This book is, in other words, metatheoretical, reformulating previous arguments in film theory according to the problem of subject-object relations, with hopes that this systematic mode of analysis may serve as a useful point of departure for future theorists with a wide range of approaches and applications. Film can be seen as the site of intersection for many voices and gazes, both diegetic and extradiegetic, and I will look at how such voices and gazes are distributed and organized according to sets of formal relations. I call the site of this intersection the *immanent field* of the film image, defining it first and foremost as an arena of possibility through which meaning can emanate, and I will focus this study on the structuring of film meaning according to relations of subject and object within this immanent field.

The immanent field ought not to be confused with the "plane of immanence" as developed by Deleuze, though like so much of this book my notion of the immanent field is indebted to his thinking and ought to be sketched out accordingly. D. N. Rodowick is apt to note: "Like many of his philosophical ideas, Deleuze's definition of the 'plane of immanence' shifts in subtle and interesting ways in different books."[6] To isolate a useful point of comparison between my immanent field and Deleuze's plane of immanence, one should turn to a Bergsonian citation from Deleuze's *Cinema 1: The Movement-Image*: "The infinite set of all images constitutes a sort of plane of immanence. The image exists in itself, on this plane. This in-itself of the image is matter: not something hidden behind the image, but on the contrary the absolute identity of the image and movement."[7] Ron Bogue astutely observes that Deleuze diverges from Bergson in his conceptualization of the plane of immanence, using it as a conflation between matter and light: "By equating matter and light . . . Deleuze brings to the fore the implications of Bergson's theory of perception for an analysis of visual images and reveals the potential of that theory for a conceptualization of the relationship between the cinematic visual image and the material world. If things are light, then what we commonly call visual images, whether directly perceptual or cinematic, are made of the same matter."[8] While I certainly consider the image as existing independently, my immanent field—unlike Deleuze's plane of immanence—does not take the film image concretely as matter but as a dynamic of relationality that produces connotative meaning through this very relationality. Complementing Bergson's theory of perception, which tends to conflate object and image, with a phenomenological model, I aim to view the moving image both *as something* and also as an image *of something*, and the relationship between these two is the centerpiece of my study. The immanent field refers to this "between," a site of potentiality and becoming, a malleable structuring of subject-object relations that makes possible an infinite variety of relationships between spectator, diegetic world, and the real, constructed according to the configurations of its formal elements. This process of configuration is what I hold to be the film image's capacity to experiment with "thinking," as I will argue through a phenomenological and then semiotic framework, and therefore provides the object of primary inquiry in terms of understanding where film and philosophy meet.

As can be concluded above, I use the immanent field to bracket off the film image as a transformative process that exists between the world of filmic meaning and the material reality of both the image's referent and the viewer. This act of bracketing has traditionally elicited skepticism in cultural studies because of its minimization of the importance of praxis so central to Marxist discourse, but hopefully we will find that my project acts instead to bolster and to add a new facet to the consideration of praxis. Moreover, I am steeled in the usefulness of this simplified methodology by the recent work of scholars such as W. J. T. Mitchell, who provides the same act of isolation in order "to shift the location of desire to images themselves, and ask what pictures want."[9] Through this concept of subject-object relations I will build a theory of the immanent field as being structured by a dynamic interdependence between the immediate intentionality of the image (the objective pole) and the point of reference or perspective relative to which this intentionality is signified (the subjective pole), a push and pull that can be boiled down to how the sound-image arranges our relation to meaning—not necessarily what the image wants, as Mitchell puts it, but how it organizes, and how it offers us ways of thinking.

This point of reference is a position that is signified as the origin of the image in order to connote a certain status of the image. It can be a diegetic subject-function (the character) or the external or absent subject-function (the apparatus) and is often a blend of the two or a permutation of their components; the structure of the image relative to these points of reference produces what I call, respectively, *subjective* and *objective* images, and films consist of a constant fluctuation between gradations of this polarity. I will hereby conflate intentionality and enunciation into an interdependent dynamic that I call a *system of reference*, which is not a concept concerning the semiotic notion of "reference" but is more akin to Deleuze's epistemological *"systèmes de référence"* (systems of reference). Deleuze equates the subjective and objective poles of representation, only "according to one or the other of two systems of reference."[10] In other words film signification can—and must, I will argue—be analyzed as a function of *how its system of reference is framed.* The immanent field is organized in a particular way to construct a system of reference, and it is through the stabilization of this sign (immanent field / system of reference) that an order of meaning, or system of logic and values, can be guaranteed, affirmed, reified. Since the actual ideological roots of cultural representation are an abstract given, postulated many times over yet difficult to analyze, I will look instead at the form of the image and how this form's internal organization of subject-object relations engenders the systems of reference that are the condition for conveying this ideology. I hope to reveal that this concept of subject-object relations is as central to the problems of Merleau-Ponty's phenomenology at the heart of cinematic realism as it is to the Bergsonian temporal philosophy in Deleuze's film semiotics. That is, I posit this book on the common ground between two disparate models of thought whose diverse methods are geared toward a similar goal: the destruction of classical divisions between subject and object, and the revelation of the relationship between the system of reference and the status of the image.

My reconceptualization of cinematic thinking has a strong affinity for the theory of human experience described in phenomenology and owes much to the long history of kindred harmony between phenomenology and cinema. In his 1945 presentation to help christen *l'Institut des hautes études cinématographiques* (The Institute for Advanced Cinematic Studies, or IDHEC, France's national film school from 1944 to 1985), Merleau-Ponty claimed that cinema shows how things signify, that it reveals to us how structures of representation produce meaning through the spatiotemporal arrangement of elements.[11] I reframe this proposition in the following way: through its organization of subject-object relations, the film image refers to itself *as a particular type of image,* implying a certain order of meaning that relates to the text's explicit meanings but also to the philosophical method of its connotative form. This book is not in itself phenomenological, but it applies a structure of phenomenological notions to a study of film signification and ultimately holds a goal not entirely unlike American film rhetoric, which considers the conventions of organization provided in film narration.[12] Yet, while questions of narration—including narrative content (the "story" of a film) and narrative structure (the ordering of narrative information)—are relevant to any film's overall meaning and specific significations, I will argue that narration is a product of the film's form and not its origin, thus associating my work more with the theories of Deleuze than with the tradition of Christian Metz and David Bordwell. It is with this assumption about the formal essence of film that I hope to provide a model that can then be applied to more narrative approaches to film analysis such as genre analysis or national cinema. After all, different film movements, world cinemas, and genres may provide us with very different manifestations of the subjective and objective poles of expression: however, each must *distribute the sensible* (as Jacques Rancière would put it); that is, each must "distribute spaces and times, subjects and objects, the common and the singular."[13] In order to do so, I believe it would benefit each to build a basic theory of this process of distribution.

Inspired by the forefathers of twentieth-century aesthetics such as Erwin Panofsky and Rudolf Arnheim, who attempt to see artistic products first and foremost as "formulations of material,"[14] I will show how these "formulations" structure the differentiation between subject and object. As such, I hope here to return the problem of film subjectivity to Noël Burch's seemingly obvious but often neglected dictum: "Film is made first of all out of images and sounds."[15] This book's conceptualization of film meaning will come to involve various individual elements and combinations of these images and sounds, including the following (in the order in which they will appear):

(1) visual composition (and, in particular, the frame), which spatially organizes the diegetic world, using the characteristics of vision to signify a source of perception, as well as to situate diegetic subjects and objects relative to the camera's operations;

(2) montage, or the conjunction between shots and image-types, which uses combinations of images to order the flow of content in a way that makes this flow attributable to a certain system of reference;

(3) the conjunction between sound (especially speech) and image, which organizes the harmony of sensory elements to provide for a totality of subjectivity; and

(4) codifications of these elements (speech/image, shot/sequence) such as the flashback (a codification of sound and image, producing meaning in a particular sequential order, to organize the image according to a particular speaking subject or point of view), which are used in order to present the film, as a whole, as predominantly objective or subjective.

I will complement this theoretical framework with the close reading of film texts, for which I have chosen as a comparative body of texts the early works of Alain Resnais and Jean-Luc Godard. Although much critical writing has been generated concerning their respective oeuvres, and although numerous theorists have acknowledged their relationship as "the two great poles of cinematic modernity,"[16] Resnais and Godard have never been placed alongside one another in an extended comparative analysis. I hope, therefore, that this dual study might also contribute an original framework for understanding the work of these two directors and an innovative approach to comparative film studies, while also providing new directions for national cinema studies and auteur theory.

GODARD, RESNAIS, AND THE POLITICS OF 1960S FRENCH FILM CULTURE

Having had their feature-length fiction film debuts within a year of each other (1959 and 1960), Resnais and Godard were both engaged in the artistic and intellectual movements of the 1960s. Moreover, each departed from the commercial scene for an extended period in 1968.[17] This justifies, despite the prolific nature of their careers (both of which are still active at the time of writing this in 2012), my isolation of the period between 1959 and 1968 for this study. Moreover, I have selected these two filmmakers for particular reasons, including the placement of their early periods at a critical breaking point in the modern evolution of both French cinema and French philosophy, as the 1960s saw a dramatic reconfiguration of French intellectualism, as well as a larger politicization that unified arenas of art and thought. The academic climate in France shifted with the proliferation of mass-market journalism as part of what Richard Neupert has termed "the new 'culture industry,'" and in the 1950s the Parisian ivory tower descended to the streets; just as Jean-Paul

Sartre, Merleau-Ponty, and others had been instrumental in wartime and postwar grassroots activism, precursors of structuralism such as Claude Lévi-Strauss and Roland Barthes found a highly receptive audience among France's urban weekly readers.[18]

Moreover, the philosophy of the 1960s gravitated toward the increasing social and political unrest of the decade. Greatly affected by Nietzschean concepts of power and history, French philosophers of the 1960s—Deleuze and Michel Foucault being the most influential—had a particularly strong faith in the present as an opening for change, as well as an unfailing belief in the interconnectedness of philosophy, social behavior, and cultural practice. In *Reading the Figural* Rodowick prefaces his chapter on May '68 by making a connection between the moment's philosophical rupture and the radical temporal disjuncture provided in Alain Resnais's *I Love You, I Love You* (1968), noting French cinema and philosophy of this period as connected within "this apocalyptic present marked by the collective belief that the passing of time is a carnivalesque Event . . . where the future is open to an infinite set of possibilities." Rodowick takes the link between philosophy and culture during this period so far as to suggest, based on Maurice Clavel's report, that French poststructuralism was "one of the primary causes of the student and worker protests" that defined the paroxysm of May '68. Nietzsche's presence in this decade's philosophy, Rodowick claims, led to the emergence in French audiovisual culture of "a new philosophy of history in images" in which "space becomes an Event defined by the force of time as becoming and virtuality."[19]

Although I will move away from the role of Nietzsche as conceptual predecessor and the Lyotardian terminology of the Event, Rodowick makes a crucial connection between the rupture occurring in French philosophy at this time and that occurring in French film culture. The changes that took place in France's film industry during this time have been well documented in a number of New Wave histories, changes that occurred as much on the textual level as on that of production.[20] While mine is not an industry study, it is worth emphasizing the important role that these directors played in bringing avant-garde practices to mainstream cinema, as the critical and commercial success of Resnais's and Godard's earliest feature films indicates an important social openness to philosophically challenging texts—they only needed a window of desperation in the old guard of finance and production to foster such an experiment.

As the eminent French scholar Geneviève Sellier notes with regard to Resnais's feature debut: "*Hiroshima, mon amour* is the first full-length fictional feature film made for commercial release that critics perceived, whether approvingly or disapprovingly, as belonging to the avant-garde."[21] Reflecting philosophy's deepening impact on the arts and the crossover appeal between intellectualism and mass-market media, these filmmakers provided systematic attempts to deconstruct classical conventions and to offer cinema as an important intersection of the arts and humanities.

Also, helping to structure this study according to a dialectical progression, these two filmmakers provide an invaluable polarity of film expression. Godard once remarked that he and Resnais were comparable to a journalist and a novelist,[22] a telling couplet of metaphors considering that I will argue that their oeuvres are concerned with challenging cinematic codes, respectively, of objectivity and subjectivity. I hope here to cultivate an understanding of their work as deconstructing conventional divisions between subject and object in order to open the immanent field as the site of dialogic interaction between discourses and agencies.[23] Representatives of a shift in European cinema toward self-reflexivity and metatextuality, Godard and Resnais reveal conventions of classical film language by reorganizing the formal basis for these conventions. Their works embody an "alternative" trend in cinema history, alternative "in so far as they transform the relations of representation and representing,"[24] relations that I will explore according to my fundamental framework of subject and object. For this their texts provided a glimmer of hope for a generation of theorists: their films both articulated and served as inspiration for theories of phenomenology, semiotics, and poststructuralism, and I hope to use their films to forge a common ground between such diverse theories. As such, their presence here serves to illustrate the problems being systematized in this study and not to *prove* any particular claim about cinema per se.

Like many such studies inspired by the experimental, I run the risk here of limiting my scope to a particular strain of European art cinema; however, Godard and Resnais provide us with the *sick* cases through which we might elucidate certain conditions and symptoms of the *healthy* cinema as it has been naturalized over time and through industrial practices, and in doing so perhaps throw into question this very distinction. The vocabulary of the "sick" and "healthy" used here is, of course, metaphorical, extrapolated from that used in Merleau-Ponty's phenomenology of perception, which often focuses on oddities or aberrations of human perception in order to explore the standards of normalcy that are implied as points of reference and to determine contradictions to them. Merleau-Ponty's exploration of the human experience is grounded in the belief that the "normal" is not necessarily the "better" but is, instead, that which has adapted to a conventional ability to differentiate between self and world, sound and image. This framework for understanding "normal" acts of perception derives great complementary strength from the example of alternatives to the norm, including clinical medical conditions but also subjective states altered, for example, by hallucinogenic drugs.[25]

In addition to Merleau-Ponty's scientific discourse, the paradigm of "sick" and "healthy" is also meant here to evoke the discursive practices of Western institutional processes of inclusion and exclusion as theorized in Foucault's work, especially *Madness and Civilization* and *The Birth of the Clinic*, both of which were, not coincidentally, published in the early 1960s and led the structuralist movement toward a widespread critique of modes of social organization, especially in terms of the dissemination of subjectivity and agency.[26] While I certainly do not want to encourage the ghettoization of any set of film aesthetics, certain norms have been historically secreted within the canon of Western cinema at the exclusion of others. The "healthy" in this book will refer to the classical norms originating primarily in the Hollywood cinema of the late 1910s and 1920s, and achieving a widespread monopoly on Western commercial practices with the ubiquitous distribution of Hollywood to Europe during the late silent period and the rigorous regulations imposed by the technical limitations of the early sound era.[27]

Though these pages aim to exonerate the virtues of the "sick," I have chosen not to address the circulation of aesthetic practices simply because the theoretical distance between Resnais's collaborative production process and Godard's origins as a critic for *Cahiers du cinéma* would greatly complicate any attempt to analyze the similarities of their influences or intentions. However, by isolating the image practices from their creative origin, I can analyze how these filmmakers provide mutations on the principles of conventional cinema as developed by Griffith and others and as outlined in the commonly used textbooks of scholars such as John Belton and Bordwell and Thompson: clarity, continuity, and logic.[28] The narrative norms (three-act structure, causality, closure), aesthetic and especially editing codes (shot/reverse shot, eye-line match, voice-over flashback), and guiding ideological principles (clear division between good and evil, male heroism) of what is referred to here as "healthy" cinema are so deeply entwined with the conventions of social structures and other art forms, and so dependent on the arbitrary historical triumph of a certain type of cinema as the mainstream norm, that it is admittedly problematic to remove this study completely from the dynamics of production, distribution, and exhibition that established and perpetuated them as norms. Such normative practices, however—which are not the same as those considered normative or conventional in non-Western cinemas, such as popular Indian (or Bollywood) or Japanese cinema—correspond not only to such material factors but also to a deep philosophical tradition that is the focal point of criticism in the works of Merleau-Ponty and Deleuze.

I acknowledge the limitations of maintaining a Western-centric corpus and can only call on experts in other cinemas and intellectual histories to take the encouragement provided here to explore similar intersections between cinema and philosophy. As I have already noted, this study focuses on a momentous period that witnessed a concurrent shift in both the praxis of intellectual culture and the cinematic division between commercial and experimental textual practices. Keeping in mind the lessons of Ella Shohat and Robert Stam's *Unthinking Eurocentrism*, I do not hope here to conflate Western cinema as all "cinema" nor merely to consider two French philosophers as speaking for all of philosophy. Instead, I hope that this study, while cordoning off a certain part of the world's philosophical and cinematic practices, will suggest that the moving sound-image provides unique formal parameters for challenging the link between traditional modes of thinking and normative artistic practices. These filmmakers used film form, and the decodification of conventional uses of film form, to challenge the ways in which normative film practices reify and perpetuate classical philosophy. This may well be what makes them so provocative to spectators, so influential to filmmakers across the world even fifty years later, and so invaluable to this book. Before launching into this study, however, let me begin by introducing the theoretical background on which this book is based, define some key terminology I will be using, clarify what I hope this book will contribute, and confront some criticisms that may be leveled against it.

Theoretical Foundation and
Central Terminology

In this book I will offer a new framework for understanding the sound-image as an immanent field of organizations between subjective and objective positions, a dualism relevant to all acts of film signification. Since this is in many ways an attempt to reconcile phenomenology with semiotics, it is necessary to consider the relationship between denotation and connotation in cinema, a relationship that will remain central to this study, because how these two are organized determines the philosophical status of the image. We can understand denotation in basic semiotic terms as the concrete meanings produced through representation: who does what, how, when, and where. What interests me here, though, is how the denotation is constructed—the form of denotation, or connotation. While I will not attempt to detach the form altogether from its contents, I will maintain in this book, in the tradition of Roland Barthes, that *there is no denotation without connotation*. It is unfortunate that Barthes, for reasons he enumerated in the early 1960s, shied away from cinema as an object of what was otherwise a sweeping web of semiotics: "it is probably because I have not succeeded in bringing the cinema into the sphere of language that my approach to it is purely projective and not analytical."[29] The importance of rejecting a language-based model for film signification will be addressed in chapter 2, as will a more detailed analysis of denotation and connotation; for now, it is worthwhile to note what Barthes believed a semiotics of cinema might entail.

Essentially, Barthes's interest in cinema manifests itself multiple times in terms specifically of film connotation. During the aforementioned 1963 interview, he continues: "How does the cinema make manifest or converge with the categories, functions, structures of what is intelligible as elaborated by our history, our society?"[30] This, for Barthes, is the essential object in a semiotics of cinema: *how* cinema intersects with modes of thinking, how it juggles sense and nonsense through the forms of its representations. This is what I will elaborate as film connotation: how the status of the image is constructed through the subject-object organization of a system of reference and the order of meaning this organization entails. While classical philosophy and sociology—according to Merleau-Ponty, Foucault, and Deleuze—insist on a rigid differentiation between sense and nonsense, right and wrong, us and them, these binaries are part of a larger order of meaning that necessitates particular configurations of subject and object that were quickly absorbed into conventional film practices. These configurations are exactly what Godard and Resnais undo, and I will ground the analysis of what I argue to be a philosophical challenge as a question of connotation, the deconstruction of formal coding and the breakdown of what is intelligible and how it should be so—experiments, as I put it, in cinematic thinking.

A study of what Barthes calls "ideas-in-form,"[31] this book looks at how we transpose orders of differentiation onto formal media, in this case cinema, and how this process extends larger philosophical paradigms that determine our understanding of experience and our interaction with the world. The means for this transposition can be found in our conventional modes of transformation, or *codes*. While this book is influenced by Barthes's notion of code, and especially his argument that all codes are formed in the connotative register, I will lean more toward Umberto Eco's formulation of the cinematic code. In "Articulations of the Cinematic Code," for example, Eco argues that structure in general exists "through a choice of operative conventions" that "rest on systems of choices and oppositions."[32] In this book I hope to give a phenomenological structure to this semiotic dualism in order to project this problem onto the immanent field. These structures of opposition, which are intertwined with the dynamic of subject-object relations, are a problem of film form: for Eco, as Julia Lesage points out, such codes refer not only to what is conventional, as far as behavior or action is concerned, but also "how to present that action in a representation."[33]

According to this understanding I will use the framework of subject-object relations to shift the focus away from the problem of referential meaning, studied by realist theorists, as well as to move away from apparatus theory's focus on the ideology behind our conventions of representation, and toward a question of how systems of reference are organized within the immanent field itself and how this process of organization corresponds to philosophical concepts, method, and purpose. The connotation specific to cinema, then, is less one of explicit value concerning the judgment of its viewed objects than it is *the connotation of the film image itself as a type of image*. In other words the image connotes itself not only as a world but also as a way (truthful, biased, trustworthy, ambiguous, certain, uncertain, indifferent, impassioned) of viewing the world and, as such, provides an important philosophical intersection between the essences explored through phenomenology and the constructions addressed in semiotics. The problems of film subjectivity and film connotation are important issues that seem to have been dismissed with the recent academic move away from semiotics in general. I hope that the regeneration of these problems, in the framework of subject-object relations and the immanent field, might reveal the kindred natures of phenomenology and structuralism in a way that will permit me to reconceptualize film as an object of their mutual concern. As semiotics falls from favor in film studies and phenomenology comes back into fashion, it would be useful to illuminate some characteristics they share, and perhaps this work might even sketch a way to extrapolate from phenomenology a metaphysical foundation with which to revive film semiotics. To do so, it will be necessary to dispel Dudley Andrew's myth (perhaps well-founded in its corroboration of popular thinking) that these two approaches are "arch-rivals,"[34] or that they are methodologically incompatible, a task that might be achieved by analyzing the film image as a process of organization.

The philosophical bookends of Merleau-Ponty and Deleuze stem from a strong recent surge in what Carroll calls cognitive-value claims in media studies: "that these arts bring about the possibility for new perceptions, that they change perception, or that they incarnate the mind or consciousness, or that they exemplify some new form of consciousness."[35] Such claims can be traced back to interwar avant-garde notions of the grand power of cinema to tap into subconscious arenas, which found a particularly focused platform in the postwar movement self-titled *filmologie*. In his oft-neglected yet seminal text in this movement, *Essai sur les principes d'une philosophie du cinéma* (Essay on the principles of a philosophy of cinema), Gilbert Cohen-Séat writes: "It is, in effect, in and during representation that the object and the new object, instituted by cinema, meet."[36] Cohen-Séat suggests here that a clue to the workings of cinema and cinematic meaning lies not in the ostensive, photographic dimension, nor necessarily in the spectator's psyche, but in what happens *in and during representation,* or within what I call the immanent field. The implication here is that, as I will not cease to rearticulate in different ways, film is a *process.* More precisely, it is a process of organization and redistribution, a system for forming relations; this is a notion that innately links even the most different representatives from a century of film theory. My attempt to situate this process according to the framework of subject-object relations must begin with an introductory review of this formulation's most influential philosophical precursor, which is the phenomenology of Merleau-Ponty.

Merleau-Ponty, Phenomenology, and Film

As indicated by a recent title in film-philosophy, *Film Consciousness: From Phenomenology to Deleuze*,[37] the two most influential thinkers on the realm of film-philosophy are arguably Merleau-Ponty and Deleuze. Yet, despite being constant points of reference, these two and their fundamental methodologies are consistently held apart as irreconcilable, if not in opposition. It is essential now to pose the pressing question: what do the primary philosophies engaged by this book have in common, and how do I aim to utilize them here? First, on the larger level of practice, these philosophers share a notion of what philosophy should serve, which is not the *status quo* but the embrace of the challenging and even (according to our conventions) the nonsensical. When discussing the role of the philosopher in *Signs*, Merleau-Ponty writes: "Our task is to broaden our reasoning to make it capable of grasping what, in ourselves and in others, precedes and exceeds reason."[38] Just as Merleau-Ponty insists on taking into consideration that which does not usually fall into the realm of the rational (the classical object of philosophy), Deleuze insists that philosophy ought to challenge the very notion of the rational. Taking this dehierarchization of the object of philosophy further, and rejecting what he considers the "sedentary" classical philosophy of representation, Deleuze argues: "Philosophy is at its most positive as critique: an enterprise of demystification."[39] I will view the works of Godard and Resnais as engaged in the very same philosophical goals, which derive from the same historical rupture and are articulated according to the same basis: the deconstruction of classical subject-object divisions and hierarchies.

In terms of influence I agree with Leonard Lawlor that all French critical theory and philosophy of the 1960s were "explicitly or implicitly in dialogue with Merleau-Ponty,"[40] and in speaking specifically of cinema, Merleau-Ponty makes an important link between twentieth-century philosophy and cinema. In his aforementioned address, "Cinema and the New Psychology," Merleau-Ponty draws many connections between cinema and his approach to philosophy, including this one: "The philosopher and the movie maker share a certain way of being, a certain view of the world which belongs to a generation."[41] Merleau-Ponty ties his generation of philosophers to the Seventh Art in unmistakable terms, and we can view here a profound contemporary sympathy bred in the 1960s spirit of rejecting convention. In his model of existential phenomenology Merleau-Ponty rejects the suppositions assumed by conventional empiricist and psychological approaches, attracted instead by the gestaltist claim that the formal structure of perception is inseparable from personal subjective experience. *Gestalt* theory, which originated with the Berlin School at the threshold of the twentieth century, focuses on the ability of human sensory perception (and especially vision) to transform external stimuli into a coherent formal structure or whole.

Influenced by this approach, Merleau-Ponty builds on the assumption that there is a process of transformation between external phenomena and subjective signification, based on formal organizations that result from the innate elements of human perception; these acts of organization, though necessary and inevitable, are also arbitrary. These organizations, for Merleau-Ponty, are where the objective world and subjective experience meet—not where they *separate*, as classical Cartesian philosophy may hold, but where they *meet*. Merleau-Ponty claims in the preface to his seminal work, *Phenomenology of Perception*, that the most important development provided by phenomenology is "without doubt to have joined extreme subjectivism with extreme objectivism in its notion of the world,"[42] a binary that for Edmund Husserl, Merleau-Ponty's predecessor, was focused primarily on the subjective side of human experience. Merleau-Ponty sets out to rectify this imbalance. As Vincent Descombes aptly summarizes, Merleau-Ponty insists on a symbiotic flow between subject and object and chooses to focus on what lies between consciousness and the thing, between "for-itself" and "in-itself," but refuses classical attempts to formulate this relationship in a rigid binary: "the alternatives of classical philosophy rejected, solution of antithesis is found in a 'finite' synthesis, an unfinished and precarious one."[43]

The terms *unfinished* and *precarious* are particularly important here, as Merleau-Ponty—like Deleuze to follow—posits philosophy's role as navigating the constantly changing and indefinite ocean of meaning in human existence, never to achieve a final and absolute understanding but instead to embrace and be a part of the constantly changing world. Merleau-Ponty challenges the logics of certainty and totality, central to classical philosophy, in terms of the fundamental paradigm of subject-object relations, what he referred to as "the subject-object correlation that has dominated philosophy from Descartes to Hegel."[44] Insisting that the subject-object dynamic "transpires within incompletion, non-coincidence, penumbra,"[45] Merleau-Ponty brackets off this organizational process for his phenomenological model, and I use this principle of bracketing as a way of applying Merleau-Ponty's methodology to the immanent field of the film image, the arrangement of which is also a necessary and inevitable, yet arbitrary, act. I will bracket off the immanent field of the image just as Merleau-Ponty brackets off the organizational process at work in human perception and, as such, argue for the validity of a transposition of philosophical method onto film theory. Furthermore, for Merleau-Ponty experience and meaning cannot be reduced to an external subject's unilateral understanding of the world but are, instead, the offspring of the subject's implication in the world itself: "I consider my body, which is my point of view on the world, as one of the objects of this world."[46] This statement leads to two important conclusions. The first, which I will explore further in chapter 1, implicates our coexistence in the world as not only a coexistence of separate beings, but instead as part of an "interworld" from which derives the symbolic and abstract meanings of our experiences; this "interworld" is projected onto the immanent field of the film image, where character and spectator meet, where subject and object coalesce.

The second implication of this statement, and the more useful at this introductory moment, is that the human being is both interior and exterior, depending on the point of reference: a subject that is at the same time an object, a body in the world and the place where exterior and interior are joined. Could we not describe cinema in the same words? As a form of representation that takes real objects as its original material, cinema provides us with a viewing subject that is also a viewed object; therefore, according to Merleau-Ponty, "cinema is particularly apt to reveal the union between the mind and body, between the mind and the world and the expression of each in the other."[47] In other words cinema can show us how the subjective and objective interact, overlap, coexist, oppose each other and are united, a meeting place between cinema and philosophy that was not lost on French film scholarship to follow. As Andrew points out, Merleau-Ponty had a direct influence on the theorists of *filmologie* such as Cohen-Séat,[48] but I will explore his relevance beyond this. Like many writers based in psychology, thinkers such as Merleau-Ponty and the anthropologist Edgar Morin became interested in cinema

for the same reasons that film theorists remain interested in phenomenology: cinema poses fundamental questions concerning the relationship
between the interior and exterior, subject and object.

The similarity between cinematic representation and human subjective
experience has led to many idealist notions of the "essential objectivity" of
the camera, a connotation fallaciously entrenched in the fact that the French
word for a camera lens is *objectif*.[49] In this way champions of cinematic realism such as André Bazin have argued that film has a phenomenological
capacity because it holds the possibility for a sort of formal *reduction* in the
phenomenological sense, a direct exposure to phenomena as opposed to a
careful arrangement of the objective world. Though aware of its artificiality as staged fiction, Bazin and others view cinema as uniquely capable
of—and indeed ontologically responsible for—representing an essential
quality that emanates from sensory appearances. We can see here a belief
in cinema's capacity not only to produce a copy of the world of external
phenomena but, actually, to uncover something in it while also respecting
its ambiguity. The question of "realism" is the crux of postwar French film
criticism's most explicit encounter with phenomenology, the work of Amédée Ayfre, whose "Neo-Realism and Phenomenology" explores the connection between this (at the time) topically popular philosophical method and
the most influential European film movement of the immediate postwar
period: Italian neorealism. For Ayfre, as for Bazin, filmmakers such as
Rossellini have philosophical implications because of their extreme humanism, and they are phenomenological because—as I will argue with
Godard and Resnais, only in less abstract terms—in their films "the mys-
tery of being replaces clarity of construction."[50]

Bazin embraces a similar argument concerning the philosophical potential of cinema, the height of which rests in the medium's ability to preserve the authentic ambiguity of nature. Ultimately, Bazin speaks of the
film image as an immanent field in the way I will approach it, but I will
distance myself from Bazin's defense of visual realism, hoping to show his
argument as an argument *for a particular type of image*—a connotative argument, a logic or philosophy. Also, this notion of the camera apparatus's
inclination toward the observational value of appearances makes it easily
comparable, through a simplistic metaphor, to phenomenology, prompting Christian Metz's suggestion that "the topical apparatus of cinema
resembles the conceptual apparatus of phenomenology."[51] I will argue

against such allegorical notions of the phenomenological nature of the cinematic apparatus, siding with later theorists who view this as an illusion constructed through the positioning of filmic subjectivity.

Furthermore, the similarity between film form and characteristics of the human subject has led many to consider film phenomenological in that its form is structured according to characteristics analogous to those at work in natural perception. Vivian Sobchack points out, for example, that film expression is an organizing activity much like human vision, which is structured and selective.[52] This position echoes two of the earliest systematic analyses of film form, Münsterberg's and Arnheim's, each of which were influenced by the *Gestalt* group and each of which attempts to define film representation through a comparison with the human subjective apparatus. Münsterberg argues that film representation overcomes the objective forms of the world by adjusting them to inner, human processes, such as attention and memory.[53] Is the apparatus of cinema therefore anthropomorphized? Some of the effects Münsterberg discusses are formal, such as depth and focus, whereas some stem from combinations of images, attempts to transpose the image onto the subjectivity of a character, such as the representation of memory through a flashback. I will ground the idealism of Münsterberg's insights with the acknowledgment, as Arnheim insists in *Film as Art*, that film is not an imitation or duplication of its source but is "a translation of observed characteristics into the forms of a given medium."[54]

These theorists mark an attempt to understand objective representation as itself subjective, transformative, and in some ways based on a formal simulation of the human subject. Later theorists such as Jean-Louis Baudry and Stephen Heath frame this duality as the starting place for an ideological critique of classical, or illusionist, cinema. Stemming from various angles of Marxism and psychoanalysis, such approaches are concerned centrally with the production and situating of subjectivity as an ideological problem. Influenced by French thinkers such as Julia Kristeva, Louis Althusser, and Jacques Lacan, these film theorists focus on the connotative structures of sociocultural institutions and mark an important historical alignment between intellectual culture and film culture in France. And, while I strongly disagree with the psychoanalytic bases for many of these theorists' conclusions, much of this book works alongside their assessment of film meaning being predicated on the signification of subject-functions, and I would agree with these theorists that the problem of film is, therefore, concerned with "the relations of subjectivity and ideology."[55] I will, however, direct this argument away from the problem of ideology and toward a more phenomenological analysis of the immanent field itself and the formal relations through which this subjectivity is constructed.

As Andrew notes, for these theorists "identification with characters and stories is based on an identification with the process of viewing itself and ultimately with the camera which views."[56] In other words there is what Metz and others have referred to as a double identification on behalf of the spectator: identification with the viewing apparatus and identification with the people viewed. This is the fundamental observation made by apparatus and suture theory that I will reframe in Deleuzean terms of the image in a state of flux between subjective and objective systems of reference. Many theorists, however, tend to merge different subject-functions—the diegetic subject-function of a character as point of identification, the camera subject-function such as is provided by camera movement, and the subject-function posited through classical editing techniques—all into one notion of what Baudry calls the "transcendental subject."[57] I will untangle this by specifying which formal configurations produce respective subject-functions and how different configurations must sometimes vie within the same cinematic moment. I hope in this book to illuminate, furthermore, the gradations by which these two identifications can shift, interact, overlap, and oppose each other. Instead of focusing on the ideology behind the image, or the psychology that governs the spectator's interpretation, I will map out the construction of this duality as an internal organization of such formal elements as the frame, montage, and the juxtaposition of speech and image.

Although I find the conclusions reached by Baudry to be invaluable to an understanding of film form and film subjectivity, his theories have inherent flaws that must be recognized, especially concerning the psychoanalytic and ideological rhetoric of his methods. Psychoanalytic theorists, Geoffrey Nowell-Smith criticizes, "cannot rest content" with the argument that meaning is produced without any subject of that production.[58] This is perhaps psychoanalysis's greatest contribution to my study: as a method it rejects the conventional myth of an internal construction that does not produce some framework of differentiation. Yet, while I agree with many conclusions reached by such theorists, and we should appreciate the critical nature of their enterprise, we must also be suspicious of a film theory that appropriates another discipline's method without skepticism, often even verbatim. In his response to this trend, Charles F. Altman takes psychoanalytic film theory to task primarily for its methodological appropriations of a master-theory (psychoanalysis) that is, itself, only a set of working hypotheses.[59] Can a theoretical approach so far removed from its object of analysis be methodologically robust?

Projecting familiar problems of film representation onto a heightened polemical arena, such theorists' political stance has also been disputed over recent years. Carroll, for example, challenges much of this theory for being focused on subject positioning as an ideological issue, when film—he claims—is not inherently ideological.[60] This critique marks a reaction, over the past thirty years, *against* the highly stylized cinema and politically polarized criticism of the 1960s, bringing under scrutiny the entire formalist project and the demystification of cinematic illusion. In this book I construct a middle ground between these. I believe very much that film is, as a sociocultural phenomenon and economic industry, without question ideological. While this does not mean, as theorists such as Daniel Dayan may argue, that classical cinema can be systematically rejected as a vessel for bourgeois Western ideology, we must nonetheless acknowledge that the formal base of cinema itself, through its modes of organizing meaning, disseminates certain values and assumptions that can be found in larger social bodies of thought and belief.

Rather than view it solely as a tool for hegemony, I view the structure of the film image as a condition either for perpetuating or challenging modes of thinking through the construction of different sets of relations. In doing so, I hope to use a phenomenological basis to establish a semiotics of film connotation, thus extending Merleau-Ponty's central method to the image-philosophy developed some forty years later by Deleuze.

Deleuze, Philosophy, and the Renewal of Formalism

The problem of subjectivity or the subject-object divide, the centrality of which I have already argued in reference to Merleau-Ponty, is pivotal to Western philosophy since Descartes and may well have reached a breaking point with the works of Deleuze, whose codevelopment (with longtime collaborator Félix Guattari) of schizoanalysis challenged the very bases of subject theory in traditional psychoanalysis.[61] Fortunately for lovers and scholars of the moving image, Deleuze did not leave it to us to transpose his philosophy onto the cinema; instead, he provided some five hundred pages, in two tomes, of the most engaging, respectful, insightful, and sometimes confusing prose ever written on the Seventh Art. Dividing both cinema history and philosophical logic into two spheres, *Cinema 1: The Movement-Image* and *Cinema 2: The Time-Image* serve up a smorgasbord of twentieth-century philosophical inquiry, auteur study of the great directors of international cinema, and an attempt to completely rework the relationship between cinema and philosophy and to reframe the overall role that cinema played in twentieth-century history.

Deleuze's *Cinema* books, which Rodowick identifies succinctly as "primarily works of philosophy,"[62] mark an important and unprecedented metaphysical turn in French philosophy toward cinema as an object of inquiry, as also evidenced in the work of Jean-Louis Schefer and Jacques Rancière, among others.[63] Instead of addressing what films say about the world (which we could refer to as the philosophical message of their denotations), the central question in French film-philosophy seems to be, Can cinema offer us new ways to think, and, if it can, *how* has it done so? Attempting to reframe the causal relationship between art and spectator according to his bipartite theory of cinematic image-types, Deleuze claims: "We can consider the brain as a relatively undifferentiated mass and ask what circuits, what kinds of circuit, the movement-image or time-image trace out, or invent, because the circuits aren't there to begin with."[64] Instead of containing cinema within the empirical premise of classical rationalism, as most Anglo-American cognitive theorists do, these French writers reframe the twentieth century as having been the locus of a great change in human psychology and existentiality. As Rodowick claims, this brand of film-philosophy seeks to "show how images and signs in movement or time are conceptually innovative; that is, how they renew our powers of thinking."[65] Deleuze serves as such an important model for new theories of cinema because his writing turns away from overt discussions of bourgeois ideological institutions and avoids any psychoanalytic or linguistic preconceptions, moving instead toward a conceptualization of cinema that rejects classical notions of fixed and rigid binary relations.

I cannot overstate, and have no doubt already revealed, the profound influence Deleuze's work has had on this book, and I must acknowledge the large amount of recent Deleuze-based film scholarship and attempt to situate my own work therein. In his introduction to the recent *Deleuze and World Cinemas,* David Martin-Jones provides a wonderfully insightful summary of the critical interest and tools that Deleuze offers to film studies, as well as a number of its limitations—its Eurocentrism and reliance on art cinema being the most central.[66] These are merited constructive criticisms that Martin-Jones makes precisely because Deleuze's film writing is so inspiring and, while providing a powerful springboard, must also be continually developed and built upon to accommodate the great diversity of industrial and aesthetic practices in world cinema. Unlike Martin-Jones's work, which seeks to make Deleuze more flexible for exploring popular and world cinemas, I hope to reveal its connections to other philosophical frameworks and to demonstrate how opening it to a larger study of film theory might help sharpen the methods of film-philosophy. Because of the innovative nature of his concepts, Deleuze provides a fecund soil for analyzing new and unconventional modes of film expression; and because of the flexibility of his somewhat uncentered film writing, Deleuze provides a powerful but often scattered beam of light for projecting larger critical movements, such as feminist film theory, beyond its original representational focus and onto concerns of the ontology of the image and the sensory viewing experience.

In *Deleuze and Cinema: The Aesthetics of Sensation,* for example, Barbara Kennedy applies problems of embodiment and intersubjectivity to what she articulates as a specifically postfeminist goal. In an innovative but slightly obtuse rhetoric characteristic of many works inspired by Deleuze, she proclaims: "We [feminist theorists] need to rethink a post-semiotic space, a post-linguistic space, which provides new ways of understanding the screenic experience as a complex web of inter-relationalities. The look is never purely visual, but also tactile, sensory, material and embodied. . . . This book seeks to reconfigure corporeality and the role of the mind/brain/body within the notions of sensation, through Deleuzean philosophy."[67] Attempting to critique the dependency of feminist theory on psychoanalytic frameworks and to provide a *neoaesthetic,* Kennedy introduces the now-trendy term *film-philosophy* as a less-than-modest concept for her own mode of "exploring 'affect' and 'sensation' through experimental visual engagements." Arguing against the masculinist concept of the fixed and unilateral subject, Kennedy claims that "a *postfeminist*" agenda is concerned with the "micrology" of "lived experiences, across and between the spaces of any fixed, sentient, or even fluid gendered subjectivity." Postfeminism, she continues, is "about more than the lived experience, but is about thinking processes at a fundamental level," trying "to bring back materiality and to understand the basis of experience as having a material and affective basis, as much as sociological, cultural or libidinal."[68]

To what degree fundamental thinking processes are "about more than the lived experience" is difficult to understand, but Kennedy's explanation of the usefulness of Deleuze clarifies the centrality of his work to this movement in general. Derived very much from his philosophical inquiries, Deleuze's cinema writing moves beyond dualistic and binary Platonist thinking processes, thus permitting us to understand the film experience as something more than just the relationship between textual meaning and spectatorial subjectivity: instead, as Kennedy asserts, a Deleuzean viewing experience is "an experience that is perceived as an event, as a processual, aesthetic event of sensation, articulated beyond subjectivity."[69] Although film works strongly on the level of sensation, I will argue that this "event" is akin less to sensory experience or perception and more to philosophical activity; and, far from functioning beyond subjectivity, it plays with the notion of subjectivity in order to experiment with modes of thinking.

Applying the politics of nonrepresentational cinema to a gender-oriented notion of sensory-evocative sound-images, Laura Marks's *The Skin of the Film* acts as an important precursor for the appropriation of Deleuzean concepts to a feminist-oriented (or, at least, antipatriarchal) position. Such arguments tend, as in Marks's and Kennedy's cases, to favor new, unconventional modes of film expression that aim to challenge clichés of cinematic language in accordance with shifting ideological norms concerning difference, identity, and the status of film criticism. These central interests have provided a new generation of scholars with the tools and paradigms with which to renovate outdated models of national, auteur, and genre cinema, as is also illustrated through the work of Martin-Jones, Martine Beugnet, Emma Wilson, Patricia Pisters, and Steven Shaviro. Soliciting a collection of films that employ "cinema's intensely tactile quality" from the last decade of French cinema, Beugnet employs Deleuze as a foundation for generating a contemporary theory of national French cinema.[70] Beugnet evokes the intellectual history of Bataille and Artaud to posit as a trans-genre national movement the near-ubiquitous presence of graphic sex and violence that is used to destabilize narrative clarity and to reconfigure traditional subject-object binaries. Although Beugnet does not necessarily cite it as such, this phenomenon can be traced to the radical manifestation of intersubjectivity and intertemporality articulated by particular films and filmmakers isolated by Deleuze—in particular, Alain Resnais. In *Alain Resnais*, Emma Wilson transforms Deleuze's focus on Resnais into a resurrected form of auteur theory. Working from Marks's and Joan Copjec's studies of the sensory nature of spectatorial trauma, Wilson focuses on the ambiguity of textual meaning and subjectivity provided through a subversion of the "status of the images viewed."[71] Like Wilson I will look primarily at Resnais's early feature film work and will return to her readings regularly in chapters 3 and 4; however, it is the gendercentric theoretical focus of these authors that I hope to avoid (though issues of gender and sexuality will be addressed), as well as the application of Deleuze's analytic tools to reaffirm traditional methodologies of cinema study. Moreover, instead of embracing Deleuze's rhetorical loopholes in order simply to apply the term *time-image* to any unconventional film practice that is of interest, I aim to provide a comparative analysis that includes specific counterexamples and conflicting discourses within the work of a director and, sometimes, within a single text and even a single shot.

While Wilson, Beugnet, and Marks explore a similar terrain of art and avant-garde film selection as my own, there also exists prolific scholarship aimed at resurrecting the critical study of popular and mainstream cinemas through Deleuzean lenses. In *Deleuze, Cinema and National Identity: Narrative Time in National Contexts*, Martin-Jones does an excellent job of utilizing Deleuzean concepts to address the alternative practices and implications of shifts in temporality in major studio films, especially those of recent Hollywood cinema. While Martin-Jones and others have demonstrated the usefulness of Deleuze to approaching highly cinema-literate and cleverly constructed films such as *Fight Club* (David Fincher, 1999) and *Memento* (Christopher Nolan, 2000), I argue in the conclusion—as I will with certain texts of Godard and Resnais— that these are ultimately plays on the denotative fabric of the text, especially the narrative structure; and, while they can provide allegorical insight into larger issues of national and transnational identity, these films fundamentally subscribe to a conventional order of meaning that reverts in the end to classical philosophical notions of subjectivity and time.

Regardless, in each case these scholars embrace the Deleuzean connection between cinema and philosophy in order to invest substantial personal and human importance in the influence of moving-image culture. Cinema's ability to affect our personal and social philosophies is based on two important aspects of its ontology and history: its fundamentally transformative form, and its historical place in the evolution of image culture. Contextualizing cinema alongside a larger development in human thought, Deleuze maps out what he calls a "natural history" of the evolution of film signs, or image-types, through which his ultimate goal is "to produce a book on logic, a logic of cinema."[72] This logic is not, however, limited to cinema but is a dynamic model of a civilization that is itself cinematic, a humanity that has been altered by cinematic form and whose image culture reflects a transformation in paradigms of thought. While the chronological determinism of Deleuze's claim to a "natural history" has rightfully drawn criticism from a number of sources, it is relevant here in that the seeds for his "logic of cinema" take root in his philosophy of the 1960s, which was both influenced by Merleau-Pontian trends and aimed to reflect a breakdown in philosophical and ideological conventions that was echoing through the alternative film practices coming to the forefront of French film culture. Rodowick notes this intersection, and Deleuze's second volume devotes much focus to the films of Godard and Resnais as exemplary of cinema's potential for philosophical thinking and, as such, "is especially useful for defining the exemplarity of French film and audiovisual culture since 1958."[73]

Even though such intersections between form and philosophy are boldly apparent in the works of these thinkers and filmmakers, drawing out this connection has met with a resistance primarily due to a suspicion of film-philosophy's abstractions and general disillusionment with formalist film theory. Addressing the latter of these points (which I hope will allow us to solve the former) brings to the forefront a problem that has been raised specifically concerning the works of Godard and Resnais. Echoing Pauline Kael's infamously disparaging remark about the snobbery and vacuity signaled by the prominence of stylistic technique in Resnais's work, David Bordwell writes: "Godard . . . raises as does no other director the possibility of a sheerly capricious or arbitrary use of technique."[74] In many ways this remark illustrates the neglect of film connotation in much film criticism, but it also provokes a question: can we not analyze the significance of how our images are structured? Should we not? Indeed, I argue in this study that the work of these film-makers raises the problem of form to a philosophical level. However, in order to promote such an argument, perhaps film form needs to be analyzed according to formats different from those used to study film narration, for example. "What does stylistic patterning offer us?" Bordwell demands rhetorically, responding: "It cannot have causal unity, and . . . seems to have no clearly designated units."[75] But does it not have causal unity, embedded in its organization of subject-object relations? And can we not designate certain units by which it can be analyzed, units concerning the interactions within and between particular formal elements that organize the immanent field in certain ways?

These questions point toward the need to reformulate the notion of film form in general, not only as a tool for supporting the denotation of a story, nor as a question of mise-en-scène and visual style or even visual symbolism, but as an essential source of film meaning. Godard and Resnais are exemplary for this argument. Raised in the Cinémathèque and film school culture of postwar France, filmmakers like Godard and Resnais grew up surrounded by the clichés of classical cinema. Yet, as Merleau-Ponty argued, they were also part of a generation disillusioned with conventional systems of thought. Fed up with the complacent and closed orders of meaning offered by classical forms, the cinema of the 1960s waged a systematic assault on conventional structures of differentiation by deconstructing the formal codes from which such structures are built.

At the heart of this assault is a challenge to the stability of our orders of meaning, the totality of any worldview—and, in challenging this, these filmmakers insist that the form of denotation itself is both significant and in need of our critical attention. As Andrew writes concerning Resnais's Last Year at Marienbad (1961) and the genre of "art" or "modern" cinema of which it is emblematic: "By taking our powers and aspirations for explanation, totality, and identification to the limit, such films bring out into the open the value, the labor, and the fragility of representation in the cinema."[76] Resnais and Godard achieve this, I argue, by shifting the semiotic focus of their films onto the connotative level of film signification and inviting the spectator to consider the immanent field itself as a dialogic source of signification. Their works resist the desire for denotative certainty, revealing the constructed basis of representation and—in the spirit shared by Merleau-Ponty and Deleuze—challenging the classical divisions between subject and object. I have selected Godard and Resnais as my examples and believe that this selection will prove itself justified, though I fully acknowledge that this is nonetheless a limited portrait of film practice, and in my conclusion I consider how such a study might also extend to mainstream Hollywood cinema and other traditions. Furthermore, in constructing a system of comparative analysis between the two filmmakers and also within their respective oeuvres, I hope here to work alongside contemporary scholars toward a method of formal and textual analysis that integrates different cinematic approaches into a common conceptualization of the dynamic relationship between philosophy and film.

Similarly, the focus of this study necessitates the marginalization of certain critical methodologies, including, most notably, spectator theory, as well as approaches, such as auteur theory, that have typically been applied to these directors. While other theories have much to offer by way of elucidating certain problems of film representation, the suppositions on which they are built make them peripheral to the primary concerns enumerated here. I acknowledge that spectatorship is largely diverse, and the spectator holds at all times a complex agency for relating to, identifying with, or rejecting the implications of any image. I do not intend to prove that filmic meaning rests solely or even primarily with either the image or the viewer: it is my purpose, rather, to reveal how the structure of the image offers different modes and levels of interaction or entrance for the spectator's agency, which here necessitates the bracketing off of the form of the image—between the content and the spectator—in order, hopefully, to expand it once again.

Synopsis

Such a critical endeavor as this one cannot work without the evidence of close textual reading, and the films of Godard and Resnais are instrumental in bringing to light the problems addressed in these pages. As my goal here is to systematize the concept of film connotation according to the phenomenological notion of subject-object relations, I begin by addressing phenomenology and the basic cinematic differentiation between viewing subject and viewed world. Chapter 1 explores the allegorical notions of the image-as-perception and the image-as-thought, reconciling such divergent theories as Eisensteinian montage and Bazinian realism under an umbrella rubric of subject-object relations. Using Merleau-Ponty to work through such phenomenological film writers as Edgar Morin and Jean Mitry, chapter 1 addresses the problem of how cinema's basic visual apparatus designates a viewing position meant to simulate the human perceptual mechanism, while also offering the possibility to nullify this unilateralism. Applying phenomenology to ways in which the visual design of the image divides viewing subject from viewed world, I perform detailed textual analyses of Godard's *Vivre sa vie* (1962) and *Two or Three Things I Know About Her* (1966). These films, I argue, illustrate a range of practices that either provide a conventional mode of visual subjectivity, in which the camera aligns with a singular viewing subject in the text, or, conversely, break such conventions down through formal deconstructions, such as through the refraction of viewing positions or the subjectification of material objects.

Godard throws the cinematic claim to objectivity into question by directly interacting with—and subverting—conventional film codes of subject-construction. Film is not just perception; it is codified perception and thus requires a semiotic approach to complement the phenomenological. Chapter 2 engages in depth with the problem of a semiotics of film based on the codification of subject-object dynamics, turning to Eco, Barthes, and Pasolini for complex notions of cinematic coding and how they might apply to a theory of subject-object relations. Using these theorists to develop an understanding of how film codes rely on the repetition and subversion of subject-object configurations, this theoretical path arrives at Deleuze's semiotic project and frames his work as a problem of connotation in order to situate it—as is rarely done—within a larger theoretical genealogy. Positioning it thus allows me to focus on two major aspects of Deleuze's argument: formalism and the immanent field. Deleuze's focus on the formal specificity of cinema shifts focus away from film content and toward its constant process of transformation between image-types, each of which can be defined through its particular arrangement of subject-object relations. These relations shift and evolve within what I appropriate from Deleuze as the immanent field, the network of formal relations existent within the sound-image whose composition determines the subject-object relations through which denotation is produced. Unlike Deleuze studies such as Gregory Flaxman's anthology *The Brain Is the Screen* or Rodowick's *Gilles Deleuze's Time Machine*, my reading aims to ground the metaphysical nature of Deleuze's concepts within a larger framework of subject-object configurations, while also finding in it the basis for a semiotic understanding of film connotation that has yet to be attributed to his work.

Chapter 3 further explores the immanent field of formal elements by including and focusing on the problem of sound. This chapter provides close readings of Resnais's *Last Year at Marienbad* and *Hiroshima, mon amour* (1959) in order to analyze sound-based subject-object configurations. I look in particular at Resnais's use of sound to deconstruct any form of absolute spatial, and especially temporal, subjectivity, including the subversion of conventional divisions between voice-overs and dialogues, diegetic and nondiegetic sound. Paralleling the shift to Resnais with a new theoretical dimension, this chapter utilizes Deleuze's Bergsonian notion of intertemporality to provide a temporal complement to the spatial intersubjectivity conceptualized in Merleau-Ponty's phenomenology. Whereas Merleau-Ponty insists on the coexistence of subjects and objects in space, Deleuze uses Bergson's philosophy of time to stress the coexistence of past, present, and future, as so uniquely captured in nonlinear cinema. Resnais's films are to Godard's as Deleuze is to Merleau-Ponty, I argue, making use of the conclusions reached in chapter 2 to add the essential aspects of time and editing to chapter 1's study of space and frame. Balancing film theory on sound with Deleuzean image-philosophy, this chapter uses a comparative analysis of Resnais's texts to include sound into the basic premise of subject-object dynamics, building on those employed in chapter 1's analysis of Godard in order to offer an approach balanced between visual and aural elements. Whereas many studies that apply phenomenology to film, such as Sobchack's *Address of the Eye*, remain very imagecentric, my work insists that sound theory must transcend its usually limited place in technical analysis and be appended to visual theory in a larger philosophical understanding of film's immanent field.

The impact of intertemporality on the classical notion of subjectivity, as illustrated through Resnais's deconstruction of sound-image codes, introduces the premise for chapter 4. This chapter is divided into three parts: an analysis of the codes for creating subjectivity in cinema; how these codes are utilized and deconstructed in the films of Alain Resnais;

and an in-depth analysis of an often-neglected gem of his early work, *The War Is Over* (1966). Specifically, I show how Resnais deconstructs what I term the *code of subjectivity* in order to experiment with understanding the individual's relationship to the world in terms of political action. This chapter challenges popular readings of Resnais as providing a cinema of consciousness or thought, which I hold to be erroneous and counterproductive analogies. Instead, I reframe his cinema as part of a connotative subversion of the implications of certainty and unilateralism implicit in classical conventions and constructions of subjectivity, and thus I position it in more clear philosophical terms—that is to say, how can cinema challenge the classical representation of linear time or chronological memory? How does Resnais reconfigure formal codes to question the conventional monistic view of personal experience?

And what about the other pole of representation? Whereas chapter 4 is concerned with subjective representation, or the system of reference that implies a direct connection between the form of representation and a character in the film, chapter 5 builds on the tripartite structure and theme of the previous chapter as a stepping stone in order to return full circle to problems addressed in chapter 1 concerning perception and objectivity in cinema. This chapter explores the connotations of objectivity in cinema and the countercinema of Godard, building a lengthy textual analysis of *Contempt* (1962), in which Godard throws into question what I term the *code of objectivity*. Unlike Resnais's film discussed in the previous chapter, *Contempt* addresses the politics of cinema as an institution and representational machine and helps to close out the larger concerns of this study of film and philosophy through Godard's extensive but unique mode of self-reflexivity. Unlike Resnais's films, which open up to a seemingly infinite possibility of meaning, Godard's cinema closes in on itself, engaging the very process of film expression in its inquiry and, in doing so, destroying any fixed illusion of certainty or containment. Confronting cinema with the problem of how it reflects on the world of which it is a part, Godard fractures the connotations of objectivity through which many worldviews are guaranteed as natural.

Setting up a dialectic relationship between two radically different but equally radical figures in international film history—linking Godard's obsessive exploration of space, vision, and objectivity to the phenomenology of perception developed by Merleau-Ponty, and Resnais's exploration of temporality, sound, and subjectivity to the Bergsonian image-philosophy of Deleuze—this book constructs a parallel and even dialectical framework for connecting film and philosophy that is built on detailed theoretical analysis and the close reading of film texts. My goal here is to use these directors' works as a sample set, based within my own area of expertise, in order to provide an interdisciplinary framework for reconceptualizing the problem of film connotation, reconstructing this concept in a way that will be valuable to all schools of film theory. The systematized formulation of the immanent field as a problem of the composition of subject-object relations could subsequently be expanded, for example, to analyses of the relationship between national traditions in international coproductions, the filmic interaction of diverse sexual identities, or the transmedial genealogy of popular narration. In other words, the ultimate goal of this book is to provide a unique fundamental structure for addressing film's formal organizations, a basic methodology that can be utilized to study other types of cinema (such as the contemporary horror film) or other problems of cinematic representation (such as race and ethnicity) than are directly addressed here.

Finally, I hope to contribute an effort toward clarifying certain problems that permeate film theory and film-philosophy today. While film studies has gradually been moving in the direction of a more historically based discipline, I hold that any analysis of film texts, of industrial history, or of the historical development of cinematic expression would benefit immeasurably from a sturdy foundation of theoretical argument. Moreover, while the focus on new media and transnational cinema seems to have taken center stage in the field of cinema studies, such approaches inherently concern themselves with the relationship between the structure of the image and the construction of subjectivity, and therefore embark on an implicit attempt to clarify different modes of film connotation. These are problems that could perhaps best be grasped if we take a step back for a moment and restore a basic attempt to understand film aesthetics according to more fundamental processes of organization. The contemporary disillusionment with structural semiotics and the move away from psychoanalysis as a model for film interpretation seem to foreshadow the watershed from which two rivers will burst: the return to phenomenology as a metaphysical model for the aesthetics of sensation, and the broadening expansion of Deleuze's film-philosophy legacy. Being inspired and influenced both by the phenomenology of Merleau-Ponty and by Deleuze's *Cinema* project, I believe it worthwhile to attempt a reconciliation between their respective approaches and, in hopes of encouraging similar enterprises, devote this work to helping weave together concerns that they share with each other and with other areas of film studies.

ONE

We no longer find ourselves before subjective or objective images; we are caught in the correlation between a perception-image and a camera-consciousness that transforms it.

—Gilles Deleuze, *Cinéma 1: L'image-mouvement*

WHEN WE ARE WATCHING A FILM, IT OFTEN SEEMS AS THOUGH we are looking through a window onto the world, or as if the camera itself were a set of eyes, looking at the world for us—perhaps both of these at once, even. The camera moves and the image shifts, or the sequence cuts to another shot, and it is as if an idea was created, a train of thought, and yet it wasn't only in our heads. It was on the screen, in the film's process of unfolding, part of the process of becoming that takes place before us. Is film a type of perception? Is it a type of consciousness? If it is, what is doing the perceiving, the thinking? Who is the "I" of this experience? Is the viewing subject absolute and set apart from the object of its gaze, or are we—as Deleuze implies—implicated in the flux between two states of perception and understanding?

In this quote, Deleuze exemplifies a tendency in film theory to describe cinema by referring to characteristics of human experience, using terms like *camera-consciousness* and *perception-image* to relate film representation to some aspect of what we consider internalized, subjective experiences: *thought, consciousness, perception*. From the early views of Jean Epstein and Sergei Eisenstein to the recent proliferation of post-Deleuzean notions of the *film-mind*, theories of cinema have been greatly slanted toward metaphors that compare cinema to human mental processes. Scholars and theorists (myself included) face here what I would say is essentially a problem of terminology, in which such metaphorical models tell us less about cinema than about our own means of describing it; to paraphrase Wittgenstein, the limits of our language define the limits of our world, and the limits of our film theory are defined by the traps we set for ourselves in our choice of analogy, metaphor, and phrasing. Yet, there clearly *are* similarities between film form and our own ways of experiencing the world. In hopes of grounding such similarities and analogies in a more philosophical bedrock, I will look here at some preliminary problems of human subjectivity as described through phenomenology and establish some basic intersections between the work of Merleau-Ponty and the construction of the primary degree of film subjectivity: the viewing subject.

Perhaps the most generic analogy in film writing is that which theorizes a type of camera-perception. As Dudley Andrew notes, many proponents of cinematic realism, such as André Bazin and Siegfried Kracauer, see "little essential difference between perception in the cinema and in the world at large."[1] However, while the subsequent assemblage of its recordings can be presented as an act of perception, a machine does not provide an act of perception but an act of recording and, then, of representing. And the metaphor goes deeper, past our instantaneous interaction with sensory phenomena and to our very psychological makeup. We may all be familiar with cross-references between cinema and human psychology, a connection made by early psychologists-turned-cineastes such as Hugo Münsterberg, whose *Psychology of the Photoplay* would be inadvertently elaborated upon in Jean Mitry's 1965 *The Aesthetics and Psychology of the Cinema*. Such approaches usually refer to the *Gestalt* model of psychology, which focuses on the perceptual apparatus as a system of organization that translates external phenomena into a set of spatiotemporal relationships that together form something more than just the sum of their respective parts. The structuring of the film image can be compared to the human perceptual gestalt: in the writings of Arnheim, Münsterberg, and Mitry, as well as Merleau-Ponty, there is a similarity between the organizational process of human perception and the manner in which the film image, interdependent on the medium's specific formal elements, organizes external phenomena into a larger worldview.

Moreover, as Vivian Sobchack writes, "the film experience is a system of communication based on bodily perception as a vehicle of conscious experience."[2] In other words, not only does film form simulate certain qualities of human psychology, but we also experience film *through the senses*, and as such it acts as a relay for phenomena to our own human apparatus, distributing the sensible once (when the film is being recorded), twice (during postproduction, when the sensory elements are being mixed and edited), and thrice (through the exhibition methods that present the final text to the spectator). However, this triple distribution is often smoothed over, rendered invisible, for our viewing pleasure—or, more skeptically, for the preservation of a dominant order of meaning. On a basic, illusionist plane I will look here at how the film image offers a mode of representation that implicitly claims its content as being directly witnessed, or experienced, because its form of presentation mimics the sensory process through which humans experience the material world. Christian Metz formulates this process as follows: the film image constitutes a source-point for the spectator to inhabit through identifying with a pure act of perception.[3] The image offers us a position for viewing, from which vantage point the visible content seems less like a cultural text and more like a chunk of some ostensible reality.

At the same time, however, as gestaltists such as Arnheim point out, film form includes many effects, such as the projection of a two-dimensional image as three-dimensional, that draw attention to the "unreality of the film picture."[4] For Arnheim cinematic realism is not a natural inclination of cinema but an affectation. As such, as is a fundamental argument of this book, one should be wary of the notion of film as itself offering an empirical or natural mode of observation. This "natural" connection is itself the connotation of a *type of image* and has been discounted as much by ideology theorists of previous decades as by a heightened cultural literacy of contemporary audiences, yet even today's reliance on video-grammar codes of truth evoke realist approaches that stipulate a natural ontological link between human observation, the camera-apparatus, and the inherent meaning of external phenomena. I will look in this chapter at the basis for such an understanding, and in the next chapter at the complications posed to such an approach by a semiotics that has a phenomenological basis. If such a theory has already been highly challenged, you may ask, why revitalize this debate? In assessing the parameters of this argument, I hope first to reveal the methodological intersection of variant theories as, ultimately, theories of film connotation; and, building from this, I aim to explore the analogy of film and perception according to the central pursuit of where film and philosophy meet, how this analogy—in its accuracies and flaws—might offer us entrance to the philosophical nature of the medium and films discussed here.

While Andrew is correct to acknowledge that the idea of cinema's being a system of signs seems to remove from it the capacity for "revelation," this same medium can still help to dissolve the division between the viewing spectator and the viewed world.[5] This does not mean that cinema is a window on the world, providing some innocent and neutral viewpoint but, instead, that it is able to perform an important phenomenological dissolution of the subject-object binary. I will thus argue for a phenomenological notion of cinema based not on the camera as a perceptive vehicle but on the flow of cinematic meaning as a dialogic openness between different subjective positions, an immanent field where the content of the image and the human manipulation behind its production meet, thus returning us to Deleuze's quote at the beginning of this chapter. To strip his claim of its metaphors: the image is neither objective nor subjective but a process of transformation that structures itself according to subjective or objective systems of reference. In other words my concern here is not the outside, or the objective world that exists anterior to any subject's experience of it; nor the interiorization of this reality, a subjective experience that renders all meaning relative; but, the image's collusion between these two. That is to say, the image consists not only of the objects it represents, nor of a particular character's vision of this world, but also—and perhaps most fundamentally—of our use of these two conditions of differentiation as the basis for meaning. These two connotative orders—the objective mode differentiating between detached apparatus and world viewed, and the subjective mode differentiating between diegetic subject and diegetic world—construct two very different systems of reference, yet both are conventionally used to divide the subject from the content represented and are thus similar in producing a closed order of meaning. Before getting ahead of myself, though, let me return to the degree zero of film subjectivity: the viewing subject as it is correlated with an objective mode of representation, and the philosophical importance of this myth of camera-perception.

FILM'S PRIMARY SYSTEM OF ORGANIZATION:
THE FRAME AND THE VIEWING SUBJECT

It is, of course, extremely difficult to claim one particular element of film expression as the *primary level* of filmic anything. I would agree, however, with most arguments that the single visual shot—the framing and composition of the shot—is the most basic unit of film expression (though we will soon find that, in the feature-length fiction film, this does not make it self-sufficient or impervious to a multitude of influences). The shot, as Raymond Bellour writes, is "le premier lieu" (the starting place) for film expression, through which the image institutes "its voyeuristic position as organizer of the real."[6] To calibrate this to my argument here: the shot is the primary unit of expression because the frame provides us with the first differentiated impression of a subjective position. It may be helpful to pause here and ask, What is a subject? Subjectivity, we could say, is an enforced system of differentiation that posits a unity of meaning or logic on one side and an object to be understood on the other. The visible elements of the image refer to the frame as a system of separation and limitation, and the frame refers to a viewing position as its origin. By enforcing the spatial system of difference in the visual image, the frame provides a system of reference, an implied subject of the gaze through which the visible is seen.

This system of reference signifies that the image is the correlation of a worldview with a subjective viewing position. The system of reference's formal praxis is the structure of the shot, the components of which—including composition, depth, movement—refer ultimately to the limitation of the image: the frame. As the defining structure of what is included in or excluded from the filmic message, we could view the frame as the film image's initial praxis for organization, a permanent system of reference that is part of any film representation. While it seems slightly monolithic, I agree with Mitry's claim that all visual elements are fundamentally attached to the frame: "All plastic significations depend on it."[7] Yet, I see no reason to claim, as theorists such as David Bordwell and Stephen Heath have, that the frame's organizational process is fundamentally narrative; although it may often be situated in a narrative context, it is first and foremost an organization of spatial relations. And, regardless of whether or not it is used in a story, the process of framing serves to differentiate between a subject and a content or object of the image.

This structuring process is a motivated simulation—engendered by the medium's forms, I will argue—of the transcendental condition discussed in phenomenology, and it would be helpful, therefore, to introduce aspects of the condition described by the phenomenology of perception so as to integrate such concepts into a semiotics of film connotation. Merleau-Ponty's most devout study of gestalt perception, *Phenomenology of Perception*, insists on the fundamental premise that an object's form and size are accidents of our relationship to it.[8] According to Merleau-Ponty, depth-of-field and vertical and horizontal relativity are arbitrary processes carried out to produce a *vis-à-vis* between a perceiving subject and the world of objects.[9] Spatial perception, we can gather, is a structural phenomenon, not an essential natural aspect, and is understandable only to the extent that it is founded in a particular subjectivity, and the positing of this anchor via the organization of the objective world according to such spatial designations is what could be postulated as the universal condition of the subject.[10] All subjects define themselves through this mode of organization.

Consequently, although symbolically, cinematic space—as constructed during a shot and according to the frame—implies the existence of a viewing subject that is the source of vision, placing the spectator in this position. As Colin MacCabe and Laura Mulvey write: "The world is centered for us by the camera and we are at the centre of a world always in focus."[11] This "centre" is defined by the frame, which functions according to an analogical relationship with real perception, a claim that is further supported by the manufactured correspondence between the horizontal-vertical ratio of the cinematic image and that of human vision. Ronald Bogue, writing on Deleuze and yet conjuring the preceding points by Merleau-Ponty, articulates this well: "Every frame implies an 'angle of framing,' a position in space from which the framed image is shot."[12] This is not an uncommon claim, but it is important to articulate here. As an organizational mechanism, the fact that the frame delimits the image creates a system of reference that, at the most basic level, refers to the frame itself as a relay for the parameters of the perceiving subject. Other aspects of film optics whose place is within the frame can also be seen as analogous to operations performed by Merleau-Ponty's human viewing subject; thus, the elements that interact with the frame imply that basic visual representation is a simulation of human vision. For example, shot scale can be used to mimic the human experience of casting attention to one particular area of vision, as in Münsterberg's understanding of the close-up.[13] In addition, there is camera movement, which grants the frame the illusion of a certain lifelike mobility, as if it were itself moving through space. Furthermore, there is the illusion of depth-of-field, which utilizes the convention of perspective in order to situate the viewer in a familiar position of relating to the world.

This effect, which I will consider in more detail in my analysis of film objectivity in chapter 5, is only part of the film image's inheritance of Renaissance artistic conventions, as Stephen Heath points out: including stability (easel), movement (*camera obscura*), and depth (perspective), these effects are meant to provide a "whole vision" that is delimited within the frame. But Heath uses these attributes, combined with the conventional purpose of framing in fiction cinema, to define the frame as "the conversion of seen into scene."[14] The continuity of the content or narrative information exchanged, however, is only the end—not the predetermination—of the frame's codification of visual perception, and, as such, I would encourage that we consider this conversion to be a question of form before it is integrated into a question of narration. The frame is not, as Heath claims, "narrated"; it is not a result of the logic of the story but is part of the mold for that narration, a channel for that message, regardless of whether it is mimetic or another type of message.

In summary: as a spatial determinant for the organization of visible relations, the frame selects the fragment of possible reality being transmitted as information. For the visible space within the shot the frame is, as Mitry puts it, "*the* absolute referent *of all cinematic representation.*"[15] Mitry, who comes from a phenomenological background, claims that the objects-turned-images are constructed with boundaries constituted by the frame and, as such, are linked to it *phenomenally* through an immanent field of formal organization. This implies a certain motivation or rhetorical nature of the form itself that is prenarrative. Because it serves as the center of gravity for what is in the image, the frame is responsible first and foremost for constructing the relationship between visible subjects and objects, thus determining the relational structure of difference within the visual diegesis. How are characters arranged relative to each other in the frame? But, also: what is allowed in the frame and what is excluded? After all, the frame not only pulls things into a common space; it also divides them. The elements in a frame, as Deleuze points out, are both distinct parts and components of a single composition, which the frame both separates and unites.[16] The frame divides its content: it is essentially selective, though there is one thing at all times both included and excluded: the viewing subject.

Second, though more subtly, the frame determines the relationship between the spectator and the visual objects, thus determining the spatial structure through which the spectator is given the visual content. This does not make such an organization essential to the object itself, but it *is* inevitable, as delimitation is a necessary aspect of any process of organization. Merleau-Ponty describes this act perfectly with regard to natural vision: "The limits of the visual field are a necessary moment in the organization of the world and not an objective contour."[17] This necessary moment, which must be seen as both motivated (in that it is selective) and arbitrary (in that this selection produces an artificial division that does not stem from the object itself) is, I believe, what is simulated in the shot. On both of these levels the process of delimitation exercised by the frame must be accepted as a necessary moment, but we should resist the naturalization of it as an objective characteristic. This resistance is of interest here because, through film connotation, such an arbitrary allotment is often given the impression of being naturally essential, objective. As Arnheim puts it: "a virtue is made of necessity."[18]

All elements of the shot—movement, depth-of-field, mise-en-scène, etc.—refer back to the frame as the center or source of this necessary act of organization, designations that assume a *vis-à-vis* of subject and world. This *vis-à-vis* is a relational system, an inherent rupture between viewing subject and visible objects that implies a condition for the spectator as being part of a division between perceiving subject and perceived world. This implication, a rhetorical effect through which the arbitrary difference implied by perception is granted an essential value, is a problem of film connotation and thus philosophical importance. "A virtue is made of necessity." Arnheim's statement summarizes the philosophical problem proposed by the previous pages' exploration of phenomenology and the film frame. The frame is the ultimate referent of everything in the image, yet it is limited by its formal determination—though different films may use different aspect ratios, the frame is always limited, and must be arbitrarily fixed. Yet this arbitrary placement defines the rational integrity of the image, like the parameters of a scientific experiment. Not only does the frame determine the limitation of information, but it also imposes a relationship of differentiation and implies that the content viewed is an absolute totality for the viewing subject. Deriving totality from limitation is a fundamental tenet of the classical philosophical order of meaning, the essence of *cliché*, and perhaps the single most challenged principle by the skeptical or subversive philosophies of Merleau-Ponty and Deleuze.

The connotative ramifications of this *vis-à-vis*, here analyzed with regard to the primary level of the shot, constitute what I will call the *myth of natural perception*. Through this phrase I hope to convey the notion that any shot signifies a point-of-view according to which it is produced, and the myth by which this image can be accepted as an act of perception is integrally linked to the implication or connotation of totality accorded to this view. As Colin MacCabe writes: "that which institutes the object as separate also institutes the subject as self-contained unity instead of divided process."[19] And, I would say, *vice versa*. The myth of cinematic perception functions according to the following convention: the screen acts as a window, and the visual content is what we see as we look through that window. The shot can deliver to us a nonsensical or unfamiliar message, but it is always one that can be seen and therefore interpreted as an image *of* something. As Metz argues, this principal effect allows the spectator to identify with him- or herself as the condition of possibility of the perceived,[20] an argument common to the psychoanalytic approaches of Metz, Bellour, and Baudry.

Although I remain suspicious of the psychoanalytic basis for such an argument, the notion of subject-formation can be traced back to the phenomenological subject-function. The shot gathers all illusions necessary to convince the spectator that, while what you are seeing through your normal perceptive process may be something that you could not see outside the cinema, you are seeing it nonetheless through your normal perceptual process, therefore legitimizing the spectacle as possible reality or what Barthes might call the *vraisemblable*, "that which the public believes to be possible and may be completely different from the historic real or scientifically possible."[21] In other words, to elaborate on an argument that is implicit even in realist theories of cinema, *any resemblance between the image and the possible—not the real, but the possibly real—lies in the form of perceiving whatever is denoted and not in the content perceived.* As Baudry puts it: "the spectator identifies less with what is represented, the spectacle itself, than with what stages the spectacle, makes it seen, obliging him to see what it sees: this is exactly the function taken over by the camera as a sort of relay."[22] The notion of the camera as relay, which is the condition for what Baudry critiques as the classical cinematic identification with the subject of visual perception, is based on the construction of a subject that, according to the principles of phenomenology, is itself a myth. The filmmakers explored in this book challenge both this myth and the assumption it produces—but first, I will further this analysis of the philosophical implications of popular analogies of the image-as-perception or image-as-thought and how such divergent theories might be reconciled by understanding their underlying methodologies as, fundamentally, problems of subject-object relations.

Shot(s): The Eisenstein-Bazin Debate

The myth of natural perception and the isolated subject is impossible to avoid in the individual shot, for the unidirectional nature of the camera guarantees just such a relational structure. But this book is concerned with the cinema: it takes twenty-four frames to complete a second of screen time, and each shot is surrounded by other shots and combined to form scenes, which are combined to form sequences. Each shot inevitably refers to its own unique viewing position; and, as Bellour writes, "film is a chain of successive viewpoints."[23] What changes with a juxtaposition of different shots? In other words, where does the viewing subject fit into the relationship between shot and editing? Positions taken in response to this question can be viewed as threefold, systematized according to the epistemological and ontological beliefs on which they are founded.

First, there is the notion that cinema has an ontological ability and responsibility to capture meanings on the surface of external phenomena, a notion developed by realists such as André Bazin. Bazin suggests that film signification ought to be grounded in the meaning produced by the objects it is recording. The formal organization should be governed, then, by its preservation of spatiotemporal unity, "the simple photographic respect for the unity of space."[24] The uninterrupted shot is therefore considered to reveal a meaning that is immanent in some presignified state, implying the film image to be an act of pure perception that offers an objective window on the world.

Conversely, there is the notion that meaning is produced by a juxtaposition of shots that gradually constructs a mental whole, or "image" in

Sergei Eisenstein's terms.[25] Cinema's specificity would lie, therefore, in its ability to mimic the process of association through which the mind reaches a dialectical understanding of the world. As such, film is aesthetically determined by its ability to organize singular ideas within syntactic relationships, its "imagist transformation of the dialectical principle": montage.[26] The sequence should mimic the act of consciousness and guide the spectator's reaction, suggesting that film is a subjective process that must produce meaning beyond the content of its individual shots.

Last, there is what I will call the *phenomenological* notion: that meaning lies in the interaction between the object and the subject of the image. This is my theory of the immanent field. I say "phenomenological" because, in this case, meaning lies neither solely in physical objects nor solely in the subjective apprehensions of these objects but in the interactive flux that binds the former to the latter, what Merleau-Ponty sought as "the synthesis of the subjective and objective experience of phenomena."[27] As Martin Jay argues, phenomenology aims to shed the Cartesian assumptions of a "spectatorial and intellectualist epistemology based on a subjective self reflecting on an objective world exterior to it."[28] In other words, and particularly in the works of Merleau-Ponty, phenomenology implies an attempt to understand both personal and artistic experience as a destruction of the hierarchy, dualism, and even the separation between subject and object. In his rejection of the transcendental subject, Merleau-Ponty dreamt of "regaining the experience of the intertwining of subject and object, which was lost in all dualistic philosophies."[29] According to such an approach, cinema's specificity would lie in its ability to dispel such a duality on numerous levels: within the shot itself, in the interaction between shot and sequence, and in its ability to change between and even integrate objective and subjective poles of representation. This is where film meets philosophy—not what films always do, but what film form is equipped to do.

Cinema helps to remind us that looking is itself an interaction with the world, and the medium can shift perspectives to alter our very notion of subjectivity. In doing so, it can open the immanent field as a praxis for the discursive interaction between characters, spectators, and the apparatus itself. Such a cinema challenges the division, or *"clivage"* as Merleau-Ponty puts it, between subject and object that is the basis for classical representation. By being able to show how we show, to bring to light how we signify and what our conventional forms connote, cinema is capable of breaking down the division instituted in our conventions of looking and offers the potential to achieve the fundamental goal of phenomenology: "to contest the very principle of this division, and to introduce the contact between the observer and observed into the definition of the real."[30]

This contact between viewer and viewed is a central topic of debate in film theory in general, and it has helped to shape many theorists' basic use of philosophy in analyzing the Seventh Art. The frame separates the viewing subject from the viewed world: what does this mean in terms of entire projects of cinematic expression and film criticism? As I propose in my introduction, this study aims at reconciling opposed approaches to film theory, and I will therefore look now at the aforementioned contrasting theories of Sergei Eisenstein and André Bazin, two examples from the canon of film theory that etch out two definitive stances on the philosophical possibilities of cinema. These positions are founded on opposing views of how cinema's transformation should mediate between world and spectator, and they offer especially good examples of how such concerns are articulated in terms of the relationship between shot and sequence—a formal binary particularly useful to rhetorical arguments that, I will argue, imply specific arrangements of subject-object relations. A detailed look at these theorists will help me to build a comparatist framework that will run throughout this book, as their differences reveal a fundamental rift between subjective and objective models, models that these theorists articulate according to a clear designation of how film's formal base *can* and *should* operate.

In "Two Types of Film Theory" Brian Henderson offers a useful platform for entering into this debate: "The real is the starting point for both Eisenstein and Bazin."[31] As Henderson continues, however, neither theorist provides a doctrine or definition of the real. Instead, their approaches are based on "cinema's relation to the real," a relation that is embedded for each in the formal interaction between shot and sequence. Polarized representatives of the duality between shot and montage, Eisenstein's and Bazin's respective theories are constructed around particular beliefs in film's capacity for simulating aspects of human subjectivity, be it as consciousness (Eisenstein) or perception (Bazin). Breaking down these analogies between formal cinematic practices and human processes of relating to the sensory world, I hope to provide a bridge between Eisenstein's and Bazin's viewpoints, weaning from the ideological trappings of each what are very useful insights concerning film meaning.

Both theorists extol cinema as an art but toward different purposes. On one hand, Eisenstein considers cinema an art only insomuch as it manifests conflict as its generative origin of meaning.[32] Conflict, realized through various levels of montage, creates juxtapositions that transcend the mere fragments of reality that one calls a shot, providing a more profound meaning than is offered by the content of a single image—as if presenting a thought or feeling. Bazin, on the other hand, views such an approach as a stylized manipulation of reality that should be avoided, as it distorts the world's original meaningfulness. According to Bazin's "Ontology of the Photographic Image," cinema is the apotheosis of art's attempt to preserve nature, to provide a replication as defense against our own mortality; and nature, for Bazin, is unified but ambiguous.[33] He thus focuses his aesthetics on a critique of montage as a manipulation of the ambiguity inherent in the photographic image's reproductive capabilities. The shot, however, is capable of preserving the complex meaning and spatiotemporal unity on the surface of external phenomena.

Henderson is perhaps incorrect, or at least exaggerating, when he criticizes Eisenstein as negligent of the aesthetics of the individual shot and Bazin for having "no sense . . . of the overall formal organization of films."[34] After all, Eisenstein wrote quite extensive analyses of the composition of individual shots, and Bazin possessed a unique ability to understand film texts according to their general aesthetic themes. Henderson is correct, though, to indicate the dichotomy between shot and montage as being central to what divides the two theorists, a division that is directly connected to their respective views on the ontology of film and its correlation to human experience. Like many of his Soviet contemporaries, Eisenstein insists that cinema is not meant to portray the world but to exceed it, to transform it: montage is, in his terms, the "means for the really important creative remolding of nature."[35] It is only through juxtaposing individual representations of nature that one can create an "image," a product (totality of juxtaposition) that qualitatively changes its factors (the individual representations that were juxtaposed).[36] Eisenstein adapts this central notion of juxtaposition to numerous elemental relations in film form, though it is particularly charged in his theory of montage between shots. The content of the frame is only a building block, the shot itself but a part of a greater whole. What is in the frame is only a stimulus to be combined with other stimuli, and the subject posited by the frame itself is subjugated to a transcendental associative subject that builds larger meanings from the juxtaposition of shots. For Eisenstein the immanent field takes shape on the level of sequential construction.

The overall effect of this interaction between elements is what Eisenstein considers a "transition from quantity to quality,"[37] as if the placement of two shots together suddenly renders each one something other than a shot, something more—something, perhaps, of philosophical impact or importance. Each shot affects the meaning of the other, and the consequent alteration of meaning further changes this relationship, thus retransforming each individual meaning once again. The final whole, or "image," whose overall meaning is not a picture but a dialectical process, Eisenstein considers analogous to human consciousness: "In the actual method of creating images, a work of art must reproduce the process whereby, in life itself, new images are built up in the human consciousness. . . . To create an image, a work of art must rely on a precisely analogous method, the construction of a chain of representations."[38]

The construction of this chain is what is known popularly as *montage*, and it provides the spectator with a constructed illusion of the dialectical process through which one gathers perceptions over time and builds composite understandings within a subjective arena separated from the objective origin of these individual perceptions. When Eisenstein refers to an "analogous method," he does not mean the analogue reproduction of material objects, but a structural similarity between the organizing process of film and that of human consciousness. Though looking at the interaction between shots as forming a larger immanent field of the image, I consider this not only as the construction of an overall system of reference but also as the interaction between multiple subjective positions. For the sake of propaganda Eisenstein avoided this interaction. Working in an overtly ideological context, he wanted to control which resultant judgment the spectator would arrive at. This manipulation consists of rhetorical practices generated through the relationship between mise-en-scène and montage. A classic example with which the reader may be familiar is from the closing sequence of Eisenstein's *Strike* (1925), which cuts from the image of Tsarist soldiers attacking a group of striking workers to a shot of a butcher violently slaughtering a bull, thus guiding the spectator to an understanding of the state police as hired murderers who treat the proletariat like animals. While Eisenstein clarifies for us the expressive potential of montage, I believe this to be a theory of how to use the image to achieve certain results, a notion of film embedded in a specific polemical strategy and not in determinants of the form itself. On a broader contextual level, Eisenstein's theories are ideologically attributable to a particular moment in history—the birth of Soviet communism and the promise of industrial utopia embraced by formalist artistic movements of the interwar period—that, in the wake of World War II, generated much skepticism as a result of how such rhetoric played out in the arena of global destruction and genocide.

Illustrating a historical intellectual shift toward rejecting the technocracy of fascism, film theorists after the war abandoned a certain idealism of what film expression could do to surpass the meaning inherent in nature and moved toward an argument that cinema was essentially meant to offer a nonbiased depiction of reality. Writing in the 1940s and 1950s, Bazin condemns the very style of manipulating reality that is central to Eisenstein's model, shifting his focus onto the camera's ability to reveal the meaning held in the source reality. In his seminal essay, "Ontology of the Photographic Image," Bazin traces the genealogy of art as the evolution of a primordial attempt to preserve humanity by reproducing it in the form of the image: "to save being through appearance."[39] For Bazin, however, this evolution was diverted by painting, which added an aesthetic aspect to this psychological desire for reproduction. This drift toward expressive manipulation was for Bazin the great sin of the Western artistic tradition, one that photography and, subsequently, cinema would rectify through the essential objectivism innate to the camera's mechanical process.[40] In conclusion Bazin claims that this "solution" lies not in the result but in the genesis of this reproduction, from which—in the case of the mechanical camera—man is excluded. For Bazin this gives cinema a particular ontological tendency toward aesthetic realism. Bazin is arguing for film as a transfer of the immanent field of reality itself. His writings extol cinema's potential to relinquish signification to its viewed source. But this leads to the inevitable question: of what does *representing reality* consist? I will argue that, for Bazin, this concept is grounded not in the content but in the form of the image—that is, it is a theory of film connotation.

Summarizing Bazin's argument, Peter Wollen writes, "Bazin's aesthetics asserted the primacy of the object over the image, the primacy of the natural world over the world of signs."[41] Bazin argues for a mode of cinema that embraces its potential as a reproductive tool, implying that the direct representation of material phenomena is a problem of form. Therefore, despite a general neglect of this facet of Bazin's argument, one could say that he is, in fact, very much concerned with film signification. Indeed, Bazin is not as naive as he is often accused of being: after discussing cinema's inheritance of photographic objectivity, he ominously ends his "Ontology" with the observation: "On the other hand, cinema is a language."[42] The impression of objectivity—like *any* connotative system—is never detached from the forms through which it is constructed. Bazin takes a particular side in his view of what cinema *should* be, an argument that takes shape according to a division between the semiotic ambiguity permitted by the shot and the semiotic certainty provided through montage, though Bazin does not himself explicitly refer to it in terms of semiotics. Bazin's most fervent formal argument is *against* the use of montage, claiming that it is an artificial dissection of the continuity of natural space-time and thus violates the precious ambiguity of reality.[43]

Whereas my book is concerned with ambiguity as being internal and essential to the image itself, and in fact very much where film and philosophy meet, ambiguity for Bazin is a criterion of realism, a property of the objective world. For Bazin the shot preserves the ambiguity of the world as it appears in natural perception, while editing tries to force one particular meaning onto a situation. Though "the abstract nature of montage is not absolute, at least psychologically," Bazin sees an absolute psychological function in the unity of the shot.[44] Bazin holds the subjective position posited by the frame as something sacred, because it allows for the ambiguity of what may pass in front of it, placing us in front of the real, whereas montage only alludes to the real.[45] We can make an important deduction from this evaluation of art and its mechanism: what is essential to Bazin's argument is not the real object itself but the phenomenological connotations of the mode of representation. Orson Welles's greatness, for example, lay not in his preservation of particular objects' essences but in his restoration of spatiotemporal continuity to the cinematic image, thus providing the spectator a certain ambiguity of perception through an unmediated visual depth.[46]

For Bazin cinematic objectivism is ultimately a matter of style (the negation of style is indeed a question of style!). Dudley Andrew frames this paradox as such: "arguing for a style that reduces signification to a minimum, Bazin sees the reduction of style as a potential stylistic option."[47] This conflict is apparent in Bazin's constant attempt to uphold the phenomenological traits of neorealism: he claims that the movement's common modes of representation know only immanence, a direct contact with sensory phenomena and the concrete world; yet he also finds it necessary to explain neorealism's individual aesthetic traits in terms of particular psychological characteristics of the diegetic subject (such as with the drab vision of bourgeois mediocrity in Rossellini's *Voyage to Italy* [1954]).[48] In other words, this stylistic reduction is still laden with signification, and one can extend this analysis to view the image as an immanent field wherein the subjectivities of the characters and of the apparatus interact. Despite many criticisms to the contrary, Bazin's view of neorealism is admittedly a connotative argument. Neorealism, he argues, is a humanism ("un humanisme") before it is a style of mise-en-scène, a worldview before it is an artistic school—a philosophy before it is a cinematic movement.[49] As such, Bazin's body of theory demonstrates how form itself, and specific formal practices, can provide the framework for a metaphysical understanding of the image.

I posit the split between Bazin's and Eisenstein's views of cinema as a connotative disagreement over whether film should be objective or subjective, as if they were approaching the image from opposite sides of the phenomenological spectrum. Whereas Eisenstein champions the subjective result of perception (the mental digestion of the seen, "consciousness" or "thought"), Bazin hopes to salvage the objectivism at the material origin of perception (what is being looked at, "vision"). On a philosophical level this divide is bridged by Merleau-Ponty's phenomenology; in his 1942 dissertation, "The Structure of Behavior," Merleau-Ponty reconciles what Vincent Descombes considers "the very French problem of the unity between body and soul" by showing that "I think" is based on "I perceive," and I will follow this lead on a cinematic level by refusing to separate the two formal elements of shot and montage.[50] Despite their differences, both signify—connote—to the extent that they imply the image to be a certain way of viewing the world, a certain type of image that provides a certain dynamic of subject-object relations. Each uses the frame to signify a subjective position; they just treat the subject of the frame differently.

This differentiation between *observing* reality and *interpreting* reality is an argument about film connotation based on the filmic distribution of subject-object relations, for observation and interpretation embody the two most common structures by which film differentiates between the image and the source of this image: the image-as-perception (referring to a mechanical viewing subject) and the image-as-consciousness (referring to a human subject). Because both of these are constructs of formal organization, it is important to remember that neither is more or less signifying than the other, more or less involved in a process of transformation, more or less genuine. But their interaction determines the order of meaning according to which the film itself becomes philosophical and, as such, can be understood in terms of how these theories breach the relationship between image and real. As Henderson notes, Bazin stops with the real, while Eisenstein goes beyond it.[51] Bazin's notion of cinema is a myth of the autonomy of the objective world, whereas Eisenstein's is a myth of the transcendence of subjective interpretation. Both of these, however, are myths inasmuch as they are conventionalized, through formal arrangements, to appear as essential aspects of the film medium. They are also myths in their implied exclusion of one another, their attempt to naturalize themselves as being total and eternal, and by being constructed according to a unilateral system of reference. In other words, they each imply a process of denotation without a formal base; they are both ultimately connotative arguments, but each one hides its connotative intentions.

These myths can be reconciled, indeed must be, as most films are a combination of the two, fluctuations between subjective and objective images, balancing acts between shot and montage. As Henderson reveals, Bazin's and Eisenstein's respective theories could be greatly enriched by an analysis of the relationship between shot, sequence, and entire film, or an analysis between filmic moments and the larger philosophy governing the distribution of subject-object relations across the text. I hope now to contribute exactly this through a comparative analysis of two films by Jean-Luc Godard.

JEAN-LUC GODARD AND THE VIEWING SUBJECT

Through exploring the philosophical ramifications of a theoretical construct (the shot as basis for dividing the viewing subject from viewed world) and the opposition of two critical standpoints regarding this element of film form, a certain polarity of the immanent field has become clearer. To make the best critical use of this theoretical construct, I now turn my attention toward actual film texts. By comparing two of Godard's

films, I will look at how a shot's system of reference can either be reinforced or contradicted through its place in a sequence and at what the
connotative ramifications of this are. Godard proves especially useful
here because, as Mitry notes, his modality of expression falls on the level
of the sequence, through which he manages (though not always, I will
argue) to destroy closed structures of meaning.[52]

Godard focuses on the sequential role of the sound-image, first as a
replication of natural perception and, later, as a revelation of the illusionary basis of this replication. It should come as no surprise, therefore, that
much criticism (usually positive, so one might call it praise) of Godard's
work revolves around impressions of ethnography, often resorting to the
critical analogy of perception. For example, the renowned scholar Marie-
Claire Ropars-Wuilleumier writes that Godard's films show "what existence offers to perception in an instant."[53] However poetic this description may be, and however much Godard himself may often attest (in
interviews and through his films) to such a goal, this is the very type of
criticism I am hoping to avoid here, as it convolutes the philosophical
importance of cinema as a fulcrum between the physical world, sensory
distribution, and human thinking. Nonetheless, Godard certainly reveals time and time again a concern for the relationship between cinema
and immediate experience. He refers in numerous interviews and articles to Merleau-Ponty's phenomenology, and his oeuvre poses many
questions concerning the relationship between human perception and
film representation. Yet an analysis of Godard's films dispels the very
myth of cinematic perception, in many ways through the constant self-
reflexive revelation of the apparatus in his films. The self-reflexive mode
developed in Godard's films finds an ebb and flow in *Vivre sa vie* and *Two
or Three Things I Know About Her*, each of which struggles—with varying degrees of success—with the notion of dialogism: dialogism, that is,
(1) as a mode of existence shown to define the relationship between characters and the diegetic world and (2) as a structure of representation between the cinematic apparatus and the content that it transforms. I will
posit this dialogism as a function of the immanent field that binds different voices and discourses.

These two films have much in common, from their technical production to their content. They were both shot by Godard's regular cinematographer during this period, Raoul Coutard, thus providing a continuity
of visual sensibility; moreover, each film is about daily life in Paris or its

suburbs, a city increasingly marked by signs of consumer capitalism and indifference to its human inhabitants. More specifically, each film regards a woman's balance of daily life as a prostitute, the quotidian struggle of an individual that is marginalized in patriarchal society. Not only are these films about prostitution "as a metaphor for the study of a woman,"[54] as Siew Hwa Beh comments, or as a symbol of *woman* as others have remarked; they are, in Godard's words, films about prostitution as a metaphor for life in Western capitalist society, where "one is forced to live . . . according to laws similar to those of prostitution."[55] Prostitution becomes an overarching metaphor in Godard's work, both on the surface and in the depths of films such as *Vivre sa vie*, *Contempt* (1963), *A Married Woman* (1964), and *Two or Three Things I Know About Her*. As Wheeler Winston Dixon notes, "Prostitution, no matter what form it takes, is an obsession for Godard,"[56] an epic metaphor that extends to characters' behavior, society at large, and the philosophical problem of subject and object as manifested by film form and the conventions of film language. During this period prostitution serves as a load-bearing issue for Godard that implicates mainstream cinematic conventions in a critique of capitalist values, while also reflecting on a more existential problem of the individual being both subject and object, having agency and being used, according to the order of meaning enforced by the cultural practices and social interactions of Western capitalism. The problem of simultaneously being subject and object is not posed only on a narrative level, however; Godard, in fact, erects it as a fundamental formal problem of the image itself and of cinema as an institution. It is this form of representation that I am concerned with here, and a comparative analysis of films with similar stories should be a fruitful way to foreground the analysis of formal differences.

It is fascinating how two films can construct very different systems of meaning out of generally similar story points: woman, prostitution, the city, the cinema. Like all films, each of these has its own unique aesthetic structure, its own balance between part and whole, and, to extend the central problems of this chapter, its own treatment of the subject of the frame. Godard claims that *Vivre sa vie* was made with nearly no editing, more or less put together in the order that the rushes were returned.[57] This claim to the low priority given to planned editing during the production shoot is supported by the film's reliance on framing and movement to guard subjectivity at all times in the eye of the camera. Throughout the film, framing and camera movements provide the spatial alienation of diegetic subjects from each other, also denying the implication that any character is motivating the movements and shifts of the apparatus. *Two or Three Things I Know About Her* reverses this system, using montage and sound design to contradict the camera-subject and to represent the characters as objects that are also free as independent subjects. This destruction of the hierarchy between subject and object is accentuated by the use of offscreen voices and direct address, each of which challenge the autonomy of the viewing subject posited by the frame. Moreover, material objects—from small to large, faucet to building—are composed in the frame as if to manifest subjective agency, objects turned subjects through the connotative potential of cinematic form. The connections between subjects and objects (and other subjects) rest in the contextual bonds implied by the relationship connecting frame, shot, and sequence, an immanent field in which the difference between subject and object is constantly in flux.

Vivre sa vie and the Classical Viewing Subject

Godard's third feature film, *Vivre sa vie* played an integral part in European art cinema of the early 1960s. Challenging traditional modes of film expression while also maintaining a certain classical aesthetic, it joins *A Woman Is a Woman* (1961) and *Contempt* as Godard's eulogy for classical cinema.

As is the case for most of Godard's films, the actual narrative substance is, in a conventional sense, quite sparse: this is the story of Nana (played by Anna Karina, Godard's wife from 1961 to 1966, and the heroine of seven of his films during this time), a young woman in Paris who works in a record store and then becomes a prostitute to make ends meet. Much in the vein of Godard's work in general, *Vivre sa vie* has been viewed predominantly as a film that "subverts conservative conventions and experiments with possibilities."[58] Reviews, almost unanimously laudatory, typically focus on the film's inherent claim to being a sort of formal liberation and point to how this complements the ethnographic approach to the story. For example, Beh writes: "In order to deal with the complexity of the subject matter, the film's structure and Godard's style are an integral part of our understanding of Nana and prostitution."[59] Beh is primarily talking about the film's narrative structure here, which is based on a transposition of literary forms (predominantly journalistic and novelistic) onto fiction film, such as in the use of chapter headings and sociological statistics. The style, however, does not help us to understand the character nor the topic of prostitution so much as it connotes its own neutrality as an image-type. I will argue, against the popular reading of the film, that *Vivre sa vie* maintains a philosophical classicism despite its progressive politics and innovative style. Few people familiar with this work refuse the opinion that it is a film of great aesthetic beauty, human tenderness, and stylistic innovation. I agree wholeheartedly. That said, and despite the film's many gestures toward its own philosophical prowess (including a chapter titled "Nana Does Philosophy," which consists entirely of a conversation between Nana and real-life philosopher, Brice Parain), it is necessary to debate romanticized readings of the text and to question certain contradictions inherent in its modes of representation, so as to consider the philosophical ramifications of its connotative order.

A principled defiance of illusionist cinema that is ironically rife with homage, *Vivre sa vie* employs Brechtian devices while retaining a visual structure that is faithful to an absolute camera-subject, an epistemological approach that places the origin of all meaning in the camera's gaze. The film is not, as Jean-Pierre Esquenazi claims (vocalizing a wealth of similar criticism), the vision of a camera "endowed with an autonomous conscience"[60] but is, instead, a network of representations meant to isolate the camera as the sole source of meaning, a camera that is, as Kaja Silverman points out, more motivated than Godard lets on.[61] In other words it is a romanticized metaphor to claim that the camera itself has a conscience, and a fantastic exaggeration to describe a machine that requires human handling to be autonomous, though the image *is* constructed to give the impression of its *being a type of image* that possesses these faculties.

The introductory sequence of the film provides a key to this connotative platform. The opening credits are interspersed with three silhouetted shots of Nana: left profile, frontal, and right profile. Belying his roots in phenomenology, Edgar Morin points out that the succession of multiple shots with the same object allows cinema to set in place a process of complementary perception "that moves from the fragmentary to the total, from the multiplicity to the unicity of the image."[62] But is this practice natural, or naturalized? I would argue the latter. This sequence could be seen to simulate an epistemological process based on the following progression: the content in the frame is the object of inquiry; the understanding of this object occurs through perception; perception occurs through the frame. According to Merleau-Ponty, understanding is built on perception; does understanding therefore imply a perceptive act? Is this the philosophical trick Godard is playing, using the tools of film form for his connotative sleight of hand? We perceive; therefore, we understand; or perhaps more accurately: we understand; therefore, we must have perceived. Should the angle of viewing this content change, but the frame's relationship to the object remain the same, it is as if there was one stable viewing subject, as if the same subject completed a circle around the object. In this series of shots we can see an attempt to construct a totality from multiple perspectives; though cutting among different positions, each shot is framed the same, refers to the same transcendental viewing subject.

The abundance of close-ups of Nana in the film has led many to view the film as a "documentary of a face,"[63] suggesting Godard's clear obsession with his real-life lover and also implying a truth-claim or documentary authenticity attached to the formal structure. While the camera may, for the most part, resist being motivated by narrative factors, it is systematically motivated by philosophical factors, to connote its resultant image as being a certain type of image. But what of the content of this documentary, the object of this humanism? In this opening sequence the character is captured in a manner that differentiates her as an object, an other being enclosed or encircled by a perceiving subject-function. The humanistic or ethnographic element of documentation is here a contradiction of method: the form acts as a sympathizing external representation of her psychological state while disposing of her independent subjectivity. Foreshadowing for us how this contradiction will be realized at the end of the film, the circle performed by the camera ends by slipping out of its own enclosed signification: the last shot is of Nana's back, in a café, thus beginning the first scene of the narrative diegesis.

The entire first scene cuts between one-shots of two people seen from behind, never allowing them in the same frame at the same time, binding them only by their separation and by the space reflected in the mirror in front of them. This denial of faces is also in a way the denial of the identity of its perceived objects. Beh claims that this framing "immediately alienates us" as spectators.[64] The frame's relation to the image actually gives us a privileged position, however, slightly hidden and voyeuristic, alienating only the characters from each other and even from themselves (that is, alienating the sound of their voices from the image of their mouths). The system of reference, one could say, is protected, affirmed, rooted. *Vivre sa vie* thrives on a connotative limitation of the immanent field, an alienation of its characters both from the camera-subject and from each other, a dual effect of the frame constantly reaffirmed by what I will call the *enclosed shift*, a hallmark of Godard's and Coutard's visual style during this period. In the enclosed shift the camera tracks slightly from side to side, often having the effect of isolating a character in the frame while that character is meant to be interacting with another character otherwise in spatial proximity; this slight movement highlights the frame's absolute nature, its impermeability and decisiveness.

Every occurrence of this effect takes place during a conversation, notable in a film that V. F. Perkins summarizes as "a string of suggestions as to how one *might* film a conversation."[65] David Bordwell cites this quote in leading to his own view that "*Vivre sa vie*'s stylistic devices achieve a structural prominence that is more than simply ornamental." Yet, in keeping with the goal of his own methodology, Bordwell refuses to assign to them "thematic meanings."[66] I would argue, however, that we should assign to these devices the thematic meanings that Bordwell rejects, as the constant use of this visual pattern has identifiable connotative significance, expressed through the film's structure of relations between the camera and the people it films. This effect heightens the tension concerning the interaction between what exists inside and outside the frame, revealing both how close two humans can be without sharing anything from their respective interiors and how the immanent field of the image can be closed. This closure, I will argue in the next chapter, is a function of the relationship between denotation and connotation. The frame seems to imply a sphere around the viewed object, like a Leibnizian monad; but, while it may provide continuity between spheres, it refuses their permeation. These two humans are not allowed to be part of the same stream of information, the same visual message. This thematic visual design guarantees the source of the frame as the origin of meaning, the subject according to which the world is organized, and everything in front of it is a series of disconnected objects. However, this monolithic system of reference is challenged a couple of times in the text, when the film grants

Nana her due subjectivity, giving us an example of the dialogism we will find to be the defining characteristic of *Two or Three Things I Know About Her.*

The best example occurs in the film's most iconic scene, in which Nana sits in a cinema and watches the Carl Theodor Dreyer classic *The Passion of Joan of Arc* (1928).[67] An intertextual montage, this sequence does not juxtapose two times or places but, instead, crosscuts between two entire connotative orders: as Nana's tears echo those of the heroine in the film she is watching, we are absorbed into a self-reflexive crystal, and the immanent field becomes saturated with a second immanent field. This is Eisensteinian montage par excellence, as it conflates the two different visual subjects (the camera watching Nana and the camera watching Joan of Arc [Maria Falconetti]) and transcends them through the subjectivity of a larger relational structure. The spectator is caught in a mode of transferred identification that is all the more powerful because it is circular, because we see ourselves in Nana, in Nana's viewing of a character in whom she sees herself (figs. 1.1, 1.2). The spectator is propelled by montage to identify not so much with Nana as with her process of viewing, her own act of identification with the tragic character, and as such Nana becomes implicated in the system of reference.

This mixture of self-reflexivity and intertextuality creates an effect similar to the Brechtian notion of distanciation, which can be found elsewhere in this film in devices—such as chapter titles and direct address—used to redirect attention toward the formal or connotative base itself. This particular scene allows a crack in the edifice of the camera-subject on two levels; the spectator is asked here to identify with Nana's process of identification while at the same time being made self-conscious of how this very process is structured for us cinematically, producing a moment of experimental thinking that provides a philosophical challenge to conventional subject-object arrangements.

One would have trouble arguing with Beh's reading of this as an intertextual commentary on the plight of women: Nana is prostituted, a martyr to capitalist patriarchy, forced to suffer for her agency much as Joan's assumption of a typically male-oriented power to act was depicted as witchery and punished with death.[68] While this is the transposition of a discursive argument (similarity of representations) onto a comparison of narrative meanings (similarity of situations), it nonetheless manages to

FIGURES 1.1 AND 1.2

In *Vivre sa vie* (1962) a captivated Nana (Anna Karina) watches the inquisition and sentencing of Joan of Arc (Maria Falconetti) in Carl Theodor Dreyer's *La passion de Jeanne d'Arc* (1928).

capture the complexity of what is perhaps the film's one great lapse in connotative obstinacy: the camera's subject-function is momentarily betrayed by the permission of an image for which it was not the implied source. The presence of Dreyer's film slips the text out of the camera's control, and the image is at this moment defined through Nana's subjective act of spectatorship.

This scene embodies the text's struggle between a nostalgia for cinema's early grandeur and a modernist disillusionment with this grandeur, attracting our identification with a representation of spectatorship that also shocks us into a sense of self-awareness or consciousness of the apparatus. Another such challenge to the monolithic, objective system of reference is offered through the point-of-view tracking shot wherein Nana dances around the billiards table. This exemplifies the immediate dialogical shift, possible in cinema, from a subjective (fig. 1.3) to an objective (fig. 1.4) representation, from the perspective of a diegetic subject to that of a transcendental subject, as if Nana's own subjectivity were being sacrificed so that she might be objectified.

The narrative theme of prostitution establishes this problem for us as a diegetic concern, though this is inseparable from the film's modes of representation: there is a reflexive similarity between the alienating effect that Nana's job has on her and the manner through which Godard relates her to the camera, one that has been analyzed according to a psychoanalytic approach that I will not necessarily adopt.[69] This particular cut makes a phenomenological connection between the character's interior view of the world and her external position as an object viewed in that world. For a moment, we are being looked at *with* Nana, from her perspective, before we go back to looking *at* her. Unfortunately, this is the extent to which Nana is granted subjective agency in the film, and the formal pretense of ethnographic representation gives way in the end to conventional narrative motivations. Just as is foreshadowed by an overt reference to Poe's "The Oval Portrait," Godard ultimately leaves his heroine dead. The film concedes its visual goals and consents to the narrative rule; as Rancière would put it, the rationality of the intrigue ends by dominating the sensible effect of the spectacle.[70] The generic cliché through which the film abruptly wraps itself up has been contested as either disappointingly extrafilmic or apt in its intertextual nature. In an otherwise praiseworthy review, Susan Sontag criticizes the end of the film for its sudden abandonment of the enclosed text, through which it is

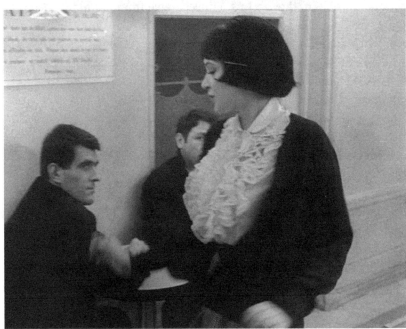

FIGURES 1.3 AND 1.4
Nana makes her way around a pool hall, looking for clients.

"clearly making a reference outside the film."[71] Beh criticizes Sontag's analysis for ignoring the intertextual practice of the entire film.[72]

I read in this debate the film's attempt to balance itself between the closed text (the film as an object of perception from one stable viewing position) and the open text (dialogic enunciation, Brechtian effects, self-conscious moments of reflexivity). Both critics, however, seem to neglect the fact that this reference to the generic closure of classical gangster films offers no indication that it is more than the invasion of the text by a narrative convention, an argument against overinterpretation that I would support and Godard himself asserts.[73] With the high level of film literacy Godard amassed during his decades at the Cinémathèque and as a critic for *Cahiers du cinéma*, and given the degree of improvisation allowed in his film shoots (ninety-minute films often based on no more than a few pages of script), it is not surprising—nor something that even the biggest fan of Godard should deny—that the director often reverts to a reliance on the type of cliché his oeuvre so successfully deconstructs. This reliance on a generic convention offers the perfect example of a closed cinematic meaning, a circular closure on the film's origin of meaning.

Overall, the textual system of shot, sequence, and whole in *Vivre sa vie* weaves a mode of representation common in filmic expression: it implies an objectivity in the representation through the connotation of a total system of reference, that of the camera. In doing so, it embraces a classical epistemology in the Althusserian sense: it arranges a differentiation between source and representation meant to "oppose a given subject to a given object and to call knowledge the abstraction by the subject of the essence of the object."[74] This is the very opposite of Merleau-Ponty's goal with phenomenology. *Vivre sa vie*, in all its unconventional stylizations, refers to a connotative system that denies the subjectivity of its viewed objects and, ultimately, closes the production of meaning off to the spectator. But this is, of course, the cinematic norm, the classical and conventional model for the film image. How might these epistemological assumptions be challenged? How could this differentiation be breached? In this film Godard offers certain clues toward such a cinema, a dialogic cinema of *being in the world* that challenges the hierarchies of conventional representation. Cinema has proven itself curious about, and perhaps even capable of, reconciling the interior with exterior, the subjective with the objective—a possibility of dialogic relations that falls short in

Vivre sa vie but succeeds more fully in what remains as perhaps the great moment of philosophical clarity in Godard's oeuvre: *Two or Three Things I Know About Her.*

Intersubjectivity in *Two or Three Things I Know About Her*

As opposed to the absolute subject of the frame that anchors *Vivre sa vie* to a continuous system of reference, in *Two or Three Things I Know About Her* the weight of signification falls to the creation of a dialogic network spread between the frame, the objects viewed, and even voices external to the diegesis. In creating this network, Godard reveals and proceeds to scramble cinema's conventional division between subject and object, a reflexive mode that demonstrates "how questions about the institution of cinema are immediately posed by a consideration of the object."[75] This film, in other words, formulates the problem of differentiation and agency as an inherently cinematic problem of the immanent field. Here, as in Godard's oeuvre in general, "consideration of the object" is extended to the consideration of *woman-as-object*, metaphorized by the social institution of prostitution. This time the story is of Juliette (Marina Vlady), mother of two, living in the tenement suburbs and being forced into prostitution by the economic demands of late capitalism. Trading the classical black-and-white composition of *Vivre sa vie* for a flattened color image, this film, as MacCabe and Mulvey point out, "marks a move away from the exotic perception of a woman's selling of her sexuality present in *Vivre sa vie* and *A Married Woman*."[76] The term *exotic perception* can be attached to the Althusserian notion of epistemology previously described, a kind of colonizing of the other inherent to the differentiation of the viewing subject and viewed object, a differentiation contested in this film.

The title itself, in all its ambiguity, introduces many of the film's themes. First, with "Two or Three Things" there is the notion of itemization, presented in the film in three forms: narrative itemization of the banal rituals that make up daily life (washing dishes, preparing for bed, etc.); itemization of the ubiquitous signs of consumerism, epitomizing the proto–pop art themes contemporaneously prevalent in works such as Roland Barthes's *Mythologies* and Georges Perec's *Things*;[77]; and, most important here, itemization of subjective experience through the sequential representation of context provided by the film's patterns of montage. Furthermore, there resides in the title the nondescript dynamic between speaking subject-function ("I") and the Paris of 1966 ("Her") that is known by this subject. This enunciating "I," vocalized by Godard's voice-over commentary, is constantly revealed to lack any totality of perspective. It is the subject of the frame, revealed and therefore displaced as just another part of the dialogic field constructed by the sequencing of shots. The rejection of a single coherent source of meaning, I will argue, is constantly "emphasized by the dissociation of sound and image and the increased use of montage."[78]

This film, as may already be clear, utilizes a radically different visual dynamic from that of *Vivre sa vie*. Immobile nearly the entire film, the camera of *Two or Three Things I Know About Her* does not duplicate or mimic human perception through depth-of-field or acts of movement, yet the frame is also rendered incomplete. The viewing subject is frustrated, but there is also no qualitative idea, building through the montage of shots, that would connote a transcendental subject. A visual design belying Godard's affinity for documentary television, the frame creates little blocks of static meaning that interact with one another through the construction of a common context: Paris and its surrounding area. The juxtaposition of images offers us a mutual space shared by person, material object, and system of representation. This visual structure respects the notion, as Merleau-Ponty observes, that the world (like the cinematic image) is an immanent field of interaction, "not only the sum of things that fall or could fall before our eyes, but also the place of their compossibility."[79] Contrary to the human condition explored in the existentialism of Sartre, Merleau-Ponty insists that the role of the philosopher extends beyond the individual, to the shared space of meaning created between us, which is where we move beyond the concrete and into the symbolic: "The question is to know whether, as Sartre maintains, there are only *men* and *things*, or whether there is not also this interworld which we call history, symbolism and the truth remaining to be accomplished."[80]

This is the philosophical—or, specifically, phenomenological—project at play in *Two or Three Things I Know About Her*; as Godard puts it in an article he wrote while shooting, the film's goal is to arrive at a representation of the *"ensemble,"* the relationships between things.[81] In terms of my attempt here to understand how this philosophical foundation is transposed onto the connotative plane, this ensemble could be seen as a reduction of the film to its immanent field of relations. Keeping true to the director's word, this film achieves what *Vivre sa vie* could not because it acknowledges other subject-functions than that of the camera. *Two or Three Things I Know About Her* combines a variety of systems of reference that Godard enumerates under four categories, which he could not have phrased more aptly for this study: "objective description of objects," "objective description of subjects," "subjective description of objects," and "subjective description of subjects."[82] Godard makes clear here, in explicitly Merleau-Pontian terms, his desire to break down the conventional subject-object dynamics of cinema and to reconfigure them according to a philosophical model, which necessitates a shift in the hierarchical relationship between form and content. Taking this ensemble further, one could argue that a nonnarrative system of montage predominates within the frame (colors, shapes), between individual shots, and also between the frame and what is offscreen. What lies outside the frame, be it an object in narrative space (Juliette's reference to clothing that the spectator never sees but is part of the open diegetic space) or an anonymous voice-over (the "I" that knows two or three things, spoken from behind the camera), persistently makes its presence known, creating a dialogism in which the frame is no longer the delimitation of the film's message.

Two or Three Things I Know About Her arrives thus at a juxtaposition between presence and absence, seen and unseen, a confession of the arbitrariness and partiality of any representation—a balance between what Merleau-Ponty might refer to as the "visible" (sensory world) and the "invisible" (meaning).[83] This critique of the shot bears the influence of Dziga Vertov's paradigm of montage, or "montage of ideas" as Mitry calls it, which denies any predetermined narrative mode of subject positioning.[84] The Vertovian source of viewing is intrinsic to the phenomenon of the visible that it reconstructs for our regard, and reproducing this cinematically cannot occur through only a single shot. Its mode of perception, Jean-Philippe Trias notes, is an "atomized perception"[85] and is therefore not comparable to human perception, refusing the implication of an absolute system of reference and rejecting the analogy of a camera-consciousness. Deleuze and, later, Rancière observe that this notion of the shot's relation to montage, as opposed to that of Bazin or Eisenstein, is an attempt to place subjectivity within the transformative process of the moving sound-image, within the immanent field, and not according to one signified position of perception or one overall qualitative meaning, thus implicating the subject in the symbiotic creation of meaning on equal terms as the object (or other subjects).[86] Through this, Godard claims not to want to uncover a universal truth but to reveal a contextualization that binds people with their objective surroundings, not some "global and general truth, but a certain 'feeling of the ensemble.'"[87]

For example, we see a macrocontext, followed by an interview with a person who functions within that context, followed by a brief scene in the microcontext where that person was interviewed. These shots are audiovisual fragments that form a sequential logic or order of meaning that, instead of constructing causal narration or economy of action, weaves a portrait of people's coexistence with their surroundings, an expression of the "totality of experience" that is, according to David MacDougall, the goal of ethnographic film.[88] This "totality of experience" is integrated into an overall textual network of signification that attempts to reveal what Merleau-Ponty calls "singular existence," wherein one hopes to describe a specific person's experience not only by watching her (as in *Vivre sa vie*) but by letting her speak and by revealing her relationship with everything around her.[89] This notion of contextualization, however, is of more interest to my argument as a question not so much of the content, which I believe Godard is referring to, but of the immanent field provided by the formal organization of this content.

Two or Three Things I Know About Her proposes the direct engagement with—and independent image of—a location in order to create ideas surrounding the conditions of its inhabitants. This juxtaposition between urbanity and humanity is performed through alluded presence (the form of montage mentioned above: a shot of a person followed or preceded by a shot of the city) and direct presence (the form of the image: a person being interviewed before an urban backdrop). In the latter a lack of depth-of-field flattens the relationship, accentuating the proximity of the buildings, the inescapable importance of context. This effect denies the difference of spatiality, merging the characters with their material context and, also, the spectator with the content of the visible image. The presence and even proximity of the city becomes part of the immanent field, a limitation of the dimensions already limited by the frame (fig. 1.5).

As Mulvey and MacCabe put it, the Parisian suburb of *Two or Three Things I Know About Her* is "filled with earthmovers and bulldozers which are changing the city's spatial relations."[90] The new space is marked by gray lines and sharp angles that conflict with the soft peachy roundness of the human forms; placing commercial growth before the

FIGURE 1.5
In *Two or Three Things I Know About Her* (1966) flattened images emphasize the shared space between human subject and urban object.

welfare of its inhabitants, it is a space of destruction and reconstruction generated by inorganic materials and machines, providing a spatial relation that negates the space of individual human agency. Moreover, it is a space in direct contradiction of the frame and the frame's immanent structuring of visual subjectivity.

This combination of architectural framing and dehumanization of the city's inhabitants implies the transformation of people into nonpeople, into what one might call objects, while also permitting the material world a certain agency—or subjectivity—to act on its inhabitants. The buildings are framed as if they exercise a social power, altering spatial relations and reconfiguring the world of their inhabitants, thus breaking down the barrier between human subject and material object. These buildings almost seem to be mimicking the frame, as if they provide their own frames and, consequently, their own subjective vantages (fig. 1.6).

As becomes clear, film form itself raises the question of what exactly the difference is between subject and object. After all, depending on how things are organized, depending on what the point of reference is, can't all things be both? As Merleau-Ponty might say, aren't humans themselves both subject, with a unique perspective of experiencing the world, and object *in* the world? And, do objects not have an agency in our interactions with the material world? The question of the interchangeability between subject and object, also present on the allegorical level concerning the role of prostitution in the narrative, is further complicated by the

FIGURE 1.6
The perceptual agency of urban architectural frames.

film's recurrent use of the close-up—not just of faces, as in *Vivre sa vie*, but of objects. The close-up poses a three-tier juxtaposition: one between spatial sizes, another between sound and image, and the last between active subject and material object. The close-up is not only capable of revealing something in microscope, but, furthermore, it has the capacity to pull an ordinary object out of relief and to give it agency—to make it the subject, or "actor object" as Fernand Léger put it[91]—and to explode it, to make it so absurdly large that an otherwise easily missed feature adopts a heavy significance. This serves a purpose beyond the epistemological usefulness of the close-up, demarcated numerous times in film theory, as the epitome of cinema's ability to view the unseen world that is hidden from the limited abilities of the human eye. In such an image, as Münsterberg points out, a detail becomes the entire visual content on which we can concentrate our senses and emotions.[92] It shatters the law of containment proposed by the frame. Inverting many popular theories of the gaze, I would argue that looking closely at a nonhuman object does not necessarily objectify it but, in fact, gives it its very own agency and allows us to identify with it. Something else happens as well, something in the immanent field itself—there is a fundamental shift in the relationship between what is viewed and the system for viewing it. The object overflows the frame, as well as the system of reference to which the frame is connected (fig. 1.7): the image becomes the object itself and not the act of looking at the object. Not only does this suggest the sublimity of an otherwise overlooked object, but it also suggests the ambiguity of what separates

FIGURE 1.7
Objects acting as subjects.

an object from a subject, both conceptually and spatially—and, moreover, it forces one to consider how the same thing can be both. This is the
very type of experimental thinking provided by Godard's formal play,
through which this film transcends the narration of philosophical ideas
and actually configures subject-object relations to demystify the classical
subject and to challenge our centered view of the world and our place
therein.

Noël Burch writes that the close-up was originally intended to avoid
"any disorientation of the spectator in respect to his or her own 'reasoned'
analysis of the spatial continuum."[93] In this film, however, the close-up
exceeds that spatial function. Rather, a material object has been transposed onto an aesthetically designated subject-function: a building that
looms and casts you into the shadows, a faucet that floods the world with
water. This is not anthropomorphism but the object's agency, its ability to
act or to affect, be it due to its three-dimensionality or its function. The
dialogic field is spread beyond that of human voices, human agents. A
more complex example of this is the famous close-up of a swirling spiral
of coffee foam, which includes into this dialogism another sensory element as well. This scene is complicated, first of all, by the fact that the
image is not attached to one source of viewing: it could be the camera's
view, but it could also be that of the man whose coffee it is, or of Juliette,
each of whom are shown in the act of looking at it (figs. 1.8–1.10).

The question of identifying the viewing subject is extended further to
the codification of speech and image, issues I will deal with in the next

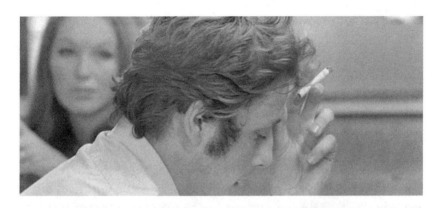

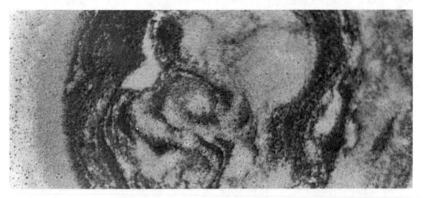

FIGURES 1.8–1.10
The legendary galactic coffee cup.

two chapters. The juxtaposition of a voice-over soliloquy, concerning the circular nature of the production of meaning in the universe, allows the image of coffee bubbles to become a visual metaphor for the entire galaxy. It is transformed once by the camera, and again by the words, an immanent field not only of different subject-functions but also of different signifying systems and different sensory elements. The audible words of a nondiegetic speaking subject transfer the origin of meaning onto the shot itself, the representation created through sound and image, which then takes on an agency of its own. This audiovisual representation follows what Rancière calls the "rhetorical-poetic principle" of the metaphor, a crisscrossing between image and sound: "words that hide themselves by making us see images that render themselves invisible by making us listen."[94]

The meaning of the words is enveloped in the image, while the original referent of the image (coffee) is effaced by the words, as if each separate signifying mechanism takes on a completely different intention as a result of its relation to the other. The combination of spoken words and visual image produces a sort of interference between themselves, or interference in our conventional way of making sense, thus destroying the hierarchy between sources of meaning. By contextually linking both sensory agents and viewing subjects, an open whole is constructed from the space that binds the parts. The nexus of this intersection is the arena of discourse that is the immanent field. Similarly, in this film the frame centralizes the speaking character as subject, while the voice-over constantly brings to the forefront the fact that this character is part of a fiction. Breaking two rules of the illusion of separation between the viewed world and the subject behind the frame, Godard's voice-over acknowledges that the content is a fabrication, and the viewed character looks directly into the camera, speaking directly to us (figs. 1.11–1.13): "*She, she is* Marina Vlady, she is an actress. . . . *Right now she turns her head to the right, but this is not important. . . . She, she is* Juliette Jansen . . ."

By adding voice-over commentary that refuses to demarcate the viewed world as separate from the structure of the image, *Two or Three Things I Know About Her* divests itself of a fundamental division between subject and object. The mixture of voice-over speech and visual direct address denies the text any singular speaking or viewing subject-function, creating a self-reflexive dialogue not only between the characters and their context but also between the represented world and the form

FIGURES 1.11–1.13

Juliette Jansen (Marina Vlady) moves her head in response to Godard's nondiegetic voice-over, pausing to look directly into the camera.

through which it is being shown. That these crisscrossing semiotic fields are deconstructed on both visual and aural levels helps to introduce many issues that I will confront in the following chapters.

Here I have looked at the primary secretion of an external viewing subject through the construction of the shot, how this system of reference maintains itself and also how it can be challenged through the sequence of shots, the organization of the image (depth, close-ups) and the use of speech. These formal elements and interactions provide what D. N. Rodowick calls the mobility of point of view in cinema, through which it "breaks with the conditions for "natural" perception upon which phenomenology is based.[95] To paraphrase Bazin, there are phenomenological aspects of cinema's immanent field, but film is also a medium of signification. While film may not be an act of natural perception and therefore necessitates more than a basic phenomenological mode of analysis, it is capable—through its inherent forms of flux and transformation—of preserving what Amédée Ayfre referred to as "phenomenological realism," pursuing the philosophical embrace of ambiguous meaning and the beautiful uncertainty of polyphony and difference.[96] The classical subject is a normative construction offered as the basis for a particular form of denoting, which *Two or Three Things I Know About Her* rejects, relieving itself of the necessity of enforcing a closed system of meaning and shifting the focus from the denotative level of signification to the connotative level of signification. The philosophical performance of this film demands that we now turn to a more devoted and detailed study of film semiotics in order to establish the intersections between phenomenology and film signification. What is the relationship in cinema between denotation and connotation, and how can we use this difference to systematize the theoretical meeting place of film and philosophy according to the framework of subject-object relations?

In a film . . . to the extent to which its discourse is treated by collectivity, there are elements in play that are not directly symbolic, but already interpreted, culturalized even, conventionalized; and these elements can constitute secondary systems of signification imposed on the analogical discourse that we could call "rhetorical elements" or "elements of connotation." They constitute, therefore, a possible object of semiology.

—Roland Barthes, "Sémiologie et cinema"

IN THE PREVIOUS CHAPTER I USED PRINCIPLES OF PHENOMENOLOGY to lay the foundation for analyzing film in terms of subject-object relations. Through analysis of Eisenstein's and Bazin's theoretical approaches, followed by a comparative assessment of two films by Jean-Luc Godard, I demonstrated that, while there are certain similarities between the organizations provided by film form and direct human experience, it might nonetheless be best to do away with such metaphors as camera-perception or image-as-consciousness. Humans are humans, and film is film. And while the latter observation may offer insights into the condition of the former, both within its constructs and through the fact that it is a technological extension of the human cultural endeavor, it would be an injustice to both to reduce them to an identical comparison. Instead, I will direct my analysis to how cinema, as a form, organizes its sets of relations and how such organizations produce and reflect orders of meaning in ways that might coincide with philosophical activity, perpetuating traditional ways of understanding the world and, possibly, even providing us with experimental modes of thinking, new ways of configuring our relationship with each other and the world around us.

We have seen, especially with *Two or Three Things I Know About Her*, that film is more complicated than the simple organization of a visual field and a viewing subject, and have thus encountered two more problems concerning the organization of the sound-image: the question of enunciation and the element of speech. Saving the problem of speech for chapter 3, I will look in this chapter at the question of cinema as enunciation and, in doing so, will build toward an understanding of the relationship between what is enunciated and the form of this enunciation, a relationship I call connotation. But what is *film* connotation, or connotation in film? I would argue that the most diverse of approaches—Eisenstein, Arnheim, Bazin, Baudry, Deleuze, for example—are all fundamentally concerned with this very issue, and while the value judgments of film connotation (in particular, those concerning race, class, gender, and sexuality) have guided much of film criticism, *how* connotation operates in film has not received systematic consideration. I will attempt to clarify in this chapter what I mean by connotation and how theorizing it would be aided by the phenomenological foundation set in place in chapter 1. But to approach questions concerning connotation, it is necessary to move beyond the phenomenological metaphysics of the human gestalt, to a study of the film sign.

The varied voices of film semiotics tend to agree on one point: there are two aspects of film signification, that which is shown in the image and the way of showing it. The first of these, denotation, provides in Julia Lesage's words "the visual 'stuff' for film."[1] While it may be incorporated into narrative structures, film denotation is first and foremost based on a code of resemblance, through which objects are presented in a form analogous to how we perceive them in the real world. This process of coding is itself part of another aspect of signification, connotation, which many have argued is the *primary* system of meaning; as Roland Barthes claims in the quote at the beginning of this chapter, film connotation— the "culturalized" philosophy that guides its construction of denotation—is not beyond the grasp of our study, and I would argue that it is the necessary starting place for a semiotics of film. After all, the power of denotation lies only in its closed form—the guarantee that its meaning be clear, which necessitates a formal totality that implies its content to be inevitable, universal, and thus inflexible to philosophical inquiry or doubt. Barthes dedicated much of S/Z to this very argument, to which end he notes: "denotation is not the first meaning, but pretends to be so."[2] Much to the chagrin of cinematic realists, such as Bazin, who hold cinema in esteem for its ability to capture the truth on the surface of reality, for its capability to produce pure denotation, Barthes and others would argue that denotation is itself a codification, the end result of a particular connotative system. (As we have seen, Bazin's theories are largely ideologically based, given that the rejection of style is itself a formal construct.) "Connotation," Judith Mayne writes by way of explaining Barthes's model, "serves to assure denotation's status as law and absolute order."[3]

As we saw in the previous chapter, assuring the status of denotation falls to the totalized construction of a system of reference and the preservation, through this system of reference, of a larger order of meaning and a fixed relationship between meaning and subjectivity. In other words, as Stephen Heath points out, the very conceptualization of cinema as a signifying system implicates the problem of subjectivity, "brings into analysis the question of the positionings of the subject."[4] Heath articulates an aspect of film theory, common in the 1960s and 1970s, in which idealist notions were reconceptualized as problems of representation, agency, and identification. In the post-Bazinian landscape of film theory there was a dramatic shift toward a nonnaturalist understanding of cinema, one that abandons the illusion of film as being akin to the duality between the isolated human subject and an external objective world. With semiotics in general, the relationship between subject and object becomes embroiled in a complex system of ideological, structural, and psychoanalytic discourse. The problem of subjectivity was, after all, the linchpin for much of Michel Foucault's sociology, Julia Kristeva's literary theory, and Jacques Lacan's psychoanalysis.[5] In short, French critical theory during the 1960s and 1970s can in many ways be seen as a large and complex extension of Merleau-Ponty's phenomenological exploration of the subject-object relationship. The problem of subjectivity ceases to be only a question of personal experience and becomes part of a larger sociopolitical concern for an individual's agency in the world. Moreover, in film theory the question of subjectivity is central to every major approach for the last fifty years, and, as such, it would be useful here to clarify the term *subject* in reference to film semiotics.[6]

Let me return to chapter 1 for a moment, specifically to the type of subject with which that chapter was concerned: the viewing subject, signified by the camera and connoted as natural perception—the subjective position dug out through a simulation of the universal human condition. In other words, I laid out how film organizes a differentiation between the viewing position and the viewed world and how this organization can be used to guarantee a closed order of meaning that adheres to classical notions of subjectivity, as well as how it can be used to experiment with our modes of thinking, to subvert traditional philosophy and to challenge the viewer to reconsider our relationship to the world—not through its content but through its distribution of the sensible. This viewing subject is, I must add, signified. For *Vivre sa vie* this subject was for the most part absolute, total. It was the viewing position, the camera or apparatus, differentiated from the world being viewed except in the brief moments in which this subjectivity was aligned with the position of Nana, which occurred in two ways: by placing the camera in her point of view, and by using montage to involve her as the point of identification. At moments she is granted a certain agency, but the final say is always held back in the camera, as if it had some greater reason for granting her this allowance. So occasionally the subject of semiotics is the viewing subject, and occasionally it is the visible or diegetic subject. In *Two or Three Things I Know About Her* this subject is fragmented further, spread across numerous levels of discourse. Here subjectivity gets more complicated, for it also involves the speaking subject. This speaking subject can refer to an actual character, as we will find in the next chapter, or to the form itself as a source of enunciation. *Two or Three Things I Know About Her* opens the immanent field to different voices, different sources of signification—an interaction I have called, after Bakhtin, dialogic.

The film sign has been theorized to relate this notion of subjectivity to the principles of visual realism discussed in the last chapter, principles that in this case assume a functional role in the image but are reformulated under the term *denotation*, a notion of film signification that isolates the content of expression from the point of reference on which it fundamentally depends. The simplicity of the naturalist model has been thrown out the window, but many theorists still swim in its bathwater. If cinema is not the perceptive act of a viewing subject, though, what is it? Film semiotics has reframed this as a question of enunciation. Lifted by Metz from the linguist Emile Benveniste, the notion of enunciation carries with it a linguistic foundation.[7] Based on the difference between *histoire* (story) and *discours* (discourse), the analysis of enunciation deals with the particular problem of where the image is coming from, and how this source reveals or hides itself, though Metz ultimately avoids such concerns in his analysis. As with the structures of subject-object relations found in *Vivre sa vie* and *Two or Three Things I Know About Her*, I will enfold this dualistic notion under the umbrella of my larger framework: the story is the narrative material and referential content of the text, while the discourse is the internal organization of this content relative to a particular subject-function, how the narrative is shaped in order to provide an origin and structure of meaning, which determines the philosophical model through which the message or meaning is produced.

But is the problem of enunciation, which implies a single discourse and a single subject of discourse, extendable to cinema, in which the immanent field involves first-, second-, and third-person enunciations? Enunciation places a subject-function as the source for the structuring of the image—but is cinema always so unilateral? This question will be difficult to answer as long as our understanding of cinema is based on a language model and, through this, remains bound to an assumption that narration is the essence of film. To move away from these methodological determinations, it will be necessary to seek another path of film semiotics altogether, one that derives from a philosophy of change and transformation and can adequately appreciate the polysemous nature and multisensory process of film meaning.

Building on the imagistic models of Bergson and Peirce, Deleuze views the moving image as a material manifestation of thought, a plane of immanence in which the organization of relations gives birth to particular configurations of signification, forever ebbing and flowing in an act of perpetual becoming. Through Deleuze I will attempt to describe film not as enunciation but as a condition for enunciation, an immanent field that can be organized according to structured relationships between the content and origin of the image: an organization of formal relations in constant transformation of its subject-object compositions. These are not Deleuze's terms, however, and to reformulate his work in this context, it will be necessary to revisit the history of film semiotics prior to Deleuze, to look at a theory of film denotation in order to understand Deleuze's connotative model. Let me continue my metatheoretical project, then, by systematizing such disparate semiotic models as Christian Metz's "film-linguistic project"[8] and Gilles Deleuze's "*sémiotique*"[9] ("semiotic") according to my general phenomenological framework of subject-object relations.

CHRISTIAN METZ, FILM DENOTATION, AND
THE NARRATIVE SUBJECT-FUNCTION

The work of Christian Metz offers a valuable bridge from the phenomenological theories examined in chapter 1 to this chapter's study of film semiotics, as Metz carries some important assumptions of visual realism over to the study of film signification. To contextualize his work within a larger body, I want to position Metz in relation to the advent and unfolding of structuralism, the historical trajectory of which his own methodological affinities follow: from phenomenology, to linguistics, to psychoanalysis.[10] Anyone who has read Metz's collective work can discern the connection he makes between structuralism and phenomenology, and he often compares the rigorous nature of phenomenological observation to the scientific claims of structuralism: "structural analysis always assumed something like a phenomenology of its object."[11] However, while I agree with the importance of using phenomenology as a structural foundation for film semiotics, that is not the same as claiming to perform a phenomenology of film.

Rewording this analogy, Metz attempts what he describes as a phenomenology of film narration, which—I will argue—he reduces to a code of analogy, or resemblance, on which he bases his theory of film denotation. Metz, that is, seems to believe that the observational reduction of the camera creates a connection between viewing subject and filmic world, which, for him, signifies a "perceiving subject" with which the spectator identifies.[12] This perceiving subject, a later development of Metz's psychoanalytic phase, stems from his earlier, quite Bazinian assumptions that film functions on the analog transfer of reality, and thus has no code except "perception with its preconditions."[13] This reformulation of the classical viewing subject I described in chapter 1 combines a Bazinian sense of visual realism with Metz's central focus on the iconic type of visual sign, the visual sign based on resemblance. This underlying principle of resemblance guarantees what Metz calls *the impression of reality* and, through this denotative form, results in the perceptive participation of an identifying spectator.[14] While it is difficult to refute, according to the samples provided, it is important to specify that Metz asserts this participation as a result of the system of reference established in classical narrative cinema, and, as such, I view it as apt for only a limited and closed order of meaning.

The influence of phenomenology was soon complemented, however, by that of linguistics, and Metz would combine the two into a notion of narrative subjectivity, linking the isolated perceiving subject to denotative enunciation. The classical, linear narrative model provides Metz with a synchronic logic that he formulates under the terms of Morin's notion of the cinematic "formula of spectacle," according to which narrative film provokes a transversal reading from the viewing subject-function.[15] This, one could say, is how Metz makes the leap from phenomenology to semiotics; I will argue that this leap provides Metz with a limited understanding of narrative cinema and a linguistic model of subjectivity. Though originally received warmly and with much acclaim, Metz's writings on film semiotics have been heavily criticized because of what could be summarized as a general animosity toward his original concern with linguistics as a starting place for the scientific study of film. This is despite the fact that much of Metz's early work is, in fact, based on illustrating how film is *not* like spoken language![16]

To place Metz's work in this study, I must consider the centrality of linguistics not merely as a methodological misstep but as an integral part of his understanding of the role of narration in cinematic signification. For, Andrew warns us, the language analogy that Metz worked so hard to dispel he then regenerates through his theory of classical narrative enunciation: "Metz seemingly spent his first years deconstructing the prevailing notions of film and language so that he could reconstruct them again in his own way, that is, systematically."[17] Indeed, for Metz (as for many others during the 1960s and since) structuralism entails the reduction of any communications system to a type of language, at least in the transposition of linguistics as a fundamental methodological framework. This historical development can be traced primarily to the fact that it was Ferdinand de Saussure's study of the linguistic sign that served as the model for the structural semiotics of Barthes, Lévi-Strauss, and many other central figures of the 1950s and 1960s. But to use Saussurean linguistics as the basis for a theory of film, as Metz purports to do, implies an essential relationship between verbal signification and the film image. This is a postulation for which Metz would be deeply criticized and that he himself would later excuse as "a methodological abstraction."[18] Before arguing against this, however, I believe it necessary to understand fully this presupposition.

Though investing much time and effort into this methodological abstraction, Metz ultimately justifies the language paradigm through his study of narration, which he isolates as the determinant of film specificity. But is narration the essence of film? My answer to this is no, and I will employ Metz, Eco, and Deleuze in the coming pages to expound on the ramifications of this question and divergent answers to it. In the meantime it is important to consider how Metz arrives here from a phenomenological approach. As I have mentioned, Metz takes from Morin the view that classical narration carves out a perceptual position for the transcendental subject, the spectator. This approach lays the film text out as a series of objects and events—in other words, as diegesis—asking the spectator to *read* the film, as if our mentally putting together point A and point B were the same as moving from left to right and adding letters together to form words.[19] That is, the linear unfolding of denotation creates an enunciating subject-function for the spectator to identify with, from which the film's significations proceed in a syntagmatic, logical order akin to language, being simultaneously spoken and read, and thus effacing their constructivist origin.

According to Metz's argument, then, film is like a language because it is narratively syntagmatic, because it follows a causal order similar to the trajectory of grammatical structure: "if the story is structurally analyzable as a chain of predications, it is because it is phenomenally a sequence of events."[20] Thus, we can view cinema as a language because it has adopted the tradition of chronological narrative and its philosophical logic is based entirely on the sequential causality of chronological occurrence. But is this adoption itself essential to the form? Metz specifies this adoption as a historical condition of cinema, a fact of civilization, a fact "that conditions in its turn the ulterior evolution of film as a semiotic reality."[21] In other words, at least starting from a certain moment in film history, narration prefigures cinema's signifying methods, an argument disputed by Eco and Deleuze. Even more specifically, Metz views the conventionalization of individual signifying practices as being directly related to this characteristic: "It is exactly to the extent to which film confronts problems of story that it leads, over the diverse course of trial and error, to constitute itself as a body of specific signifying procedures."[22] Metz makes a relevant point here: the dominant conventions of classical film expression are those that help to provide narrative stability, a particular logic that is part of a greater order of meaning. This is very much what we saw with Godard's two films in chapter 1: whereas one preserved the subject necessary to a coherent narrative and the totality of a closed system of meaning, the other deconstructed this same subject and refused the closed narrative form of denotation.

That narration and the viewing subject of classical cinema are undeniably linked in this theory of denotation, however, does not necessarily mean that cinematic specificity exists in its structuring of narration. Nor does this prove, as Metz claims, a link between cinema's narrative essence and its similarity to language. Speaking not of duration but of the juxtaposition between different images, Metz writes: "To pass from one image to the next is to pass from image to language."[23] Is this true? Does the combination of images create a language? This brings me back to the debate between Eisenstein and Bazin, through which I concluded that signification is not, in fact, limited to the juxtaposition of shots or images but occurs within them as well. This position is argued perhaps more clearly by Eco, who views a system of articulation more complicated than language to exist already in the individual shot. Attesting to the affinity he postulates between language and classical narration, Metz bases his model of cinematic grammar—"The Grand Syntagmatique of Image-Tracks"—on the taxonomy of combinations provided through classical narrative sequencing.[24] Indicative of Metz's general exclusion of the aesthetics of the visual sign, one finds here the conjunction of two of his central concerns: classical narration and the attempt to reconcile film expression to a language-based model of conventionalized denotation. As Andrew points out, Metz's Grand Syntagmatique turns out not to be an abstract grammar of film signification but, rather, a master code for understanding a certain type of cinema.[25] Metz looks at mainstream modes of film expression, according to which he designs a semiotic model in which the syntactical logic of narration and the enunciating subject-function are inseparable. Choosing to subordinate film semiotics to "the question of why one unit of narration is preceded or followed by another,"[26] we could say that he paved the way for David Bordwell's cognitive approach to narrative analysis. Unlike Bordwell, however, Metz places this narrative essence in the history of film as an industry and not as an interpretive aspect of spectatorship, which he reserves for psycholinguistic (as opposed to cognitivist) analysis.

Regardless, this obvious preference for a particular mode of cinema is not in any way lost on my study. After all, we can view Metz's understanding of narration as fruitful to the extent that he considers denotation as a mode of producing narration that posits images as acts of natural perception, natural in that denotation implies the isolation of the representational content from any connotative concern for its system of reference. In defense of Metz, Martin Jay writes: "Even throughout his most semiologically formalist phase, he never lost sight of the fact that the coded language of the film was based on the simulacrum of lived experience produced by its analogical, denotative foundation."[27]

Analogy is, for Metz, the underlying code of film expression, "a means to transfer codes."[28] This is the basic myth of the reproductive apparatus, and it is based on this connotation that film can present us with a denoted story that we accept as realistic or *vraisemblable*. Yet resemblance itself is guaranteed in different ways, and this condition produces the double-nature of film signification as creating meaning on both denotative and connotative levels. In the quote above, Jay's use of the word *simulacrum* indicates a critique of the purity of denotation that arose with later theorists, but which is to a large degree stifled by Metz's focus on classical cinema.[29] Despite his acknowledged division of film signification between denotation and connotation, however, Metz excludes the latter and focuses on the former. For Metz denotation is provided for the spectator via "certain modalities of representation," or signifiers. He points out, echoing Barthes (under whom Metz studied), that the intelligibility of denotation is guaranteed by the total set of forms of denotation (i.e., connotative systems) that constitute an analogy between film and the real world, such as perceptive codes and codes of identification.[30] So Metz clearly is not delusional concerning film's mythological status, though he may well have been nostalgic for a time when he was. Still, in any case, connotation does not fall within the interest of Metz's scientific inquiry.

As Mitry and Barthes understand it, connotation is the "how" of denotation, its form: it is the way in which the referential content of the image is structured. Though Metz seems to follow this point to the conclusion of setting denotation aside as a mode of signification privileged for analysis, he does not fail to grasp that it is built from a connotative base: "If cinema arrives at connoting without necessarily needing specific connoters, it is because it makes permanent and constant use of the most essential of connoters, which is the choice between various ways of constructing denotation."[31] Yet Metz dismisses film connotation as being too general. According to Bill Nichols, Metz pushes connotation to the side, only "treating his denotative level as matter, material for analysis."[32]

For Metz only the level of denotation is quantifiable, possible of analyzing scientifically. I hope here to go beyond this limitation, turning my attention to the immanent field through which this denotation is realized.

Perhaps the greatest critique merited by Metz is that, like many other theories focusing primarily on classical narrative cinema, he views the denotative as a separate level of signification, indeed as that which is *essential* to the medium. One could say that, for Metz, the chain of signification leads from the diegetic, internal sign (the filmic) to the external sign (the cinematic). I will argue the opposite, however, siding with theorists such as Eco, Heath, and Deleuze. As Lesage points out, the narrative story is less an origin of meaning than an anchor for connotative meaning: "it limits the polyvalent image to a certain range of emotional and social interpretation."[33] This limitation, this enforced rigidity of film meaning, is a heavy but often transparent philosophical act that determines how we can understand the medium's relationship to thought. Moreover, the assumption that denotation is the basis for film meaning works on the supposition of denotation as a naturalized state of reproduction, a supposition that is itself part of the connotative register. As Judith Mayne remarks: "The very notion, in other words, of a neutral system (denotation) which forms a support for richer, more complex associations, must be challenged. This is because these connotative associations affect our notion of what constitutes a primary system in the first place."[34]

Thus, this book argues that a semiotics of film should occupy itself rather with the connotative level of signification, where film and philosophy meet.

DEMYSTIFYING THE DENOTATIVE ILLUSION OF CLOSED MEANING

The guarantee of closed denotation is the very object of critique in suture theory, which analyzes the means by which a transcendental viewing subject-function is signified into the text in ways that efface the constructive origin of that signification.[35] As many have pointed out, conventional film editing and camera movements imply something absent, something behind the camera; that "something" is the transcendental viewing subject that has been theorized to be signified in film expression. Adherents to the movement known as suture theory, many of whom view Metz as politically negligent, nonetheless make his perceiving subject the focal

point for analyzing what Stephen Heath enigmatically calls the "historic-
ity of ideological formations and mechanisms in relation to the processes
of subject-meanings (meanings for a subject included as the place of
their intention)."[36] In other words suture theory is interested in the production of film signification as part of an implied system of reference.
Suture theory marks an important step in this book, away from Metz's
and Bazin's interest in denotative meaning and toward an understanding
of film based on its organization of subject-object relations.

Daniel Dayan, who popularized the French theory of suture for Eng-
lish-reading theorists, considers suture to be the practice by which an
invisible subject-position is created through formal editing conventions.
Basing his approach primarily on Lacanian theories of the implied subject of language, Dayan looks at how the shot/countershot convention of
classical editing secretes a subjective position into the visual production
of discourse.[37] Dayan translates this secreted subject into a transcendental subject that we may recognize from Baudry's "Ideological Effects of
the Basic Cinematographic Apparatus," going so far as to claim, "Narrative cinema presents itself as a 'subjective' cinema."[38] This idea links up
well with Metz's claims and echoes certain implications of my analysis
from the previous chapter. But Dayan's notion of "subjective" here is not
the same as the one I hope to develop in this book. While Dayan makes a
sharp insight into the transparent nature of classical editing, I believe
that this formulation can be misleading because a transcendental subject
and a diegetic subject can be very different things built from very different
formal structures, and films use a range of different systems of reference
including both of these. After all, cinema may very well posit itself as the
organization of space and events according to relative points of view, but
this only implicates the otherwise widely accepted point that any signifying act is by definition subjective.[39] But, as this book argues, film representation is not only the unilateral product of one subjective position but
is a dialogic fluctuation and interaction between many.

My goal here and now is to untangle the manner in which such approaches conflate different types of subjectivity, just as others have challenged Dayan's generalization of cinematic practices and his postulation
of an ideological homogeneity among classical texts.[40] Nonetheless, suture theory helps bring to light many of the problems I have discussed
up to now, including many of the critical missteps I hope in this book to
rectify. One of these is, of course, the confounding of phenomenological

and semiotic principles. The notion of suture has led to great misunderstandings in phenomenological approaches to film, especially with regard to the notion that this practice posits a perceptual body within the text.[41] This neglects the codifying nature of suture, the fundamental process by which suture provides the spectator with "a falsely harmonious whole by encouraging [the spectator] to identify seriatim with . . . gazes which seem to come from centered and unified subjects."[42] Suture theory's goal is, after all, to reveal that the "harmonious whole" is false or faked, and mine is to add to this a study of the variety of harmonious wholes, fractured wholes, and partialities, to introduce into this debate the principles of demystifying and subversive philosophies.

According to the suture argument, classical modes of representation give the illusion of an alignment between the image's view and a single coherent visual subject-function, yet it is purely a relational configuration of signified source and represented world—in other words, a composition of subject-object relations. Shot/countershot editing conventionally works to organize the visual space so that the spectator is placed in alignment with an absent one, the position of looking. Yet the spectator is not really looking directly at the content but is being fed a visual message. Suture is a question of producing a position for which the spectator is implanted into the text as subject, implied as the origin of meaning in a representation from which he or she is actually excluded. It is, ultimately, an act of positioning or relationality, based on an inherent classical fallacy—that the act of vision is a unilateral act on behalf of the viewing subject, as opposed to a dialogic experience between viewer and viewed—that Merleau-Ponty's phenomenology tried to rectify. Nonetheless, classical editing procedures, as well as suture theories of them, rely on the unilateral relationship between subject and object. The denoted world is closed, and we are given the impression that it is our vision, our presence, that encloses it. As Heath writes, "The suturing function includes the spectator as part of an imaginary production."[43] But includes them how so, and to what extent? To build on problems confronted in chapter 1, I would say that suture enforces a connotative order that opens the image to the spectator while closing the spectator off to the production of meaning, enveloping the spectator into the process of differentiation created by the organization of spatial relations and, through this subject-object dynamic, giving the spectator the impression of producing meaning. The spectator is given the illusion of being in a position in which to experience the sensory world through his or her own perception, but it is nothing more than a signification of—and identification with—that position. "Suture," Heath concludes, "names the . . . conjunction of the spectator as subject with the film."[44]

Suture theory clearly indicates a strong affinity with my own approach. However, the centrality of subject positioning to suture theory comes mainly from the influence of psychoanalysis and the notion of subject-formation that is at the center of Lacanian psycholinguistics. Like Metz's linguistic project and subsequent turn to psychoanalysis, suture theory is founded on a conceptualization of subjectivity rooted in suppositions that are in no way cinematic per se. This methodological appropriation rendered theorists such as Metz and Dayan the targets of much criticism. "Without analogies of this sort," quipped Charles F. Altman only a year after Dayan's essay was published, "the entire structuralist and post-structuralist critical enterprise would not exist."[45] Though maintaining ties to psychoanalytic theory, Stephen Heath provides a useful criticism of Dayan's comparison of suture editing to verbal language. Classical editing may imply a mode of *enunciation* that perhaps resembles language in ways, but a theory of film connotation must rise above the connection that such words have to language and linguistics. As Heath puts it: "What is at stake here, the real problem, is exactly the understanding of cinema as discourse, of *enunciation and subject of enunciation* in cinema."[46] While one single subject of enunciation may be impossible to isolate for what Nowell-Smith calls the "meta-discourse" that is an entire film text,[47] it is important to note that each individual discourse itself consists of an organization of different enunciations, each of which consist of a dynamic, interdependent relationship between composition of enunciation and subject of enunciation.

In this way the overall discourse of the film resembles my notion of the dialogic immanent field, a field of expression in which various voices are interwoven, the level of meaning-production wherein film and philosophy meet, and where cinema can, in fact, provide us with experiments in structures of thought and understanding—not understanding the world necessarily but understanding our relationship to it, our ways of organizing meaning within and from it. A film, a sequence, and even some shots could thus be seen, as extrapolated by Deleuze, as a combination of such compositions. Indeed, as I argued in chapter 1, a film's overall treatment of its content could be analyzed according to the connotative system at the base of such a set of combinations. This is the semiotic model I hope here to develop, concerning how a film permits or prohibits interaction between different poles (the interaction between diegetic and transcendental subjectivity, for example, which was denied in *Vivre sa vie* and yet was a central aspect of *Two or Three Things I Know About Her*). Suture theory, although grounded in certain psychoanalytic presuppositions that many hold to be problematic, succeeds at reformulating Metz's essentialist view of narrative denotation as a problem wherein discourse necessitates the signification of enunciating subjects. It is concerned, I would say, with film connotation as a question of subject-object relations. Moreover, Heath in particular opens this analysis to the fabrication of *different types* of subject-function but ultimately retains a notion of narrative determination that I hope to do away with.

How might we avoid this determination? The centrality of narration is abandoned in the approaches of Pier Paolo Pasolini, Umberto Eco, and especially Deleuze, who shift the focus of film semiotics. With less linguistically oriented models of film semiotics we can locate an attempt to move away from a view of narration as being essential to film meaning. Some such approaches share with Metz and Bazin a more essentialist view of visual reproduction than that of suture theory, yet they place cinema's basis in visual resemblance—often referred to as the iconic sign—within the context of understanding film as a dialogic space of organization between the content and the transformative apparatus. Pasolini, for example, argues that the denoted level of expression consists of "a whole complex world of significant images" that prefigures cinematic communication.[48] This is undeniable, isn't it? That is to say, the content of a film, even of a shot or image, consists of a selection from the possible range of people and things, actions and words, modes of signification that exist outside of cinema's capturing of them. Or, more simply: cinema's articulations are constructed from the building blocks of other significations. Yet cinematic form produces significations that were previously impossible.

For Pasolini this brute visual transformation of the external world of significant images makes cinema an irrational type of signification (much like for Mitry it makes cinematic symbolism an unconventional type of symbolism).[49] But Pasolini also discusses this reproduction of the world of signs as a sort of overlapping of different subject positions. Referring to a notion of film's phenomenological potential altogether different from Bazin's, he concludes that cinema's use of the signifying world as the signifier for a greater discourse means that cinema "is at the same time extremely subjective and extremely objective."[50] That is to say, he reiterates a phenomenological theme that should be becoming familiar by now: film is both something to be looked at and also a transformation of its content into particular cinematic modes of looking at it. But Pasolini's manner of articulating this is particularly useful to this study.

Referring to Bakhtin's theory of the novel, Pasolini conceptualizes this dualism according to what he calls "free indirect discourse," which incorporates a subjective view into the objective image. Free indirect discourse, for which Pasolini uses Godard as his example, resembles my own conclusions concerning *Two or Three Things I Know About Her*. Pasolini uses this phrase to theorize a sort of cinematic dialogism, as Ronald Bogue points out: "Pasolini, following Bakhtin's analysis, argues that this is not a simple mingling of two fully constituted subjective voices, a narrator's and a character's."[51] In other words, it is not necessarily a harmony of subjects, or a duet, but a dialogue. I am not interested here, however, in trying to imply an authorial voice or estimate an artistic intent in the text. While this authorial voice has been debated by many, I am concerned with a model that brackets off the image from such questions of authorship, a model offered by Deleuze.

Deleuze, also using Godard as his exemplary case, reformulates Pasolini's notion as a question of "a construction of enunciation, simultaneously operating two inseparable acts of subjectivation,"[52] hence Deleuze's quote, cited at the beginning of chapter 1, about the image being caught between a perceptive act and the consciousness that transforms it. The agency of the image consists of the organization between the camera-subject (the objective) and the subjects in the viewed world (the subjective). However, one must ask: is this only the case in reflexive (what Pasolini calls "poetic" and Bordwell calls "art") cinema? Is this not the case for all film expression, a system of articulation in which we find both the subjectivity of characters and the subjectivity of the apparatus, which occasionally align and occasionally are set in opposition? It certainly is. The only difference seems to be that classical (or "mainstream") cinema tries to refuse this dialogue as much as possible, to preserve the unification of the origin of meaning so that the meanings themselves are grounded, certain. Godard and Resnais, on the other hand, build their films from this dialogic principle, arriving at a polyphony of subject-functions and promoting an experimental way of viewing the world that has profound philosophical ramifications.

Looking through the image to the significant world beneath, the danger of Pasolini's approach lies in its attempt to view film signification as being without a code. Other theorists, such as Metz and Wollen, have formulated similar notions of film signification, and especially the iconic sign, as "a language without a code," for which Ronald Abramson criticizes them as taking for granted a "natural code" that should be analyzed instead of ignored.[53] Writing in many ways in response to Pasolini, Eco offers us a way out of this by incorporating the codification of real-life signifying acts into the codes of cinematic signifying acts, in what Nichols summarizes as an "account of the visual rhetorical codes found in the image."[54] As Constance Penley remarks, Eco diverges drastically from Metz's pseudo-phenomenological model of mimetic representation: "He [Eco] points out that there are so many transformations involved from the object to the representation of the object that the image has none of the properties of the object represented, but that, at most, the iconic sign reproduces some of the conditions of perception."[55] Moreover, Eco insists that this resemblance carries with it another layer of significance or signification. As such, Eco addresses film as a process of transformation in which the image of the real by definition carries with it another level of meaning. To make this argument, he constructs the model of what he calls "articulations" in order to direct his theoretical investigation beyond the denotative, to what I call the connotative. Bringing me back to the question of Pasolini's semiotics of action, Eco points out that "we find the universe of action transcribed by the cinema already existing as a universe of signs."[56] This notion of an articulation concerns the formal codification of an already coded source material, regardless of any narrative context. Again rejecting the Metzian model (and contradicting those of Dayan and Heath), Eco "introduces the notion of cinematic articulations at the level of the image rather than at the level of narrative."[57]

Not only does Eco help us to detach film semiotics from narration, but he actually insists that the image is itself an articulation *beyond* language, for it is built from combinations of signs, which are themselves constructed from individual figures. Cinema, therefore, signifies through a form that cannot be reduced in any way to the model of language—after all, language is one of its building blocks, one of the codes of expression that are cinema's source material. Language is an element in this imma-nent field. Thus, as Eco says, "the cinematic code *is the only code carrying a triple articulation.*"[58] Through the combination of sign with sign, cin-ema produces what Eco calls "a sort of 'hypersignificance,'" an overall cinematic meaning beyond language or iconicity. In other words there is that *something else*, that something cinematic. This is what I refer to as the moving sound-image's immanent field, wherein the signifying acts of the source material and the signifying acts of film form interact. This third articulation arises from the fact that cinematic form has no denotation that is not connotative, no way of showing that does not also refer to a way of showing—no statement that is not, whether conventional or alter-native, also a message. Every image-type, regardless of make or model, carries with it philosophical ramifications, attaches itself to an order of meaning; to fully understand the dynamic relationship, both historical and instantaneous, between film and philosophy, let me now turn to the philosopher who has been most engaged in specifically addressing this intersection: Gilles Deleuze.

DELEUZE AND FILM CONNOTATION

Arguably no single writer of the past thirty years has been more influen-tial on film studies than Deleuze, whose *Cinema 1: The Movement-Image* and *Cinema 2: The Time-Image* revolutionized how we understand film meaning, film history, and the intricate evolutionary and conceptual re-lationship between cinema and philosophy. This is not the place to sum-marize Deleuze's cinema books, which has been strongly accomplished elsewhere;[59] instead, I hope in these pages to offer only cursory summa-ries where necessary in order to build something new from a Deleuzean genealogy. In terms of the intersection between cinema and philosophy explored here, I understand Deleuze's work as a formulation of how cin-ema has helped to illustrate and also to catalyze what Rodowick suc-cinctly labels "a tectonic shift" in a larger common worldview that evolved over the twentieth century,[60] marked by a breaking point that occurred with World War II and after which the strict logics of classical cinema and classical thought began to unravel. For Deleuze the order of mean-ing enforced by cinema is of great philosophical and even ethical impor-tance, in terms of cinema's ability to reject or to embrace the qualities of change, transformation, and becoming that he sees as essential to film, philosophy, and life itself.

We could say that, for Deleuze, cinematic form has no agency beyond the volition of image-types and their ontological evolution. As such, Paola Marrati clarifies for us, the film image is not the doubling of an ontological condition but rather the revelation of various types of image in which "cinema places before our eyes perceptions, affections, relations of thought that cinema knew to create."[61] Cinema, in other words, is fully cinematic. Strangely enough, this is a rare admission in film theory but one of the underlying assumptions of this book. That is to say, film is not perception, nor is it linguistic, nor is it ultimately at the mercy of its artists or of its stories. Cinema engenders the specific possibilities of its own images, and the signification produced by this form stems primarily and essentially from the agency of cinematic image-types and their combinations. Deleuze's project is, Marrati concludes decisively, "a properly cinematographic semiotics,"[62] and as such is immensely inspirational to my own work here. Moreover, instead of reducing the film image to a subject of enunciation or a camera-based subject of perception, Deleuze analyzes it according to fluctuations between subjective and objective images, so my goal in this chapter is to position Deleuze within the theoretical corpus discussed thus far.[63]

Deleuze derives the foundations of his project from Bergson, who focuses much of his work on the dualism between mind and matter, interior and exterior—a dualism that Bergson attempts to deconstruct as being imposed by a certain idea of subjectivity. The attempt to move away from analyzing subjectivity itself, and toward what Temenuga Trifonova clarifies as "the conditions under which subjectivity is formed,"[64] draws a connection between Bergson and Merleau-Ponty, whose phenomenology uses perception to deconstruct the very same dualism between person and world. In reading Deleuze, one finds that the concept of subjectivity is not necessarily abandoned as much as it is shifted, reformulated. Trifonova provides a very useful insight concerning Deleuze that could apply both to Bergson and Merleau-Ponty, as well: instead of destroying the idea of subjectivity, Deleuze, in fact, redefines it, "eliminating the inside/outside opposition that has always underlined the idea of subjectivity."[65]

In an attempt to dispel this dualism, Bergson claims that a thing is inseparable from the perception of that thing; as I pointed out in my introduction, they are one and the same image "but related to one or another of two systems of reference."[66] These two systems of reference could be called subjective and objective: one is the system of reference of the thing itself, alienated from all others, whereas the perception of that thing is its image in relation to an other singled-out thing or image. As I will draw out further in chapters 4 and 5, subjective images reveal a diegetic world according to a person in that world, whereas objective images view that world from an external perspective. However, characters and the external apparatus itself can be implicated as both subject and object depending on the formal arrangement of relations, as with the buildings, coffee, and the "I" and "Her" of *Two or Three Things I Know About Her.*

As Marrati observes, Deleuze's *Cinema* books are based on a precise assumption: experience is irreducible to natural perception; therefore cinema is irreducible to one subject's perceptive position.[67] This is particularly evident in Deleuze's division of the *movement-image* among what he calls the *perception-image*, the *affection-image*, the *action-image*, and the *relation-image.* Built from what is perhaps an excessively complicated attempt to reconcile Bergsonian image-ontology with Peircean imagistic semiotics, Deleuze bases this taxonomy of image-types on how the image is constructed through the arrangement of subjective and objective positions, or subject-object relations.[68] The film image is for Deleuze a dialogic immanent field of numerous currents of meaning, the dynamic of which is defined by such relations, and in which such relations are constantly changing. In Bergson's image-ontology, all people and things are perceivable entities that are, at all times, in a state of transformation, coalescing forms of light, matter, and movement. Everything is an image, and images are things. Yet not all images are constructed the same, and their construction belies the infusion of a particular organization of relations. From this ontology Deleuze founds his critique of classical cinema, which he views as being arranged according to a particular order of meaning, manifesting connotations of this order of meaning through various types of formal relations. This is the movement-image, in which representations are usually structured according to a conventional logic of clear-cut and absolute differentiations.

The eye-line match, for example, follows a logical editing pattern across cuts and between shots, in which the apparatus itself is attuned to the motorized actions of the diegetic subject. This logic of editing is part of the overall image construction, the preservation of a fixed meaning and central subjectivity that emanates from what Deleuze calls a "sensory-motor logic," a logic that extends also to the larger philosophy of narrative models. The structure of causal narration, which begins with a situation and then ends with the transformation of that situation as the result of a character's subjective agency, is the narrative extension of this logic.[69] These are both aspects of the movement-image's logic, and both formal conventions of the transcendental subject and the linear narrative model are parts—one could say they are formulations—of the movement-image's order of meaning, the philosophy that is structured by this network of formal organizations—the philosophy, one might say, of this image-type.

One aspect of this model that is most unique is that it illustrates how, unlike most understandings of classical narration, Deleuze views the narrative order as originating with a particular image-type, as opposed to the image-type originating with an enunciating narrative agent or syntactical order. Deleuze rejects narration as the fundamental determinant of film signification and ties this to a general rejection of language as a model for understanding cinema. As this may imply, Deleuze posits his *sémiotique* (his unique play on *semiotics*) in opposition to the Metzian tradition, and assessing this difference will help both to clarify Deleuze's method and to define my own project. Between Metz and Deleuze one finds a similar polarity as that between Eisenstein and Bazin, except that instead of an argument between shot and sequence there exists here an argument between denotation and connotation, between whether narration or form is the origin of film representation.

Although Deleuze rarely discusses other film theorists, he does explicitly confront Metz in a passage that is central to the opening of the second book and is arguably Deleuze's most substantial and overt discussion of previous film semiotics. First, Deleuze refutes Metz on methodological terms. As Greg Flaxman puts it, Deleuze is fundamentally opposed to Metz's manner of treating the cinema "by analogy (cinema is *like* a *langue*, the shot is *like* an utterance)."[70] This is not only a specious mode of methodological appropriation; Deleuze rejects Metz's linguistic model, most importantly, because this analogy has certain consequences. The worst of these consequences lies in ignoring cinema's essential uniqueness and formal specificity. As Bogue notes, Deleuze's adamant autonomy from the conceptualization of *film-as-language* is necessary "because the notion of film as language tends to privilege narrative as the fundamental dimension of cinema."[71] Deleuze criticizes this analogy for enabling Metz to make a specious jump from fact to approximation, thus permitting a decisive imprudence: the selection of narration—instead of movement—as being the defining characteristic of cinema, the specificity of its form.[72] Narration is, after all, a characteristic common to many arts, although in each one the method of narration is directly governed by the medium's formal specificity. Deleuze views narration as related to notions of realism, and Deleuze's dismissal of narration as the specific essence of film expression is contracted with a criticism of the Bazinian tradition of film criticism. As Deleuze writes, such interpretations "do not take into consideration the form of films, thus forgetting that in cinema as elsewhere in art realism is an aesthetic choice and is defined by formal criteria."[73]

In further building toward an understanding of the division between denotation and connotation, one could say that denotation and its general contents are common to all signifying mediums, whereas connotation (the form of denotation) is specific to each. Considering narration to be the impetus behind the film image grants to denotation a founding role in film signification, when it is really, I argue, a product of the connotative order. Instead of considering narration to be the inherent given of cinematic images, the engendering basis of cinema's underlying structure, I intuitively side with Deleuze: "Narration is nothing but a consequence of independent images and their direct combinations . . . images that are apparent and sensible in and of themselves, as they define themselves beforehand."[74] That is to say, narration—and even the readability of film syntax as proposed by Metz and Bordwell—is a secondary consequence of the combinations of image-types and their organization of relations. Transcending most narrative theories' limitation of film selection to a certain period of classical cinema, Deleuze holds this as true for any type of image, born from any connotative foundation, as can be seen in his continuation of this argument: "What is known as classical narration unfolds directly as a composition of movement-images (montage), or according to their specification as perception-images, affection-images, action-images, following the laws of a sensory-motor scheme. We see that modern forms of narration unfold from composition and types of time-image: even 'readability.'"[75]

Thus, narration should be seen as a symptom of the agency of various types of image, not as their catalyst. As Bogue puts it: "The regularities and continuities of narrative have as their condition of possibility the regularities and continuities of . . . space-time."[76] In other words the possible dynamics of the immanent field of the image are determined by the relationship of formal elements. The film image, before being part of a narrative or syntagmatic structure, is fundamentally a process of organization according to a larger order of meaning; the image can build itself through a story but does not originate from it. "Narration," Deleuze writes, "is founded in the image itself, and [is] not a given."[77]

Whereas Metz and others build their model from the logical order of classical narration, Deleuze starts with the specific form of the components, "beginning with images and their combinations, not as a function of language-based determinations."[78] I view here a decisive break with the semiotic approaches of Metz, Dayan, and Heath, though in the next chapter I will try to reconcile sound and especially spoken language to Deleuze's nonlinguistic model. Though he dismisses narrative structure as the origin of film representation, however, Deleuze is clearly interested in montage, the "combinations" of images, as an ontological problem. This focus seems reminiscent of Eisenstein's conceptualization of the image as the qualitative product of the juxtaposition of multiple representations, and it is important to acknowledge that the immanent field is not limited to the organizational principles of the single shot. This focus on montage merits a degree of criticism. David Martin-Jones argues for the necessity of tapering Deleuze's focus on montage, positing the early silent films of Méliès and the role of spectacle in film as an important counterbalance in film texts that, for industrial reasons, do not employ editing in conventional manners.[79] It is important to complement the role of relationality with that of spectacle, as Martin-Jones elucidates through his subsequent study of the spaghetti western,[80] but I hope here to assert Deleuze's notion of "combinations" as congruent with Merleau-Ponty's notion of the *"ensemble,"* helping to bridge the phenomenology of space with the philosophy of time in a larger theory of connotation revolving around structures of relationality. As we saw in my analysis of *Two or Three Things I Know About Her,* and as will be central to the coming chapters' analysis of Alain Resnais, Deleuze offers an approach to montage that is connotative as opposed to denotative: a question of the types of images being assembled, through what system of reference they are realized, not according to their narrative function but according to the order of meaning that emanates through the organization of formal elements.

In other words we could say that Deleuze uses the word *combinations* in reference to an understanding of montage as a form of relating one image-type to another, not in an additive sense but in a more abstract sense that I hope here to ground in a phenomenological framework. These image-types, I would argue, are composed of different compositions of subject-object relations. The overall structure of montage, the fluctuation between subjective and objective poles, precedes and supersedes the organization of what Bogue calls "narrative, motivic, or discursive continuities."[81] For Deleuze, I would conclude, the origins of the image lie in its connotative regime, and the only permanent or transcendental element of film is the immanent field itself. In understanding Deleuze, one can see that he is central to my enterprise here, indeed any enterprise that endeavors to understand the problems of film connotation, film subjectivity, and the intersection of film and philosophy. But Deleuze's notion of film subjectivity requires clarification, as it is not the subject of enunciation delineated by most semiotic models. In conjunction with refusing the preliminary importance of narration, Deleuze also rejects the principle of cinema's being merely describable as enunciation, thus distancing himself from suture theorists such as Dayan. For Deleuze the singular notion of film subjectivity provided by suture theory's analysis of classical editing is insufficient for cinema, which both engenders and is built on the interaction of different organizations of subject-object relations. The film image is not enunciation, but the condition *for* enunciation: "it is not an enunciation, or even enunciations. It is an enunciable."[82]

As revealed in the films of Godard and Resnais, cinema provides the condition for the construction of subjectivity but is not fundamentally subjective or relatable to one absolute division of subject and object. For similar reasons Deleuze proffers these two filmmakers as models for his notion of the time-image, a cinematic order of meaning that abandons the classical mode of subject-object differentiation for a more dialogic immanent field. As a connotative system, then, I view Deleuze's time-image as both a crisis in the stability of thought and a crisis in the stability of the codes that guide the conventional organizations of film meaning;

the time-image is thus a deconstruction of the totality or unilateral isolation of any one system of reference. This is, in fact, the very place where film and philosophy meet, and the capacity in which these directors provide experiments in cinematic thinking. As Deleuze argues, in the films of filmmakers such as Godard and Resnais the relationships between subjective and objective poles of expression, reality and fiction, past and present, lose their duality. Greatly influential to my own approach, Deleuze views filmmakers like Godard and Resnais as deconstructing the cinematic myth of a unilateral subject of enunciation, and their texts illustrate a resistance to classical formal divisions between subject and object in every sense (viewer and viewed, agent and receiver, producer of meaning and means of that production). The time-image presented by these filmmakers, in Rodowick's terms, "presumes a Nietzschean aesthetic" that is defined by what Deleuze calls "powers of the false": indiscernibility between real and imaginary, inexplicability of narrative difference, and undecidability in temporal logic—all of which result in what Rodowick summarizes as "a transformation in the problem of judgment."[83] Instead of the isolation of singular subjective perspectives from linear stories governed by spatiotemporal causality, the time-image engenders film texts that are lost to more irrational and interchangeable structures, thus forcing the spectator to develop alternative formats of meaning—or, as Deleuze might say, carving out new folds in our brains.

Working on the supposition that narration is film's essential characteristic, theorists such as Metz do not take into account what happens when conventional hierarchies break down, when the causal logic both of story and of representation unravel and expose themselves. This crisis, which Deleuze analyzes on filmic, artistic, historic, and philosophical levels, is centered on a rupture in the traditional dualism between subject and object. This is the conclusion I hope to have clarified in my reading of Deleuze's project and that I hope to bring to light through this book's analyses of Godard and Resnais. The *Cinema* books lead us to a different understanding of the subject-function's role in film signification, refusing the notion of a singular or monologic subjectivity that guides the imaginary or diegetic discourse. The constructed nature of this division highlights Deleuze's view of narration as secondary to the process of organizing relations; and, as the duality between subject and world becomes less distinct, less enforced, the unraveling of narrative causality as a denotative illusion is merely a result. As I have mentioned, in place of the subject of narration the time-image erects what Deleuze explains to be the subjectivity of time itself.[84]

Deleuze thus introduces the Bergsonian notion of time into the problem of cinematic narrative tension, and while the "subjectivity of time" is very unclear in its formulation, I hope to elucidate it by placing it within the larger philosophical genealogy connecting Bergson and Merleau-Ponty. Bergson's philosophy of time is central to this book in that it aims to deconstruct the notion of precise, impenetrable divisions of temporal subjectivity. I hope to clarify this notion by analyzing the problem of filmic intertemporality in terms of the diegetic speaking subject. This intertemporal division of the subject can be viewed as parallel to Merleau-Ponty's dissolution of the barrier between subject and object in the act of perception, and my particular reading of Deleuze's semiotics will permit me to incorporate intertemporality into my concept of the immanent field. Deleuze is certainly not a phenomenologist, yet these different philosophical methods can be reconciled on the grounds of their mutual rejection of the hierarchy born from classical views of the division between subject and object. Moreover, one can draw connections between the two theorists based on Merleau-Ponty's insistence that time is not a chronological line but a network of "intentionalities."[85] Such "intentionalities" can be seen as compositions of subject-object relations, systems of reference that I will look at in the next chapter. I hope gradually to illustrate that, together, Merleau-Ponty and Deleuze help to illuminate the notion of the film image as an immanent field in which both spatial and temporal divisions can be transcended, thus challenging the classical philosophical notion of a singular and isolated subjectivity.

THREE

SOUND, IMAGE, AND THE ORDER OF MEANING

The relationship between things is more important than the things themselves.

—Jean Mitry, *Esthétique et psychologic du cinéma*

IN CHAPTER 1 I ENGAGED WITH THE PHENOMENOLOGICAL relationship between the film image and human perception; in the last chapter I moved away from strict film analysis to dive deeper into the connection between philosophy and film semiotics and, more specifically, where they might meet in a theory of film connotation. This meeting place, I will continue to elaborate here, is intricately and inevitably linked to the relationship in film between an order of meaning and a system of reference. An analysis of Godard's films led me to conclude that the transcendental subjective position is only one of many possible origins of meaning within the immanent field of the film image and that the organization of such subject positions can be considered a function of what I have called connotation. This connotative foundation, as we have seen, prefigures narrative and linguistic functions of film, and thus it is with the immanent field of the form itself that we must begin an analysis of film and philosophy. But doesn't film form include more than just visual elements?

In this chapter I will focus on codifications of speech and image and how they are built according to connotations of the relationship between the diegetic speaking subject, the status of the image as a function of time, and the representation of memory. I will argue that time is as important a factor as space in the construction of filmic subjectivity, and I will invoke Deleuze's philosophy of cinema to extend Merleau-Ponty's concerns of spatialization and vision to an analysis of temporality and the sound-image code, a theoretical step that I will illustrate through a close reading of the films of Alain Resnais. Introducing the philosophical notion of intertemporality into film semiotics under the heading of the "crystal-image," Deleuze elaborates on Bergson's principles of time: the past coexists with the present that it once was *and* preserves itself in each new present as "the past"; and, binding these two, time doubles itself at each instant into the present that passes and the past that preserves itself.[1] This nonclassical conceptualization of time resonates within certain forms of film editing, such as the flashback, which themselves typically rely on the codification of speech and image to provide a particular order of meaning: an "order of meaning" in that speech evokes a complementary meaning in the image or vice versa, and an "order of meaning" in that such patterns are conventionally built to maintain a stable connotative relationship between system of reference and worldview. But Resnais offers many variations on this code, and in his films these variations saturate the immanent field with a dialogic interaction of different subject-functions, thus forging new formations of interaction between subject and world, experiments in cinematic thinking based on distributing the sensory roles of vision and sound across an intertemporal crystal.

In "Is the Film in Decline?" Roman Jakobson suggests that the difference between auditory signs and visual signs rests not in their degree of importance but in their function.[2] In a way, though, they both lead to the same end. That is, in the framework of this book I can rectify this difference through their mutual attempt to organize subject-object relations. Yet there is some truth in Jakobson's assumption, voiced by others as well, that vision is spatial while sound is temporal, at least in their means of constructing sets of differentiation and organizing relations. And, following Jakobson's suggestion that sound be understood primarily as an element of montage, let me consider to what extent film signification—as a product of montage within the image, between shots, and as an entire order of meaning—is based on the division and unity of aural and visual expression.

Comparing different compositions of the flashback (and, later, the flash-forward) in light of Bergson's claims about time will help to illustrate how speech and image interact in the representation of intertemporal modes of thinking such as memory. The sensory elements are divided among different gradations of objective and subjective discourse, and the calibration or dissonance in this interaction is essential to the stability of a system of reference and, through it, the preservation and perpetuation of an order of meaning. Although Deleuze does not necessarily frame Bergson as such, in this chapter I will look at Bergson's intertemporality as an insight into the dynamics of film's immanent field, a key link between film and philosophy that is particularly prominent in Resnais's films.

Having looked primarily at the absent viewing subject of the apparatus, I will now look at the human subject as represented *in* the text, a character that is implied as the source of the image or its elements: the diegetic subject. Whereas Godard deconstructs the detached subject of objective representation, Resnais does so with the diegetic subject and the subjective mode of representation. Resnais's films are particularly interesting here because of the great diversity and scope with which they use speech, different codes—dialogue, voice-over, offscreen voices—struggling for domination of the text's order of meaning, thus reflecting on a range of formal problems concerning the organization of the image and its source of enunciation. To expand this study, it will be necessary once again to add to my arsenal of formal concerns. While I view Martin Schwab's criticism that Deleuze is "insensitive to the specificities of cinema" as an exaggeration,[3] I do believe that Deleuze's analysis of types of image-combination is indeed incomplete in its ocularcentric focus on the visual aspect of cinema. However, Deleuze does devote the last chapter of his second book to the relationship between speech and image, indicating that his film project would be well complemented with subsequent consideration of how these elements interact.[4] While scholars such as Patricia Pisters and Gregg Redner have made recent contributions to the study of Deleuze and sound,[5] I hope to ground this intersection in a more systematic view of how sound and, in particular, speech, functions within the immanent field and is crucial to the configuration of subject-object relations.

The relationship between language and film is a problem that has long been dominated by two focuses: the question of meaning created through dialogue, and the question of whether film is itself a language. That is to say, most critical analyses of speech in cinema, especially concerning Godard (whose use of language has been called a "frequent resort to a kind of verbal delirium"),[6] have had less to do with the relation-ship between speech utterances and the moving image than they have with basic analyses of what people say, the content of dialogue. And, at the other end of the spectrum, as we have seen, much of film semiotics has been dedicated in one way or another to understanding the relation-ship between film and language as signifying systems.

Inspired by Eco's notion of cinema as possessing a third articulation, however, I prefer to situate the relationship between cinema and language as a more formal problem that is centralized within the question of cine-matic codes and, on the level of signification, the attempt to reconcile sen-sory data to internal thought, or to use spoken words to create, to contradict, to support, or to alter the meaning of visual images. An analysis of shot and montage must be integrated into an analysis of film as a speech-im-age construct, just as the objective mode (signifying a detached transcen-dental subject) must be reconciled to the subjective mode (signified in the form of a character). For, these systems of reference coexist as modes of discourse within the same image and as image-types within the same metadiscourse, problems I hope to elucidate through a comparative anal-ysis of two films by Resnais, *Hiroshima, mon amour* (1959) and *Last Year at Marienbad* (1961).

SPEECH-IMAGE CODES AND THE HIERARCHY OF SENSES

Before extending these concerns to larger referential metacodes (the code of subjectivity and the code of objectivity), I will in this chapter redirect my analysis to focus on the codification of speech and image, the conven-tionalized relations between spoken word and visual image that guaran-tee the coherence of filmic subject-functions. I hope to use the notion of code to extend this work beyond psychoanalytic and ocularcentric studies of the apparatus and toward the problem of when the image is structured as the implied product of a diegetic character and not just a transcenden-tal subject. While it may not be fully self-evident, and is not frequently acknowledged, the filmic relationship between speech and image consti-tutes a code on the most basic level: the transposition or passage of sub-jectivity and signification between one sensory element and another. This includes any method by which speech and image are aligned in order to permit some form of transformation between the two sensory systems, whether from the aural to the visual or vice versa—a code at work, for example, in the immanent field of the galactic coffee cup from *Two or Three Things I Know About Her*.

In his *Aesthetics: Lectures on Fine Art*, Hegel considers hearing and seeing together as rational senses, what Heath translates as "senses of the distance of subject and object."[7] There is a ring of the phenomenological here: these senses help us to orient ourselves, to organize the subjective pole relative to the objective pole—what Hegel might call rationalizing our relationship with the world, and what I would call constructing an order of meaning. In nature perception is contextual, and these senses help us to organize spatial relations; in cinema this contextualization is an operation based on specific formal techniques (sound perspective, visual focus, etc.), and these senses don't only organize space but also help to signify a source of signification, an origin of meaning, and the harmony of this sensory orientation is crucial to the stability of its order of meaning. In real life, sound and image are often harmonious in a multitude of ways. For example, to hear a voice and to see a person's mouth opening and closing would be an expected sensory conjunction (which Michel Chion calls "synchronism"); similarly, we see a bat hit a baseball, and we expect to hear a crack as opposed to a splash (which Bordwell and Thompson refer to as "fidelity").[8] In more complex configurations people use words to point to an object we can see; also, we often hear descriptions and consequently imagine a visual image of what is being described. Such natural conditions are simulated by cinematic codes that use conventionalized relationships between sound and image to provide a subject of sensory harmony and, to the chagrin of theorists such as Panofsky and Arnheim, to produce a heightened connotation of realism in cinema.[9] Couldn't we say that this harmonious relationship connotes that the subject-function signified by this denotative fidelity is itself a coherent, monistic subject?

That I began my analysis in chapter 1 with the visual side of this problem is indicative of the preferences demonstrated by most theories of film and modernization. For example, film scorer and historian Hanns Eisler considers that, whereas the human eye "has become accustomed to conceiving reality as made up of separate things, commodities . . . the human ear has not kept pace with technological progress."[10] The suppositions on which this declaration is founded can be traced to a larger historical phenomenon. The cinematic century unfolded alongside what many call *the visual paradigm*, according to which both our sciences (empirical as well as philosophical) and mass media have set vision aside as a privileged sense, an ocularcentric dominant ideology that, as Martin Jay argues at the heart of *Downcast Eyes*, was challenged by the twentieth-century French philosophy for which Merleau-Ponty and Deleuze form two crucial pillars. I hope to extend this challenge here to tendencies in film theory, and in this chapter to balance out the focus on cinematic visuality that I developed in chapter 1.

My ultimate aim here is to deconstruct the popular association of vision and the image with cinematic meaning. Film may have started as a visual form, and may often favor visual expression, but is this really an accurate portrayal? Does not *Two or Three Things I Know About Her* confront us with the very fact that the immanent field of film representation is a dialogic site for the interaction of different sensory elements? If we pay attention to the construction of meaning in a film, we find that sense is often made as much—if not more—through the use of speech, which we could consider as the diegetic form of pure enunciation: a character speaks, and we listen. Not only do *we* listen, but the apparatus listens, and often the image acclimates itself to the words issued. This is the case with verbal narration, in which a character's words denote what is then provided in visual form. My interest lying not in the content of what is said but in the manner in which the sound-image is organized through subject-object relations, it will help to focus on patterns or conventions of ordering speech and image, such as the voice-over flashback, that construct a subjective position to be passed from the apparatus to the spectator in the form of a diegetic subject and thereby fix the meaning produced. How are speech and image distributed to order subject-object relations?

Psychoanalytic models, such as Chion's, answer this question according to the Lacanian argument that words make order of things and give them names, and thus words are the discursive tool of an enunciating subject-function posed as the origin of meaning.[11] However, this causal linearity from word to image, what we could call cinema's *nominative practice*, is as inadequately monolithic an assessment as was Heath's: after all, sometimes created visually and sometimes aurally, film meaning rarely follows the trajectory of only one specific order of sensory discourse. Both senses are part of the immanent field, which is in a constant state of flux as the sound-image bends and transforms. While the psychoanalytic notion of subject-formation can be useful, I am looking at film in Deleuzean terms, as a communications-based model of information and, as such, prefer to put this in terms of denotation and connotation. Roland Barthes argues, in his study of photograph captions and advertisements, that "the primary function of speech is to immobilize perception at a certain level of intelligibility . . . fixing its level of reading."[12] Speech in film is often used in a similar way, and could thus be viewed as a life preserver for film denotation. Reviving Lesage's metaphor from chapter 2, speech helps to "anchor" the text's meaning, or as Paul Willemen puts it: "verbal language is there to resist the unlimited polysemy of images," to stabilize the meaning of the film sign.[13]

In extending my claim concerning the relationship between denotation and subject-object relations, one could say that speech helps to guarantee coherence to the referential content by adding a sense of subjective totality. Speech and image are conventionally coded to preserve both a stable meaning and to guarantee the coherence of the source of that meaning. Reaffirming my understanding of this codification as a sociocultural phenomenon, a process of mythologization, Colin MacCabe and Laura Mulvey assess it as a function of conventional cinema's estrangement of the spectator from the production of filmic discourse: "This [process of mythologization] requires a fixed relation of dependence between soundtrack and image whether priority is given to the image, as in fiction films (we see the truth and the soundtrack must come into line with it) or to the soundtrack, as in documentary (we are told the truth and the image merely confirms it)."[14]

While these patterns are not necessarily fixed to fiction or documentary films per se, they *are* codified so as to collaborate in the signification of a particular system of reference that may be used to connote a certain order of meaning, for example the omniscient neutral narrator of documentary reliability. Does this imply the cohesion of subject-functions to the voice as an aural element, as Chion argues? Aren't MacCabe and Mulvey suggesting, rather, that there is no specific, inherent fixed order but that an order in either direction is constructed and with certain connotative consequences?

As Maxime Scheinfeigel points out, the visual paradigm has particularly strong roots in cinema, which has been considered "a visual art" ever since its first, silent decades.[15] As part of the formalist challenge to cinematic mythology in general, however, many theorists have tried to resist the *kingdom of images* and the *myth of visual purity*, denying the

dominant position of the image in the semiotic hierarchy of filmic expression. This denial became a central tenet of ideology and apparatus
theory, "to call into question what both serves and precedes the camera:
a truly blind confidence in the visible."[16] I believe that this study would
benefit greatly from rejecting such questions of hierarchy altogether and
by looking, instead, at how the senses are ordered in the structuring of
the sound-image. Film production techniques, as Mary Ann Doane observes, offer many practical industrial manifestations of an arbitrary hierarchy between the senses (for example, sound technology has been
developed primarily with the goal of making certain visual effects possible in the shooting process).[17] However useful such analyses have been
for revealing the ideological foundation of mainstream cinematic practices, though, I disagree with drastic conclusions such as Chion's "there
is no soundtrack."[18] Speech is not *always* swallowed by the image, as we
will soon find, but considering it so has led many to limit their analysis
of film.

Hoping to resist such a bias in film criticism's historiography, I will
now turn my ears toward an analysis of how spoken language is situated
in relation to the visual image and how this relationship contributes to
the construction of cinematic subjectivity. Moreover, how can speech—
the organization of aural meaning, not the content of words—permit
film to transcend the classical binaries of self and other, interior and exterior? Where does speech fit into the dialogism of the immanent field?
Chion claims that, in cinema, sound does not change dramatically in its
own right, but "what changes is the relationship between what we see
and what we hear."[19] This relationship is the speech-image code. And, as
Mitry points out, as holds true like a gestaltist signet for this book: "the
relationship between things is more important than the things themselves."[20] How can experiments with the sound-image code challenge
our classical understanding of how we interact with the world and even
with ourselves?

SPEECH IN, OF, AND FOR THE IMAGE

In film the use of speech changes according to how the words are connected to the visual image. This is particularly relevant to my analysis of
film signification because of its demonstration of the link concerning
structures of causality and the order of meaning, leading us to a new

twist on one of the great apocryphal philosophical quandaries: what came first, the vocal utterance of the word *chicken* or the image of the chicken? Cinema answers this question in many different ways, each one with its own connotative organization of the relationship between the speaking subject and the visual image. Many feminist critics with whom I strongly agree view the codification of sound and especially speech, therefore, as a problem of great sociocultural and ideological importance.[21] After all, since enunciation is conventionalized in conjunction with the alignment of speech and subjectivity, the notion of film as the condition for enunciation is complicated by any alteration to, or subversion of, this alignment. I find it useful to divide filmic speech into two categories: that which is part of the image, and that which is not. This does not mean diegetic versus nondiegetic, or onscreen versus offscreen; it is also slightly different from ideas such as "fidelity" or "synchronism." I hope to suggest a connotative difference between speech that is coded harmoniously with the image and speech that is coded in dissonance with the image, at least in terms of classical philosophical and cinematic conventions. There is the use of speech that implies subjective totality, and there is the use that, in what Deleuze calls "the disjunction of the sound-image,"[22] creates a dialogic interference within the image itself.

Speech can play an important connotative role, defining the logic by which subjectivity is constructed and the order of meaning that unfolds. The voice-over flashback, for example, is a codification of speech and image used for two major effects: to shift the temporal setting of the story, and to shift the discourse itself into the narrative position of the speaking subject. The immanent field is derailed by one particular character, one voice, signified as speaking subject by the fact that the constancy of this character's voice renders the temporal shift perfectly coherent. The voice-over's order of meaning is particularly intriguing because it is used to align the visual content as an expression of the speaking subject's verbal agency. This presents the construct of a new type of subject, the human subject within the image: the film becomes a simulation of that character's subjectivity. There is yet another articulation beyond Eco's, a fourth articulation, as the image is itself a representation of the objective world via a diegetic character's subjective experience of that world. After all, the voice-over seems to open the human agent to us, implying that the image has a privileged position relative to her or his subjectivity: we are allowed entrance to the interior of the character. The voice-over signifies the representation as attributed to a particular source, a spatiotemporal coherence that links the character's voice to the perspective of the filmic image. This source, differentiated from the objects seen in the image but not from the act of looking, is what I have been calling the subject; only now we can see it constructed in a different way.

And *how* does the voice-over provide this process of differentiation, of situating? Chion writes quite a lot about the voice-over or the voice without visual body, which he calls the *"acousmêtre."* Describing the *acousmêtre* as neither inside nor outside the image,[23] Chion performs a thorough technical analysis of the voice-over, assessing the recording practices and specific audio characteristics that engage the spectator's identification with the voice-over, or I-voice.[24] Through timbre, acoustics, and other technical elements, Chion helps us to understand, on a level of form, how this audible subject is created for us. Reminiscent of the thoroughness and attention to technical detail of Mitry's writing, Chion provides a perfect example of how a formal analysis can offer insight into the codification of filmic subjectivity, how the structuring of the immanent field determines from what position it will be entered, experienced. In doing so, one could say that Chion is trying to explain *how* this codification constructs a certain *feeling*, or *mood*, an indication that the image is a type of image. In other words, he focuses on the connotation of film sound.

Mary Ann Doane suggests that the voice-over has a "presence-to-itself".[25] This claim refers to the disembodied voice that, through its signifying process, posits a "phantasmatic body." I agree partially with Doane but must point out that such a "body" is a metaphor based on the system of reference, a metaphor especially familiar in semiotic and phenomenological approaches, though I will reword this to say that the voice-over signifies a particular composition of subject-object relations: the aural subject-function. As such, this formal cinematic process offers a new level on which a cinematic code constructs a filmic subject-function, how the interaction of two elements provides a particular differentiation between subjective and objective poles. Whether it is structured as inside or outside the image, the voice-over is always within the immanent field, capable of erecting a subject-function while erasing any specific visual identity thereof; instead, the visual representation is signified as being the image projected from the position of discourse that is demarcated by the voice. This is connotative—the voice-over is a form of denotation, a way of framing how the content is offered.

With the problem of spoken language and visualization, one finds the immanent field once again linked to the importance of order, both hierarchical and causal, just as it is in suture theory. As with Jacques Rancière's notion of audiovisual metaphor, this process can be seen as directly related to the interaction of speech and image inasmuch as speech tries to make things seen and images try to make things heard, contradicting both Heath's and Chion's respective hierarchies. However, as Rancière notices, "the problem is that, when a word makes us see, it no longer allows us to listen. And when the image makes us hear, it no longer leaves us to see."[26] In other words, he concludes that secreting a formal element into a code of signification seems to erase the element's formal, constructed origin. It erases its own footprints, sews together the seams of its construction, and—sutured into that fabric—we believe that we are part of an organic whole, a totality of experience taking place in the structuring of the image. We believe ourselves to be set before a denotation with no connotation. And what happens when this code breaks down, when it is revealed as a construction? As Scheinfeigel points out, conflict in the speech-image code disturbs both the image's and the spectator's conventional access to cinematic meaning and narrative logic.[27] In other words the system of reference is disturbed and the denotation rendered unstable.

How can this process be assessed? By isolating and analyzing a particular speech-image code and looking at what happens when it unravels. Here I will look at the voice-over flashback, which is perhaps the most common cinematic simulation of memory, a representation of memory as a particular composition of subject-object relations. Luckily for us, Resnais offers a wealth of films in which variant modes of representing memory are central. This also permits me to establish a dichotomy between the two filmmakers in this study. For, whereas Godard's cinematic reflexivity concerns the transcendental subject primarily as a problem of space or spatialization, for Resnais the deconstruction of subjective unity is forged through temporalization, the intertemporal fragmentation of the diegetic subject.

This shift to Resnais and the intertemporal also permits me to systematize two thinkers who are generally seen as quite disparate. Both Merleau-Ponty and Deleuze, I argued at the end of chapter 2, have the same basic goal of destroying the division of interior and exterior that is central to the classical notion of subjectivity. As a marvelous complement to

Merleau-Ponty's claim that an individual's interior is bound to other subjects and objects through its exterior existence as a body in the world, Deleuze elaborates on how the human subject is also in a state of dialogism with his or her own self at other times in the virtual past and future. Deleuze illustrates this condition through a reading of films, such as I will look at here, that rely on the subjective narration of a character. Subjective narration usually takes the form of recounting a memory. Since memory is by definition an individual's impression, and thus classically viewed as divided or isolated from the external world, Mitry points out that it is *always* subjective.[28] Yet in cinema a human's memory is also part of the immanent field; that is to say, this subjective representation of the past is being narrated in the present-time discourse of the non-subjective moving sound-image, the film itself.

This doubling of time provides a perfect example of where film and philosophy meet, as the relationship between screen-time and story-time provides for a folding of temporalities that makes cinema uniquely capable of challenging classical notions of the human experience of time. As Bergson claims, memory is not just a moment in the past, but it coexists in the present, and its representation is tied directly to the establishment of the relationship between a film's system of reference and its order of meaning. I will analyze the signifying code of the flashback according to my phenomenological framework of subject-object relations. The fluidity of the flashback, which supplies an overlapping of temporal planes due to its having started, and usually returning, to a stable present, is an organization of subject-object relations challenged by an individual's fragmented recounting of memory in *Hiroshima, mon amour*, a collective production of memory in *Last Year in Marienbad*, and, in the next chapter, a person's anticipation of virtual futures in *The War Is Over*.

ALAIN RESNAIS AND THE INTERTEMPORALITY OF DIEGETIC SUBJECTIVITY

Having begun his career in documentary film, Resnais offers across his oeuvre great insight into the filmic construction of time and memory, both of which are often considered overarching themes of his work. In *Muriel* (1963), for example, sequential shifts between past and present serve as a method for addressing a collective sense of shame (the war in

Algeria) by acknowledging that the cause of this shame is still present. The memory remains, both in the form of our silence and in the form of tangible suffering, as well as in the form of the moving image. The exploration of memory is more formally complicated in *I Love You, I Love You* (1968), for example, wherein the recurring presence of the past splinters the present into a cycle of interpretations contingent on a past that no longer has the anchor of subjective certainty.

Such temporal issues are especially resonant in Resnais's use of the voice-over flashback, a codification, as I have argued, of speech and image used to align the film message with a particular character's interior experience. Mitry notes that the use of subjective commentary as a framework for film narration goes back to more classical films like *How Green Was My Valley* (John Ford, 1941) and *Brief Encounter* (David Lean, 1945). These films used this code to preserve the totality of discourse as referring to one subject-function, a speaking subject who is also the hero of the story being recounted.[29] Such a structure gives the impression that the film is a simulation of the character's memory, using the stability of a system of reference to guarantee a consistent order of meaning. Remarking on even earlier uses of the flashback, Hugo Münsterberg refers to the flashback as an "objectivation of the memory function" in which the image is structured according to the laws of the mind over those of the external world.[30] But does our memory follow the neat and tidy logic of the conventional flashback? I agree with Noël Carroll's claim, for example, that the conventional flashback's sequential nature is "phenomenologically disanalogous with imagistic memory."[31] This statement is relevant here particularly because of its claim to a phenomenological perspective; however, I would argue that we can explore it more in terms of subject-object relations than in terms of instantaneous perception. I will use Resnais's work to illustrate a systematization of these two positions: Resnais offers an experimental mode that, while revealing that this "objectivation" is based on the specific codification of film elements, produces a connotative structure meant to refer to a type of subject different from that of the classical flashback, a subject imagined by Merleau-Ponty's phenomenology and Deleuze's film-philosophy.

To assess Resnais's codification of the speech-image relationship, one must consider the variety offered by his texts. Built systematically around the recounting of memories, *Hiroshima, mon amour* and *Last Year at Marienbad* set in opposition two modes of speech-image codification: codifications in which the words and images complement each other, refer to each other, lead into each other, or explain each other; and, codifications in which the images and the words are in conflict, rupture, the unanchored flux that is essential to film's moving image but not always allowed in its final products. In the first case, predominantly in *Hiroshima, mon amour*, speech is used to transfer information from one character to another (and to us, the viewers). The words often complement—and, in many cases, illustrate—the images, or the visual sequence unfolds according to the verbal narration. The speech-image code provides narrative unity and a source of identification in the central character as the subject of discourse and agency. However, this totality of discourse begins to come undone. Whereas in *Hiroshima, mon amour* the voice-over is part of a diegetic conversation, in *Last Year at Marienbad* it becomes lost in a dialogic cross-fading of possible pasts and uncertain presents. The immanent field begins to open up, to include not only multiple subjects but also multiple temporalities. The first film produces a logical and linear mode in which the voice-over signifies a speaking subject via its causal agency over the visual representation; the other codifies speech and image so that the referential content cannot be traced to a specific, isolated subject-function.

I would like to reiterate here that this is not an aesthetic comparison; making use of Sacha Vierny's exquisite cinematography and Resnais's signature pacing, both of these films offer a lush black-and-white visual beauty and a ruminative rhythm. This is not an argument that one film is better than the other but, instead, a comparison to establish how the nuanced shift in subject-object configurations can have a dramatic philosophical impact on the larger connotative structure of a film. Much the same as with the comparative analysis in chapter 1, the first of these films offers the possibility of radical subversion, a challenge to classical connotation that it retracts at the end but that is fully realized in the second film.

Hiroshima, mon amour and the Speaking Subject

Hiroshima, mon amour, Resnais's first feature-length fiction film, heralded the director's defiance of traditional cinematic expression. The film was instantly seen as a cinematic breakthrough. Marie-Claire Ropars-Wuilleumier summarizes the majority view: "*Hiroshima* precipitates a rupture of codes; through a forceful cinematographic *écriture* it dismantles the conventional order of cinema."[32] Although I will avoid the metaphor of *écriture* (writing) that she develops with regard to what is often seen as Resnais's novelistic tendencies,[33] this observation is a useful introduction to how the film, and indeed Resnais's work in general, has been viewed. The dismantling to which Ropars-Wuilleumier refers, I will argue, revolves around the problem of subjective stability raised through conflicting speech-image codifications of memory. A film about the communication and incommunicability of memory, *Hiroshima, mon amour* challenges the myth of subjective autonomy, showing the fragility of a unilateral source of signification whose totality is guaranteed by a linear temporal order. What can be said about film's subject-object relations when such quintessential codifications of diegetic enunciation as the flashback cease to adhere?

As with most of Resnais's films, the story here could be seen as a springboard for experimenting with the representation of subjective time; in fact, Mitry proclaims *Hiroshima, mon amour* the first work to make existential time and memory the basis for the film itself.[34] But this is not simply a film that *talks about* memory and time; it *shows* and *speaks* them, a cinematic show-and-tell that is achieved by focusing on the connotative level of signification. The progressively unconventional obscurity of the film's forms of denotation directs attention to the immanent field. Yet I strongly disagree with Roy Armes's claim that *Hiroshima, mon amour* "has no story to tell in the normal sense."[35] The film does tell a clear story, even if it is not told in a conventional way. In fact, the unconventionality of the film arises from the formal conjunction of *three* stories: (1) the present-tense story of an affair between a French actress (whom I will call "Nevers" [Emmanuelle Riva] as she is dubbed at the end of the film) and a Japanese architect ("Hiroshima" [Eiji Okada]), both of whom are married; (2) Nevers's self-narrated past, which involves her love affair with a German soldier during World War II, his death, and her long-endured punishment by family and community; and (3) the story of the nuclear destruction of Hiroshima and the new scale of warfare introduced by the atomic bomb.[36]

These three stories are interlinked in a complicated form of denotation, a shattered network of sound-images to mirror a shattered world—a postgenocidal and postnuclear trauma of representation that Jacques Rivette claimed to be Resnais's primary obsession: "the fragmentation of the central unity," which I understand as the unity posited through

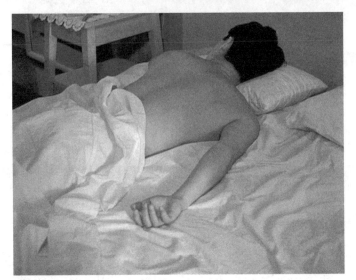

classical philosophy's notion of subjectivity.[37] This network of representations is not merely a question of narration, as many would argue, but concerns spoken narration as a means for ordering the image as a type of image. In other words it is a problem of connotation. How are these image-types constructed? Present dialogues use present images as triggers for the representation of memories, memories that begin as spoken words only to transform into image-sequences. Many argue that this is a novelistic convention of cinema, a narrative flow of temporal dimensions that we may recognize quintessentially as the thematic basis for Marcel Proust's *Remembrance of Things Past*. For example, the position of Hiroshima's arm, as he lies in bed, reminds our protagonist of the position in which her first lover died, thus thrusting her back into the past (figs. 3.1–3.3)—which, gradually as the film unfolds, thrusts her into narrating that past.

For Mitry this evokes the Proustian notion of the present as "a privileged instant between memory and forgetting."[38] I would translate this poetic but unclear claim to say that in cinema the present is the temporal praxis for the immanent field through which other temporal subjectivities emanate. The present is privileged as the praxis for enunciation, and this moment is privileged for the speaking subject, who can view herself, her own experience, as a product of her own enunciation. Linking the present with the past through a simple visual shock, she transforms this connection between sensation and memory into a formal cinematic code: the voice-over flashback.

The voice-over flashback, I have argued, reduces the film image to a shared mental image—shared between the narrator, her lover, the viewing subject set in the past, and the immanent field that ties these together—at once both a memory and the communication of a memory. In other words it is an image that within itself casts shadows on multiple points along the scale from subjective to objective. Moreover, it is also, Mitry notes, her own act of looking at herself as an object, which for Mitry is central to memory in both real and cinematic terms. Echoing Münsterberg, as he often does, Mitry refers here to the flashback as an "objectivation of the subjective," an objective rendering of a subjective experience, which Mitry compares with Proust's writing in order to

FIGURES 3.1–3.3

In *Hiroshima, mon amour* (1959) Nevers (Emmanuelle Riva) flashes back to her past.

illustrate a novelistic aspect of this codification between speech and image.[39] Wolfgang A. Luchting poses a complex argument to this effect in "*Hiroshima, mon amour*, Time, and Proust," in which he systematically dissects the film according to a narrative structure of different temporal cases (real time, subjective time, etc.), and thus as a complicated representation of "the order of things."[40] This "order of things," however, avoids the fundamental question of *how* this order is constructed, not as a sequence of temporal unities but as an immanent field, a collection of interrelationships of specifically cinematic formal elements and interwoven processes of organization. Although narrative experimentation is part of *Hiroshima, mon amour*, such an analysis does not fully acknowledge how this narration is unique or unconventional: how is this connoted, and how is it cinematic? Beyond the film's implicit commentary on nuclear warfare, memory, and forbidden love, how do its sound-image forms provide experimental ways of understanding our relationship to the world and to ourselves that transcends the content or object of the text's analysis?

The film's focus on history and subjectivity inclines one to follow up, respectively, on more allegorical or psychoanalytic interpretations, such as those offered by Luchting, Ropars-Wuilleumier, and Emma Wilson. While Luchting focuses his analysis on the moral ambiguity of adulterous love, Ropars-Wuilleumier argues that the subversion of codes is an allegory for the sublime and inexpressible magnitude of Hiroshima as a historical event.[41] Wilson reformulates this allegorical understanding of the flashback according to a psychoanalytic framework, as "an unwilled returning hallucination or memory that takes possession of the victim of trauma." Wilson goes on to suggest that the film consists of subjective representations from "a traumatized mind" and that this opening function of the connection between the images of arms exemplifies the importance of bodies and the representation of the haptic in Resnais. She affirms this argument for a visceral reading based on the fact that, in its context in the film, this flashback "serves no explanatory function in the narrative."[42]

Wilson is correct in that, at this point, we don't know who the dead man on the ground is or what the context of that image is. I would argue, however, that this sequence does serve a different explanatory function, as it introduces the film's paradigm for subject-object relations, the form through which its denotations will be presented. This fleeting cut accommodates us to the system of reference on which the narrative will be founded, easing the film's immanent field into an alignment with the subjective position of a particular character. In Metzian fashion Wilson makes the connotative analysis secondary to a denotative argument based on the experiences of the film's main character. On the connotative level, *Hiroshima, mon amour* is guided by an order of meaning for the most part making use of conventional cinematic codifications of memory. Maintaining aural agency over the unfolding of images, Nevers projects herself as an object in the past while guarding her subjectivity in the present. Typically viewed in film criticism as a text based on fragmentation and struggling discourses,[43] *Hiroshima, mon amour*, I argue, as with *Vivre sa vie*, poses challenges to classical representation while, in the end, reverting to conventional codifications of subjectivity.

This is the case beginning with the opening scene, in which the film presents abstract images of two intertwined bodies, each of which glimmers with sand crystals, and quickly drifts into a voice-over dialogue (it is a voice-over to the extent that it is assumed that, while the speaking couple may be intimately conjoined, these are not their actual bodies). The sequence unfolds according to a cyclical progression from speech to image, the images following Nevers's voice-over. She is, quite literally, denoting. Each time she claims to have seen something (first the hospital, then the museum, then the newsreels), we see what she is describing; this image is sometimes even given from the perspective of a moving camera that is directly looked at by people in the frame (fig. 3.4), implying that the shot is constructed according to the individual perspective of a mobile subject.

Hiroshima, to whom she is saying all of this, frequently interrupts to say: "You have seen nothing," forcing her *acousmêtre* back to the praxis of the diegetic present, back to the visual context of their bodies. Armes describes this scene as a counterpoint between subjective recollection and documentary modes of representation.[44] According to my framework I would argue that here we have an overlapping of different systems of reference. We are seeing images similar to those presented in documentary forms, and sometimes even images from a documentary film, but *as* the mental image of a character, her memories, as codified through the speech-image relationship. And, the immanent field constantly shifts between documentary-style images of Nevers's past and objective images of the couple in bed.

Nevers introduces cutaway images with "I saw . . . ," leading many critics to conclude that the film is about seeing things.[45] But the film is

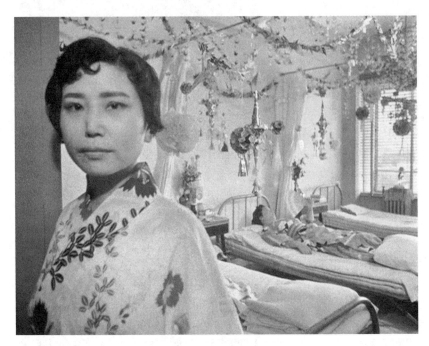

FIGURE 3.4
The camera of *Hiroshima, mon amour* glides through visualized memories.

less about *having seen* than about *showing*, about using a particular codification of speech and image to create a narrative discourse in the diegetic present. It is crucial that the logic of ordering begins not with the
visual manifestation of the concept or act of seeing but with the words *I
saw*—a phrase that, importantly, begins with *I*, a subjective pronoun es-
tablishing a system of reference before any claim to action or evidence of
this act is provided. While Nevers's ability to show is manifested in her
signaling of subjective images, Hiroshima's interjections constantly
bring us back to the objective pole. This struggle between audiovisual
discourse and the physical body raises questions concerning the relationship between signification and physical existence, between the subjective and objective in cinema. Jean-Louis Leutrat, among others, argues
that the central theme of the film is the theme of skin, hands, impressions of the tactile.[46] This tactile aspect constantly interrupts the codification of speech and image. Nevers is a being in the world, as Merleau-
Ponty might say; but our knowledge of her being is coded through film
form. The structure of her being is part of the immanent field.

Redirecting these theorists' argument, then, one could rather see this as Nevers's coexistence at once as the subject of her own narrated story and as an object in a physical context (which is the text that we are watching). Though it contributes to the dialogic notion of film, this reading of the speech-image code proposes a conventionalized overlapping between perception, memory, and communication (what she has seen, remembers, and tells). Christian Metz's suggestion that a flashback is like a striptease is particularly poignant here: the more that she reveals, the more that she posits herself as an object of her own narration, the more subjective control she has over the text.[47] This codification begins to display its own fragility, however, as the protagonist proceeds further into recounting her own traumatic history. She tells of her German lover and of her incarceration in the family cellar as punishment for the shame caused by her affair with the occupying enemy. Denotatively, this sequence is particularly moving for its allegorical representation of the repression of female sexuality and the dualistic nature of fascism as a function of what Noël Burch calls "the stupidity of the provincial bourgeoisie" during wartime. Burch observes, furthermore, that Nevers's story unfolds a-chronologically: we see the events not in the order that they happen but in the order that they occur to her, "the stream of her impressions and associations."[48] Burch's point upholds the common understanding of this enunciation as a conventionalized representation of her attempt to represent her own experience.

We should, however, view this breakdown of denotative linearity as a question primarily of formal—not narrative—subversion. For the sequence to unfold as it does, it must be engendered to do so by the construction of subject-object relations in the form of the speech-image code. During this scene *Hiroshima, mon amour* encounters short-circuits in the flashback process, blips in the speech-image code that connote imperfections in conventional systems of reference. This is a contradiction between temporal sources of speech and image: the image of the past is still dominated by her voice in the present. We are in the present with the couple. Her voice ushers the visual track into an image of the past, but an objective relationship with that past is never established. The voice-over flashback does not fulfill its role as a code, does not transfer the image from her subjectivity to an objective image set in the past. Resnais's experimentation with the simultaneity of sound blends objective and subjective poles in a manner that challenges our conventions of understanding and representing memory. The images begin slightly to contradict her narration: she tells about hearing "La Marseillaise" overhead, and we see soldiers passing silently. The speech-image code, whose coherence of enunciation is meant to connote a particular order of meaning, is beginning to splinter.

The division of subjectivity represented by the shift in temporality proves to be too much for the psychological stability of the character. Herein lies the connotative trauma that Wilson's analysis could have followed through with, as the state of narrative limbo is fundamentally a breakdown in the formal codification of speech and image. As if deeply disturbed by the abovementioned fragmentation of speech, sound, and image, Nevers begins to narrate her memory, a recounting of the past, *in the present tense*, fracturing the spatiotemporal coherence of her enunciation. The speech-image codification, which is the cinematic sign of her psychological stability, begins to come undone: the image ceases to be linked to her speech.

We should therefore understand this as a connotative rupture—not as a rupture in the narrative, which remains relatively stable, but instead with the philosophical ramifications of how the story's telling is structured, what its telling tells us about the individual as an intersection between past and present and what it is suggesting as alternatives to conventional theories of memory. That is to say: a rupture in the form of denotation, a formal rupture between aural and visual elements that offers us a new way of understanding human subjectivity. This enunciating subject-function begins to splinter further between the past she narrates and the present in which she is narrated, in a scene that takes place between Nevers and her reflection in the bathroom mirror (fig. 3.5).

Her entire discourse deteriorates here into a polysemy of pronouns. She speaks to herself about herself, addressing herself as the first person "I" and also the second person "you." Beyond addressing herself as possible interlocutor, she interchanges her past and present lovers in the mix of discourses, each of whom at numerous points assumes the mantle of "you" in the present-tense discourse. But her schizophrenia—and therefore the image's—goes beyond the content of her words. This decomposition manifests itself on the formal level of the speech-image code, as her monologue (or conversation with herself) fluctuates between diegetic speech and voice-over speech. The same thread of speech is continued in these two aural forms, thus presenting the same voice as the source of

FIGURE 3.5
Nevers's doubled image: a split subject.

two different modes of enunciation, a subject split between discourses. The immanent field spreads its wings to mend and encompass the division of the interior and exterior of the diegetic subject.

I should acknowledge here the psychoanalytic importance of the fact that this exchange is happening in a mirror reflection.[49] According to Lacan, the mirror phase—one of the most frequently recurring psychoanalytic concepts used in film theory—attests to the stage in human subject-formation in which the infant succeeds at identifying itself as both a visible object and coherent subject. As can be gleaned from the language of the previous sentence, Lacan's theory projects Merleau-Ponty's existential philosophy onto a psychoanalytic framework of mental development. In filmic terms this is similar to Mitry's assessment of the flashback, in which the character verbally posits herself as a visible object in the imagistic representation of her own verbally narrated recollection. In this particular example the codification of that recollection becomes apparent, as if cinema itself were acknowledging its own duality between subjective and objective poles. This mode of self-conscious,

FIGURE 3.6
Despite Nevers's aural narration to the contrary, Hiroshima keeps his distance.

reflexive cinema, constructed by Resnais and Godard in very different ways, could well be described as cinema's mirror stage.

After this scene Nevers attempts to gather the composure of her conventional subjectivity. She walks down the sidewalk with her lover only steps behind, depth-of-field adding yet another mode of organizing the division between them. She tries to reclaim the authority of her enunciating subject-function by reinforcing the causality between her voice-over and the visual representation. "He will walk towards me . . . take me by the shoulders. He will kiss me," her voice-over says as they walk. However, he remains distant (fig. 3.6).

Her voice-over is not supported by the visual world of action; she is revealed to be powerless in the present, and her control over the narrative is revealed as a coded representation. This fully rejects any illusion that the image is essentially or naturally connected to the words being spoken. Her interior is made exterior, and the representation is caught between aural subjectivity and visual objectivity, a site for the dialogic overlapping of reference points.

In a textually circular fashion, however, evoking this nominative process marks the film's return to its original speech-image code, the reconciliation of speech, image, and body found in the opening. In the final scene, after having passed the entire film anonymously, the two characters name each other: she names him "Hiroshima," and he names her "Nevers." This act of naming reconciles the film's speech-image irregularities in a way that supports the conventional subject-function challenged in certain sequences: in the end the human subjects are defined by a nominal logic of differentiation and returned to the objective system of reference held in the apparatus. Just as we saw with Nana's death in the final scene of *Vivre sa vie*, *Hiroshima, mon amour* ends by nullifying its experimental philosophy and returning to an order of meaning founded on traditional rules of thinking.

Last Year at Marienbad and the Dialogic Subject of Collective Memory

Last Year at Marienbad is quite different from *Hiroshima, mon amour* in that it is not simply divided between the present and the past *but between all possible pasts and their contingent presents*; moreover, its embrace of an unconventional order of meaning, which does away with the hierarchy between real and imaginary, certainty and confusion, owes the realization of its philosophy to the complex system of reference set up in the film's immanent field, a transforming flow between the apparatus and two diegetic subjects. This terminology admittedly owes much to Deleuze's conceptualization of cinematic time, which uses Bergson's principles of temporal overlapping to understand the temporal fragmentation of a diegetic subject. Indeed, just as *Hiroshima, mon amour* serves for Mitry as the model for a new type of cinema, *Last Year at Marienbad* holds for Deleuze a special place: it is "an important moment" in the deconstruction of classical codes and a constant point of reference in *Cinema 2: The Time-Image*'s exploration of a new film-philosophical outlook that rejects classical paradigms of logic, representation, and the subject-object binary.[50]

A film about the struggle between two people over a memory of something that may or may not have happened, *Last Year at Marienbad*, Ronald Bogue points out, can be said to represent a "malleable, non-personal virtual past" composed from the slightly varied repetitions of "memory suggestions."[51] By "non-personal" we can understand Deleuze's concept of nonspecific film subjectivity, what I have reconstructed as a fluctuation between positions, which is illustrated by this film's combination of image-types in an overall network of collective memory that includes both the apparatus and multiple characters. Bogue extends Deleuze's analysis to posit the images as "coexisting strata of time," a flux that I would describe as the coexistence, in the present, of multiple possible memories.[52] This fluid movement between past and present would be impossible without keeping one foot in the present while stopping the other in the past. To do this, a code must be ruptured and divided between the two elements that compose it.

This rupture is accomplished by splicing the speech-image code. We have seen how in *Hiroshima, mon amour* the splice in this code can permit a sort of time travel, as long as the subject-function driving this time machine is coherent, stable. I will look now at what happens when this time machine loads up on turbo fuel, loses its GPS device, and gets hijacked by another driver. *Last Year at Marienbad* is built from a system of montage in which the conventional narrative organization of shots is replaced by an interweaving of temporal moments, using certain formal relations to connote the permeable nature of temporal continuity, as well as the crystalline or multilateral nature of film enunciation. This crystal, like that constructed in *Two or Three Things I Know About Her*, reveals the dialogic capabilities of film's immanent field. Nowhere is this more apparent than in the synapses between speech act and mental image, a relationship that we could isolate as the central basis for *Last Year at Marienbad*'s philosophical experiments. The film's screenwriter and champion of the *nouveau roman*, Alain Robbe-Grillet, himself wrote in the published version of *Last Year at Marienbad*: "The entire film . . . consists of a reality that the hero creates from his own vision, his own speech."[53]

The film is about the attempt to denote a visual reality through the use of spoken words; however, the film does not unfold neatly. *Last Year at Marienbad* is composed of a wide variety of speech-image relations, rarely maintaining a conventional code of present-speech/present-image or even a clearly defined code between present-speech/past-image. But let me start out more simply, with an overview of the film and its critical reception. Though there is admittedly little "story" to go on, there *is* a general theme of seduction, refusal, and persuasion—what Jean V. Alter aptly calls "a conflict of wills."[54] This conflict of wills manifests itself through opposing mental acts, an audiovisual phantasmagoria that unsettles most conventions of film storytelling, leaving viewers to ask: "*What* happened?"

As a result of its unique stylistic extravagance and its cryptic order of meaning, *Last Year at Marienbad* has inspired no shortage of commentary and interpretation. Wilson, for example, views the general unreality of the film as being "about the role of fantasy in supporting desire."[55] Working from Slavoj Žižek's reading of the film, Wilson interprets the experimental narrative as manifesting the characters' desire and fantasy: the struggle for volition, according to Wilson, could be seen from this angle as a rape fantasy. Although I will not take a similar psychoanalytic approach, Wilson's interpretation could be viewed as a variant on my notion of the immanent field, in which we find an interaction between image-types built according to different subject-object relations, struggling to guide the philosophical logic of the film's metadiscourse. While metaphors of fantasy and dream dominate most readings of *Last Year at Marienbad*, my model would systematize these alongside more narrative approaches, such as Neal Oxenhandler's analysis of the text as a symbolic representation of emotion.[56]

For those familiar with the film, it is without question complex and fecund for interpretation. And, while *Last Year at Marienbad*'s system of meaning is so vastly open that a multitude of allegorical, psychoanalytic, and symbolic interpretations could be applied to it,[57] I will defer to the filmmakers' insistence that the text is, fundamentally, a reflexive experiment in film form.[58] Regardless of whether the unfolding scenes are memories or fantasies, dreams or alternate dimensions, critics such as Jacques Brunius and Haim Callev point out that this debate is made possible by the fact that the film perpetuates no clear system of reference.[59] *Last Year at Marienbad* is constantly unsettled by a fluctuation between the subjective and objective poles, and we are never given a clear structure of subject-object relations; the film dismantles the coded divisions between subject-functions, constructing a reflexive parallelism that implicates in the immanent field the signifying processes between person and person, between character and text, and between text and spectator. As Merleau-Ponty might say, it shows how we show—to others, and to ourselves.

The opening sequence in *Last Year at Marienbad* introduces the connotative principles that will prevail throughout the film, including audiovisual motifs as well as the thematic instability of the code that binds the audio and the visual. On the visual level the film opens with long tracking shots that capture the luxurious frescoes and gilded trellises of the chateau where it is set, an ornate visual design accentuated by

Vierny's black-and-white photography and a vast array of mirrors and re-
flections (Lacan, incidentally, first presented his mirror-stage theory at a
conference held in the town of Marienbad in 1936). The tracking shot,
usually attributable to a specific source, is not attached to an identified
subject of vision, so we turn to the audio for such an anchor. But the
images flow by hypnotically, apparently without any motivated connection to a soundtrack that is saturated with conflict, an ebb and flow between two aural elements: an organ and a male voice-over that describes
the labyrinthine grandeur of the locale. Taking turns fading each other in
and out, the aural elements constantly exchange places in the forefront of
the sound mix. This produces what David Bordwell calls "the cocktail-
party effect,"[60] referring to the difficulty of following two aural discourses
at once. Though Bordwell relegates this effect to "spoken discourses," it
could be applied here to the disparate sources of enunciation, as these
overlapping soundtracks vie for the production of different systems of
reference: one that is narrated by a character and another, accentuated by
organ music, projected from the apparatus.

At this point, however, neither the voice nor the organ has a diegetic
source in the film: we see no organ, we see no body. One could argue that
the voice-over, in fact, belongs to the male protagonist (who, following
Robbe-Grillet's script, I will call "X" [Giorgio Albertazzi]), but this is unclear at this stage, as the audience has not seen him. Continuing her argument of the tactile in Resnais's work, Wilson claims, "Words precede images here, as if the extraordinarily tactile, sentient world of Marienbad . . .
is called up, imagined as a result of the words we hear narrated."[61] However, the scene does not necessarily unfold in this nominative manner:
the words follow a cyclical, not linear—or explicative—trajectory and are
constantly faded in and out by the music. What I termed cinema's nominative practice earlier in this chapter, in which the visual image is conjured
or described directly by spoken words, is frustrated further by the constant, interruptive return of the organ. Neither of these aural elements ex-
erts a causal agency over the flow of images. The voice-over speaks of being thrust back through rooms and halls, yet the visual pictures are not
necessarily connected to the words. For example, the organ softens slightly
as the voice-over fades in at a random point in its cycle: " . . . the lengths of
these corridors . . . " As his voice continues, the shot cuts to a different
tracking shot. The new tracking shot moves fluidly as the voice then fades
out and the organ fades in: the shift between the two aural tracks has no

connection to the cutting between tracking shots. Voice-over narration, nondiegetic music, and the tracking shot are all normally characterized by their fluid formal continuity. But here one continues as the other breaks, shifts, or restarts, thus accentuating the rift between them, belying their own respective lacks of totality. This introduces what Leutrat views as the film's central theme of repetition and difference.[62]

This theme escorts us into the scene that follows. The guests at the villa are paired off into couples or trios, and the camera slowly moves through the rooms while the sound records fragments of often unattributed conversation. Following the theme of repetition and difference, a collective discourse is interwoven among the different groups, basic themes of conversation that continue unimpeded from one group to the next. Each group engages in a variation on the incertitude that will come to dominate the interactions between X and the female protagonist, "A" (Delphine Seyrig). "We met . . . ," " . . . when . . . ?," " . . . where . . . ?" Watching this clarifies Wilson's observation that the guests "function as part-animate props" to provide molds for how the film will use speech-image codifications to represent the phenomenon of collective memory and the role of verbal narration therein. A certain process of collective interaction permeates the immanent field: the signifying system from which this film builds its articulations consists of what Wilson refers to as "the social codes which construct identities and social interchange" through repetition and circulation.[63] Fleeting claims about "when we met . . . [and] where . . . " are confirmed not by images or even firsthand description but by the narrative assertion that "I heard . . . " As I will show, however, in this film, being recounted, being narrated, does not make something factual, does not always lend it certainty. These conversations weave in and out of the voice-over of X, who has now been given a visible body (at least, a body we assume to be his, as he is the only person we recognize in numerous images). His voice-over, too, extends its own permutations on this collective discourse.

This scene introduces A, the female protagonist about whom these hushed voices may or may not be talking, via a conflict between speech and image. Wearing a black dress, A stands in a doorway. Presumably speaking of her, and also to her, we hear X's voice-over utter the words: "Always the same." The image cuts to A, in the same position, only now wearing a white dress, thus ironically following the speech-act with the visual contradiction of its meaning (i.e., in the second image she is not "the same" as in the first). In *Last Year at Marienbad*'s dance of repetition and difference, the film tells us up front, we will have to get used to our expectations being dashed. This signals a split that I will argue in chapter 4 is characteristic of Resnais's oeuvre in general and, in chapter 5, is manifested in different ways in Godard's *Contempt*. This split occurs between the sensory aspects of the sound-image, keeping both visual and aural elements present in the immanent field but detaching them from a solitary system of reference. This split signifies a struggle for subjective agency, a multiplicity in the film's origin of meaning and therefore an experiment in the classical model of logical thought and the totality of meaning. This sensory split, like the aural discourses of *Two or Three Things I Know About Her*, reveals the text itself as a field for the interaction of possible subjective positions. But in *Last Year at Marienbad* the sequence of images is not only a site for this interaction: it is a battleground for the war of speech-image agency. This struggle for a closed audiovisual image, for a singular subjective position, takes the narrative form of persuasion: X's attempt to convince A of their mutual experience by conjuring up an imagistic past with his verbal discourse in the present. But the present is not stable in the midst of forking pasts, possible memories, and conflicting temporal discourses.

This instability results from the fact that, while these temporal fluctuations are linked through the transformation of speech codes, these links do not provide a stable subject of discourse. There is never a definite logical order of meaning infused into the relationship between speech and image: the mode of discourse is constantly changing and, thus, never stabilizing a single subjective agent, nor even a single sensory agent. As Christian Metz writes: "In *Last Year at Marienbad*, the image and the text wrestle. . . . The battle is even: the script creates images, the images provide a text: it is this game of contexts that provides the contours of the film."[64] These contexts consist of a constant overlapping between speech functions and visual functions. Contrary to Metz's assertion, though, I view the film rather as a *failure* of words to make images and *vice versa*. The subject-functions of visuality and speech are kept from conjoining, thus denying each other any corroborative certainty or confirmation. For the majority of the film X struggles to convince A of their previous meeting by garnishing visual support for his words, but this agency constantly finds itself at the crossroads of overlapping subjective and objective poles.

We find A, for example, wandering through an open hallway as X's voice-over speaks of her clothes and gestures. At this point the image

FIGURE 3.7

In *Last Year at Marienbad* (1961) X's voice-over narration becomes dialogue as he joins A in the frame.

seems to be a mental image constructed by his verbal description. That impression is soon shifted, however; the camera zooms in and pans slightly to reveal X himself in the image, his voice-over suddenly becoming an onscreen voice (fig. 3.7). This formal alteration to the immanent field abruptly shifts the system of reference from subjective (though it is unclear according to *whose* subjectivity) to objective.

Yet this is not the code he wants, for it does not assume an alignment between his speech and her imaginary. It does not align the immanent field to signify him as its unique system of reference. So, again, X returns to conjuring images according to his voice-over. When he gets this wish, however, it is not without its consequences. We see A outside, awkwardly trying to position herself according to X's description. His voice-over describes how she was standing, and in the image we can see her attempt to accommodate his description. That is: A, in an image that is coded to be set in the past, responds directly to the speech act that is attributed to the present, fully breaking the illusion necessary for a stable denotation either between the characters or between the film and spectator.

This sequence provides the first truly self-conscious rupture in the conventionalization of temporal divisions, self-conscious in that the text acknowledges that it is supposed to work *a certain way*, that there is a conventional way of structuring film meaning through the order between speech and image that this film is currently violating—it is consciously experimenting with cinematic thought, performing philosophy not through written words but through the tools and codes of cinematic form. The code is brought to the surface; the myth that X is attempting to create is re-vealed as exactly that, a myth; and the frustration of a closed denotation directs attention toward the film's connotative base. This myth is then naturalized in the form of an objective image of the two characters, and objectivity is thrown into question by the fact that their conversation con-tinues in voice-over. Again, when one sensory element follows X's attempt to organize a system of reference, the other sensory element deconstructs it. He tries to keep A at the mercy of his aural agency, the power of his voice-over narration, which exists only through the ability of his words to conjure images. The film returns to the diegetic "present," in which X's description of the statue by which they were standing is interrupted by Frank (presumably A's husband [Sacha Pitoëff]), who explains the histori-cal basis for the statue and, thus, offers yet another subject or source of meaning in the film, another system of reference intersecting in the im-manent field.

The centrality of the statue to the multicharacter discourse has led many, including René Prédal, Leutrat, and Suzanne Liandrat-Guigues, to make the argument that *Last Year at Marienbad* is, in fact, a film about the statue itself.[65] In the context of my analysis, however, at most the statue can be seen as a microcosm for the film's meditation on interpre-tation and relativity, and merely plays the role of an object of discussion around which the multiple voices can vie for subjective agency. My own argument can be posed as such: there is a problem of denotation, which can be traced to the instability or lack of specificity of a single system of reference, the interruptions and feedback of multiple discourses. The vi-sual tracks begin to intersect here, and it becomes unclear within which system of reference the image is being signified. Does the image belong to A or to X? Even as it seems that she is beginning to remember, her memory is still not the same as his. In this way *Last Year at Marienbad* offers us a simulation of collective memory, two people trying to recon-cile their mutual present to a nonmutual past. As Deleuze observes, Resnais "discovers the paradox of one memory shared by two people."[66] It is important to note that Deleuze uses the word *mémoire*, which means memory as a mental function, and not *souvenir*, which refers to one spe-cific memory. These two people have different understandings of some time-space continuum that they may, in fact, have in common; it is just a question of how it is seen, what the logic may be through which they con-nect to the world—in other words, what their philosophy may be.

This paradox, formally realized through a juxtaposition of aural and visual elements, presents a struggle for authenticity on the level of the speech-image code: subjective agency rests with the character who can determine some sort of sensory causality or harmony, who can establish an affinity with the immanent field, align his or her imaginary with the film image. But in *Last Year at Marienbad* this codification never succeeds: what began as a singular attempt to persuade becomes a collective challenge to remember. To follow up on Deleuze's "memory of two," we slowly realize that the memory being debated, regardless of whether or not they both experienced it at some point together, is "a memory that is communal because it relates back to the same givens, affirmed by one and denied or rejected by the other."[67] This very opposition, manifested in the formal sharing of visual representations, reveals a bond between people. But who is telling the truth? Is there any such thing as absolute certainty, or truth, in the classical notion of subjectivity, which—according to Deleuze—by its very essence implies the divergence of consciousnesses and, between them, the impossibility of consensus?[68]

The suspense concerning their possible shared past builds toward a climactic confrontation over that pivotal night during which a tryst is claimed to have happened, and a sexual assault is implied as a possible alternative. Standing at the bar, X describes to A his entrance into her room. There is a quick crosscutting between the present moment of description and the past that is being described. In the present A looks at X, finally beginning to adopt his verbal descriptions as her own memory. He speaks of entering her room. In the bedroom A looks up, as if at someone who is entering, and laughs (fig. 3.8). The sound of her laughter resonates through the temporal division provided by the code of montage, continuing on the soundtrack as if escorting the image—and therefore her and us—back into the present, back to the bar, where a female bystander's laughter replaces that of A (fig. 3.9). The two sounds merge into one experimental sound-bridge, blending two temporalities into one filmic utterance; the immanent field binds the temporalities through its inclusion of formal elements.

The aural element of laughter is continuous, providing an intertemporal unity or totality that breaks A out of the trance of X's agency, as if from fear of being consumed by his claim to subjective power. The sound-bridge of laughter carries her from the collective imaginary back into the present, where she is terrified at the potential power of his verbal

FIGURES 3.8 AND 3.9
The sound of laughter provides a sound-bridge between possible past and apparent present.

subjectivity. At this point it becomes wholly apparent that these temporal shards, or what Deleuze calls *nappes*, are not independent of each other: in their Bergsonian coexistence these temporally different sound-images create what Deleuze refers to as a sort of "feedback" similar to that produced by electricity interfering with itself.[69] It is through this feedback of multiple utterances, each of which is composed of its own subject-object configurations, that the system of montage deconstructs the conventions of the classical subject and signifies what Resnais refers to poignantly as "a universal present" in which all temporalities collide.[70]

Terrified, A recoils, bumping into the bystander and knocking a glass to the floor. Her fear in the present is then transferred to her representation of the memory, in which she now expresses fear. In the bedroom A, recoiling in fear, knocks over a glass (fig. 3.10).

FIGURE 3.10
The affective continuity of fear provides a transition from apparent present to possible past.

Shaking with the reverberations of this feedback, the speech-image code struggles with a transition created by the sentiment of terror being directed from the present backward. In this case, as Deleuze observes: "The characters exist in the present, but their feelings plunge into the past."[71] In fact, both the characters and their sentiments alternate between past and present, present and past, but one is never exclusive of the other. Both emanate through the immanent field. The past affects the present, and the present affects the past—it is all a matter of what, at a given moment, is the system of reference according to which the text is structured.

This sequence marks a turning point in the film because it is here that A begins—as if in desperate self-defense—to challenge X's dominance of the speech-image code. Whereas we saw before that she would attempt to accommodate his voice-over by shaping her mental image accordingly (such as the placement of her arm on the balustrade), she begins now to struggle against his agency. At one point, from within the mental image that is being constructed by his verbal description, she pleads with him to leave her alone, an intertemporal plea to the present from this convoluted past. The speech-image code reveals its own constructed nature—and, as a construction, it reveals itself as a site of the struggle for agency, an agency that she can assume just as well. Resisting his description of her room, A briefly takes control of the voice-over description, going so far as to contradict aspects of the image that were not even a part of his verbal discourse. "I don't know this room," she argues, "this ridiculous bed, this fireplace with its mirror." But he had mentioned no fireplace, no mirror. She is now implicated in the unfolding of images, is now fully complicit in the discourse—be it to her advantage or disadvantage, she has commandeered agency through controlling the sound-image logic. She claims that there was a painting above the chimney as opposed to a mirror, and the images follow suit (figs. 3.11–3.13).

A has momentarily appropriated the agency forged in the speech-image code of voice-over flashback. She begins to correct X, which sends him into a spiral of self-doubt. Wilson observes that X is not satisfied by A's remembrance but is instead threatened by her speech-image agency: "the relation between them begins to become more disturbing to the man and his fantasy less protective."[72]

One could certainly consider this development from a feminist point of view as the empowerment of her character, not only as a narrative agent but also on a more sweeping connotative level. Manifesting a systematic subversion like that evoked by Gledhill and Doane earlier in this chapter, A uses speech to subvert the patriarchal order of the visual. She has usurped the formal code from which his agency was formed, much as the montage of close-ups of material objects permits *Two or Three Things I Know About Her* to subvert the code of frame and composition in order to destroy conventional divisions between subject and object. Unlike *Hiroshima, mon amour*, which transposes a subjective position conventionally given to men onto a female character, *Last Year at Marienbad* presents an intersubjective dialogue between two subjects, each afraid of being objectified by the discourse of the other.

I will stop here, though *Last Year at Marienbad* certainly provokes many chapters and even books worth of formal analysis and possible interpretation. This particular moment in its unfolding brings my analysis to a breaking point, though, a pinnacle of illustrating how formal codifications provide first and foremost for the production of an image as a type of image rooted to a system of reference, structuring the immanent field according to an organization of subject-object relations. Moreover, we can see how the immanent field extends itself, how these subject-object compositions interact, as Deleuze might argue, on a level of montage. Wilson again manages eloquently to preclude my own conclusion: "The effect of *Last Year at Marienbad* as it continues is to make us increasingly uncertain about the limits of the subjectivity and desire of

FIGURES 3.11–3.13

A takes control of the verbal narration and image production in *Last Year at Marienbad.*

these lovers. This effect is in part created by our uncertainty over the status of the images viewed."[73]

The deconventionalization of speech and image makes us question whether the images are meant to be memory or fantasy, the mental image of one character or another, or an objective representation external to both. Any quest for denotative clarity is rendered impossible by the fragmentation of the images' systems of reference through the decodifications of speech and image. We therefore can also see, through this analysis, a specific way to articulate the underlying relationship between speech and diegetic subjectivity that I have examined in this chapter. Regardless of how one might interpret its sexual politics, *Last Year at Marienbad* prohibits the illusion of an autonomous diegetic subject or transcendental subject as anchor for a totality of vision or an absolute order of meaning. This injunction restores to the film an inherent polysemy that not only acknowledges a dialogic collectivity between the characters within the text but also between the referential content and the implied source of the representation. This dialogic space is the immanent field, and I hope now to be closing in on an understanding of Resnais's and Godard's reflexive cinema as a general rejection of the division between subjective and objective poles that is central to my concept of the immanent field, a theory capable of linking the philosophies of Merleau-Ponty and Deleuze and constructing a foundation for exploring where film and philosophy meet.

FOUR

ALAIN RESNAIS AND THE CODE OF SUBJECTIVITY

The photoplay tells us the human story by overcoming the forms of the outer world, namely, space, time, and causality, and by adjusting the events to the forms of the inner world, namely, attention, memory, imagination, and emotion.

—Hugo Münsterberg, *Hugo Münsterberg on Film*

AS I HOPE HAS BECOME APPARENT IN MY READING OF DELEUZE, this book is not an indictment of subjectivity or filmic subjectivity. As Martin Schwab points out in discussing Deleuze's film writing: "the subject is not an anomaly—it is cosmic normality, no matter how unlikely its emergence."[1] But between the theories of Bazin and Eisenstein, Metz and Deleuze, and between the cinemas of the classical era and those of Godard and Resnais, there exists a striking difference among arguments of *how* film subjectivity should be constructed, what it should resemble, how it should be organized and how the process of its constitution engenders the text's fundamental relationship to meaning, message, and logic. In the last chapter I extended this study of film connotation and subject-object relations to the construction of a diegetic subject-function, which I hope to expound upon here through an analysis of what I call the code of subjectivity, to be complemented in the next chapter with a study of Godard and the code of objectivity.

Schwab continues: "the subject is the place where a certain differentiatedness achieves the status of self-feeling and projects a world picture."[2] The connection here between differentiation and a world picture is important, as it indicates how central the classical subject-object binary is to the manufacturing of philosophy, morality, and ideology. The process of organization through which the individual subject-position is differentiated from—and reconciled to—the objective pole of representation has been considered a basic premise of film representation, as is firmly indicated by Münsterberg's quote at the head of this chapter. Arguing alongside suture theorists, yet not going so far as to place my inquiry in a specific ideological context, I am interested here in the connotative structure through which human subjectivity is simulated and how this renders cinema capable of performing a philosophical function. One way to analyze this, as I have done thus far, is to look at examples where it is decodified. In the opening chapters of this book I looked at the transcendental subject, or subjectivity in the position of the apparatus itself, to which I will return in chapter 5. And, in the previous chapter, I attempted to extend this to the diegetic subject, which led me to assess modes of film in which characters themselves are linked to the distribution of the sensible in the moving sound-image; these modes, such as the flashback, are what I call subjective modes of representation or elements of the code of subjectivity.

With *Hiroshima, mon amour* and *Last Year at Marienbad* we found that the construction of diegetic subjectivity is often dependent on the audiovisual coding of the relationship between past and present. This brings time, temporality, and narrative chronology—all of which, I will argue more fully here, are problems of the form of denotation—into the framework of subject-object relations. Stephen Heath asks rhetorically: "What is a film, in fact, but an elaborate time-machine, a tangle of memories and times successfully rewound in the narrative as the order of the continuous time of the film?"[3] Heath's question provokes me once again to wonder what film is, essentially, other than a temporal organization of events, narration. In response to Heath's question I would say: everything. This ordering, or reordering, of time is only a problem of narrative structure and sequencing and is not always "successful," nor does such an understanding consider the fluctuations between different image-types from which such a juxtaposition of moments (or "tangle") might be built. Heath's question is particularly interesting at this point in my study because it could summarize the general consensus concerning the work of Alain Resnais. Indeed, I can locate here the root of a problem that has led most critics to view Resnais's work primarily as a reflection, through montage, on the nature of time. But aren't Resnais's systematic experiments with sound and image, and his unconventional structuring of temporality, only parts of a larger connotative project? Is Resnais interested in the nature of time or our relationship to it, to each other, and to ourselves?

Let me clarify, rekindling my reading of Deleuze from chapter 2: editing, or the assemblage of images and shots, is not essentially narrative. It is, first and foremost, formal, a means for organizing the immanent field, a relationality of different compositions of subject-object relations. In certain types of representation this juxtaposition produces a harmonious alignment of subject-functions; in others, as with *Last Year at Marienbad*, it produces a constant conflict or feedback of agencies, a contradiction of points of view. Because of the centrality of editing to Resnais's works, critics from Raymond Bellour to Emma Wilson have drawn comparisons between him and Eisenstein.[4] No two filmmakers, however, could have more dissimilar philosophical functions for editing. Whereas Eisenstein uses montage as a means for guaranteeing the spectator's interpretation of a film, for producing specific meaning through the signification of a monolithic transcendental subject, Resnais's use of montage offers a completely different connotative meaning. Contrary to Eisenstein's precise and certain worldview, Resnais's films aim for uncertainty, a polyvalent signified produced through a dialogic system of reference, leaving the image in a state of ambiguity and the spectator in a position of critical awareness.

And, while Resnais's films are clearly concerned with problems of temporality and memory, these are secondary functions, much like the problem of time is secondary for Bergson's *Matter and Memory*—secondary to, and instrumental in, reformulating the problem of the division between interior and exterior and the notion of subjectivity on which this division is based. Many theorists have reduced these interweaving interests of time and subjectivity to a representation of thought itself. I would argue, however, against the reduction of Resnais's work to a metaphor that in most cases does not include thorough explanation, much as we saw in chapter 1, with allegories of perception concerning the works of Godard. Instead, I will reformulate this metaphor as a question of subject-object relations, and of the codification of subjectivity in cinema. To this end Wilson writes: "Resnais is fascinated by mental or subjective images, the virtual reality which makes up individual consciousness and is itself composed of both what we have known and what we have imagined. This interest in the finest workings of the mind . . . calls for an extraordinary reshaping of cinema and rethinking of the capacity of film to show us reality as it is imagined, as well as lived."[5]

The crucial phrase here: "as it is imagined, as well as lived." In other words Resnais is concerned with the connection between our subjective experience and our coexistence as an object, our being in the world. This dualistic nature of human subjectivity, phrased here in very Merleau-Pontian phenomenological terms, also reflects Deleuze's understanding of the image both as the representative of something and as something in and of itself. While Wilson uses this aspect of Resnais's work to address the visceral in his films, I will focus more on how this problem may permit us to investigate the cinematic construction of new circuits of thinking in which subjective and objective poles are displaced, confused, exchanged. In previous chapters we saw that image-types are conventionally combined not only to provide a sense of narrative logic or temporal cohesion but, more fundamentally, to construct a stable system of reference for the overall text. Be it in the relationship between depth and framing, between a shot and editing, or in the speech-image codification known as the voice-over flashback, the sound-image's meaning varies according to the alignment of its significations with the source of enunciation.

In the previous chapter I introduced Resnais's work as a deconstruction of the division between these objective and subjective poles, showing that in the immanent field the human subject is never fully isolated from its objective and intersubjective context. Keeping these problems in the forefront of this study, and drawing on a broader analysis of Resnais's work during this period, I will now extend my conclusions from the previous chapter to what I call the code of subjectivity, part of a study of meta-codes in which this and the next chapter function as a complementary pair. The code of subjectivity is a network of formal codes and signifying practices that merges processes of identification with those of subjective imagery to create a bond between the spectator, apparatus, and a character. The character and immanent field are linked both externally (we watch the diegesis as a function of the character's actions) and internally (we watch the diegesis through the character's eyes), bridging the emotional gap, as Alex Neill might put it, between sympathy and empathy.[6]

This code, however, has also been deformed in certain modernist cinemas as a means for subverting its connotations of certainty, such as one finds in Orson Welles's *Citizen Kane* (1941) or Akira Kurosawa's *Rashomon* (1950), films that provide multiple viewpoints of the same action or story and act as prototypes for recent developments in Hollywood genre cinema (see Pete Travis's 2008 action thriller, *Vantage Point*, for example). This subversive tendency is particularly resonant in the work of Resnais, who was influenced by—and collaborated with—writers from the *nouveau roman* or "New Novel" movement, who were engaged with codifying a new type of psychological realism in literature.[7] In reference to the relationship between Resnais's stylistic innovations and the problem of cinematic realism, René Prédal describes Resnais's work in terms that combine my philosophical argument with more conventional terminology of representational analysis, claiming that "through the will to present all facts on a level field," Resnais produces "a total realism that situates itself beyond the tradition of cinematic realism."[8] To the extent that I will engage with the problem of realism, suffice it to say that Resnais's films subvert the connotative foundations of conventional cinematic realism, shattering the denotative consistency necessary for a traditional model of verisimilitude. This rejection of stable denotation manifests itself in terms of two definitive extensions: the system of reference through which it is realized, as well the narrative clarity it helps to guarantee.

Resnais deconstructs the code of subjectivity to represent a mental world in which there is no dominant subject-function and, consequently, no clear causal narrative logic. In more Bergsonian philosophical terms Resnais's code of subjectivity produces a subject that does not adhere to the division between interior and exterior. This deconstruction is based heavily on the recurrence of certain formal interactions, including alterations to the speech-image code, camera movement, and the constant interruption of denotation by varying types of insert sequence. Revealing the code of subjectivity to be based on conventionalized forms, it could be argued that Resnais liberates the image from the anchor of denotation. He draws our attention to the immanent field, wherein a multiplicity of subject-functions meet. His films therefore permit the spectator to assess the text critically and even to learn from it new paths of thinking—or in Jean-Albert Bron's words, "to validate or eventually to modify her consciousness of the real, and through a ricochet effect to validate or invalidate the film in terms of its representation of the real."[9] Through this reflexivity Resnais provokes the spectator into a position outside of the typical comfort zone provided by the secreted transparency of mainstream cinema; as he himself once stated, in very Barthesian terms, Resnais wants to address the spectator in a critical state: "for that, I must make films that are not natural."[10]

As I have pointed out, this formal challenge to cinematic convention can be seen quite clearly to reverberate on the level of denotation. Resnais (and Godard, as I will explore in the next chapter) produces a two-tier frustration of what David Bordwell describes as classical cinema, wherein "cause-effect logic and narrative parallelism generate a narrative which projects its action through psychologically-defined, goal oriented characters."[11] Beyond the mere breakdown of narrative causality and clear character motivation, however, one finds with Resnais a systematic rejection of the myth of the absolute subject and its foundation in the sensory monism provided by conventional formal relations. Resnais's films are particularly telling in this regard because they focus on the problem of representation: spoken representation as communication between two people and, also, cultural representation as a discourse on history and the present. Resnais's texts thus pose a diegetic problem for his characters, as well as an extratextual problem for the image, and the two are frequently merged as mental images to cast the characters' internal projection onto the screen.

The Code of Subjectivity

The code of subjectivity, as I have mentioned, is a set of signifying practices that provides for the structuring of subjective images that can be transposed from a character to the image and, thus, to the spectator. I will outline this metacode as playing two roles: (1) using formal tools specific to film signification, it molds its objective images to imply a privileged identification between the apparatus and a particular character; and (2) it provides for the transfer of this character's experience to the spectator by aligning the film with that subject. In short, the code of subjectivity binds the spectator to the diegetic character by implying an affinity between the immanent field and that particular person. Furthermore, the code of subjectivity acts to transfer the character's signifying processes onto that of the formal apparatus itself.

This code operates in numerous ways and has many possible contributing elements. For example, most conventional cinema has embraced this code on the purely quantitative level of narrative focus, considering a story through its influence on—and reaction to—a particular character, the hero or protagonist. Through the concentration of screen time placed on this character, and the character's centrality in the causal logic of the events, he or she becomes the primary source for spectatorial identification.[12] This mode of identification is reinforced by formal links organized between the diegetic subject and the form, such as with a following shot in which the camera follows a character as he or she walks, thus implying a direct link between the change in the image and that character's trajectory. Kaja Silverman explains this as being an indexical signifier, in which the form itself seems to be attached by extension to its object.[13] The character carries a privileged position in the immanent field, both in terms of physical presence and importance. Mitry refers to this as a semisubjective image, or "associated image," an image in which the visual elements are constructed in order to give one character a bias in the representation.[14] The objective pole of the recording machine is affected, we might say, by the subjective pole of the diegetic character. In addition to the moving camera, this code includes conventions of framing, in which one character is spatially dominant, bigger, or in a position of prominence in the composition, as if the character is given a place in the spatial organization that indicates his or her uniqueness from the rest of the space, that indicates his or her differentiatedness.

Sometimes the subjective interior of a character spills over into the objective markers of the image, such as when the plastic attributes are altered to represent the psychological state of the character or diegetic world. This is the case in Bazin's aforementioned analysis of bourgeois mediocrity in *Voyage to Italy* and is also the governing principle of neorealism's stylistic opposite, German expressionism. In the 1920s German cinema of Lang, Murnau, and Weine, the visual world of extreme plastic exaggeration helps to produce an overall mood that, in turn, connotes a motivated relationship between the immanent formal field and the characters within it. Taking this one step further, formal functions such as framing and movement often act to ease the transition from the objective image into a subjective image, in which the image-type aligns the apparatus with the character's subject-position. An exemplary case would be the point-of-view tracking shot, in which the camera assumes the position of a moving character. As I have argued is the case in *Vivre sa vie* and *Hiroshima, mon amour*, the diegetic subjectivity of the shot is enhanced by using a moving camera that is looked directly into by the people it passes. The camera is signified to *be* the character, and the viewer is in turn signified to be the camera, thus allowing for a clean and unfettered passage of meanings and worldviews.

Other elements of the code of subjectivity are editing based, such as examples of suture wherein codes of editing create a subject-function that binds the image to a filmic position. This can include a *speaking* subject, as I analyzed in the last chapter, or a *looking* subject. The eye-line match, for example, cuts from a character in the act of looking. This cut sutures the point of reference into the perceptual act of the person looking and signifies the next image as the subjective gaze of that person. This is what François Jost calls "internal ocularization": the camera has made the character's gaze its own and, consequently, *our* own.[15] Another term for this, though with only a slight alteration (the addition of a third shot, returning to the viewing character), is the point-of-view shot; the point-of-view shot is an example of what Mitry calls the "analytic image," in which the camera views things from the diegetic character's place, "identifies itself with her gaze."[16] The immanent field's organization is justified, in this case, as the visual operation of the character. This transfer from the camera to the diegetic character produces an alignment between what is happening and how it is being shown, as is explained in Heath's slightly more complex description: "The look, that is, joins form of expression—the composition of the images and their disposition in relation to one another—and form of content—the definition of the action of the film in the movement of looks, exchanges, objects seen, and so on. Point of view develops on the basis of this joining operation of the look, the camera taking the position of a character in order to show the spectator what he or she sees."[17]

Because of this dualistic nature or purpose of its operational function, the point-of-view shot has been analyzed in many ways. For Dayan and Baudry, whose approach is concerned primarily with the ideological role of connotation, it is the extension of a bourgeois value system and artistic tradition. William Rothman and other Anglo-American writers, as I mentioned in chapter 2, see this convention rather as a rhetorical filmic device, narrative in its nature but incapable of being fully classified as ideological.[18] Supporting Rothman's position with a detailed textual investigation, Edward Branigan's "The Point-of-View Shot" offers a thorough analysis of this practice as a strictly functional narrative device.[19]

Similarly, Heath points out that the point-of-view shot is only subjective to the point that it assumes the spatial position of a character. For Heath there is no great difference between subjective point-of-view shots and objective non-point-of-view shots, merely an "overlaying of first and third person modes."[20] Such a code does not for Heath necessarily assume anything beyond that, such as the character's psychological experience. This observation provides me with an interesting point regarding the code of subjectivity as it is used classically: it does not necessarily change the image qualitatively. Mitry reiterates this: "A completely subjective cinema (on the visual level) is nothing other than that which 'objectively' relates the vision of someone who is effaced behind that which she presents to us."[21]

Mitry points out, in terms that conjure the analyses of Baudry and Dayan, that this perpetuation of the subjective representation's objective characteristics effaces the character at its source—at least this is the implication, an implication nearly always reinforced in mainstream practices. This effacement, frustrated on numerous levels in the works of Resnais and Godard, is itself an effect of the organization of the immanent field. While there may be no noticeable difference between the two types of representation, there is a subtle difference in their systems of reference, which is of utmost interest to this book. Though Heath may have a point, the film is still being systematically altered, as Deleuze might say, according to the image's origin. Moreover, I have found that the qualitative similarity is not maintained, for example, when the shot is taken out of a linear context or when stripped of conventional codifications of sound and image.

In other words, I would argue that, though Heath is accurate that the point-of-view shot does not always indicate an aspect of the character's subjective transformation of what is being viewed, this effect does play a role in affirming or challenging a text's connotations as a function of its system of reference. While the form of content may not be altered, the system of differentiation upon which the denotation is based assumes a particular dynamic. Nick Browne attempts, in "The Spectator-in-the-Text: The Rhetoric of *Stagecoach*," to understand another possible effect of this alignment, which is the identification with a character through the eyes of another character—that is, the unrolling of images through which our process of identification differs from the position in which we view, or how the point-of-view shot can provide contradictory systems of reference.[22] This helps me to iterate a duality with which the code of subjectivity is infused: within the subjective there always remains the objective pole as well.

While the structuralist mode of analysis employed by Dayan and others may differ from the rhetorical narrative analysis proposed by Branigan and Browne, one can locate a fundamental similarity in their attempt to understand the point-of-view shot as an organization of images via a fluctuation in the images' implied source. That is, the self-imposed polarity of their approaches can be reconciled through the framework of film as an organization of subject-object relations. But can the point-of-view shot be the only type of subjective image, the only level of diegetic subjectivity in cinema? Of course not: there are many degrees of the subjective image, as Mitry elaborates to great extent.[23] There are also internalized subjective shots in which the image assumes the imaginary realm of the character—the dream sequence, for example. We see a character sleeping, followed by a sequence of shots; the transition between an objective representation of the sleeping character and a subjective representation of that character's imaginary is usually indicated by some sort of audiovisual effect, such as a wavering image or the plucked notes of a harp. This effect *signifies* that what follows is a dream sequence. These formal tools serve a connotative role: the immanent field shifts its origin of meaning onto the subject-position of the diegetic character. Such editing-based conventions of the code of subjectivity become more complicated when another sensory plane of expression is added, as seen in the previous chapter. The voice-over flashback merges the narrated and the narrating: the subjective mode and the objective mode are linked by the bridge of a codification of speech. In most classical practices this subjective past slides seamlessly into the objective past by shifting the plane of verbal signification from the voice-over to that of diegetic conversation. This aligns the subjective with the objective by granting both the enunciating character and the transcendental subject a certain relationship with the image. They are interchangeable, linked through their inextricability from the immanent field, their relationship with the formal base.

In the films of Resnais, however, such constructs are wafer thin. Resnais's work is particularly useful here because it incorporates a variety of devices that make up the code of subjectivity. For, whereas Godard attempts to describe a subject's interior by contextualizing its objective exterior, Resnais tries to turn a character inside out: "he begins with the interior of the character and moves toward the exterior."[24]

ALAIN RESNAIS AND THE CODE OF SUBJECTIVITY

It is through the use and deconstruction of the code of subjectivity that Resnais explores his most regular themes of the human condition: the relationship between the past, present, and future, and the inherent struggle between the real and the possible, between personal imagination and collective reality. Evoking an opinion common to all writing on Resnais, James Monaco describes these films as attempting to deal "with the way we comprehend the world."[25] But what does this mean, and how might we understand this in more concrete terms? Resnais's work should be framed not according to the representation of *consciousness*, or some such metaphor, but according to its philosophical organization of subject-object relations in a cinematic deconstruction of the division between interior and exterior.

I agree with skeptics of formalism that Resnais's stylistic endeavors would be of less interest if they were not used to engage historical problems and the social and moral issues that arise alongside them. But they do, and that is why so many people find his work moving, important— "philosophical" in a conventional use of the word, meaning how movies can make us think about deep stuff. Directing this reflection toward contemporary geopolitical problems, as well as questions of how culture constructs history out of such problems, Resnais's films between 1959 and 1968 are uniquely engaged with history as a process of representation, combining international events with the problem of recording, representing, and preserving history between individuals (such as Nevers and Hiroshima, X and A). I say "uniquely engaged" because Resnais's vigilant consideration of contemporary historical events (the Holocaust, nuclear warfare, the colonial war in Algeria, the Spanish Civil War) is unique to this period of his work, after which his cinema becomes more theatrical, less topical, and his dedication to films with a sincere conscience places him among a minority in film history generally.

Resnais's films from this period manifest a recurring conception of history and memory as being interrelated in some form of linguistically paralyzed sublime, in which the ability to name or to conjure images through words is constantly frustrated. As such, there is an overriding uncertainty in his signifying systems, an ambiguity and a polyvalence that refuses the straightforward production of denotation (which often frustrates viewers seeking an easily decipherable storyline). But, again, let us demand: *how* is this achieved? It may help to begin with Resnais's arrangements of speech and image, as introduced in the previous chapter. In most cases Resnais uses the voice-over flashback to construct a subject-function through the representation of memory, in which the coexistence between past and present provides a coherence of representation that is posited as an enunciation from a position of subjective unity. This ranges from the unilateral narrating subject to the Bakhtinian communication process in which a subject constructs itself in constant reference to an implied other, a range of possibilities introduced in my analysis of *Hiroshima, mon amour* and that I will extend in this chapter's analysis of *The War Is Over.*

Resnais's work does not always focus on the voice-over; however, it does rely to a large degree on other experiments with editing. Alternative examples I touched on in chapter 3 include the coexistence of two parallel stories, such as one finds in *Muriel.* This film uses the juxtaposition of images to show the remnants of the past in the present of a particular character, not in terms of an allegory but in terms of the juxtaposition of image-types. A similar premise is provided via the narrative foil of a time machine in *I Love You, I Love You,* which revolves around a man's attempt to come to terms with his wife's untimely death. The last film Resnais made before his five-year absence from commercial filmmaking, *I Love You, I Love You* is often considered his text par excellence because of its frenetic experiments in montage and temporal order, which could be analyzed as a constant deformation of the conventional organization of subject-object relations.[26] Robert Benayoun calls *I Love You, I Love You* "an editor's sinecure: a film where montage becomes a philosophical tool, a dialectical manipulation of the most fundamental degree."[27] The focus herein on the importance of editing belies the influence, discussed by Resnais himself, of Marcel Carné's innovations with narrative editing. In films such as *Daybreak* (1939), Carné alters the conventional temporalization of the story in order to produce what Resnais calls "moments of uncertainty,"[28] a rejection of denotative stability that would be infused throughout Resnais's organization of subject-object relations.

Carné's model of what is better known as "poetic realism" offered one of the first systematic attempts to reorder classical narration according to a particular character's point of view. Resnais takes this tradition of narrative editing one step further. Beyond merely frustrating the narrative, he uses editing to challenge the unilateral and absolute vision of any one individual, a tendency that aligns him with other modernist filmmakers such as Luis Buñuel.[29] Resnais, however, must first encode a subject in order to deconstruct it, which he does through traditional means of the code of subjectivity. Aside from such experiments in temporal narration, Resnais's thematic visual style is perhaps best known for its epic use of

the tracking shot, so prominently placed in Resnais's connotative order that it inspired Godard, in talking about *Hiroshima, mon amour*, to
comment: "tracking shots are a moral issue."[30] This formal tool is central
to Resnais's earlier documentary work, such as *Night and Fog* (1955) and
All the Memory in the World (1956), and continues into his early fiction
films. Resnais's tracking shots, almost always moving forward, provide a
physical sensation of pressing through the world. The tracking shot, as
we saw in *Hiroshima, mon amour*, is a marker for the subjective nature of
memory; only, Resnais uses it to construct a subject-function that he can
subsequently divide.

As in *Last Year at Marienbad*, the tracking shot does not imply an unlimited movement or transcendental omnipresence, as Baudry argues in
his theorization of the transcendental subject,[31] but quite the opposite:
through its relation to framing, montage, and sound, the tracking shot
reveals the limiting aspect of the frame—it insists on the partiality of the
image, the lack of a specific subject-position to associate with the visual.
Moreover, Resnais's tracking shot usually follows no narrative motivation: as Alain Fleischer puts it, "The camera seems to displace itself for
nothing, dispossessed of drama."[32] Somewhat similar to the Vertovian
system of montage that I argued for in my analysis of *Two or Three Things
I Know About Her*, Resnais's tracking shot removes the camera's perspective from a fixed spot and transfers subjectivity into a public space: it is a
"subjective tracking shot without [a] gazing subject."[33]

It is not, however, fully objective either. Roy Armes tends toward familiar rhetoric when he describes Resnais's tracking shot as "an attempt,
still very crude and primitive, to approach the complexity of thought, its
mechanism."[34] Again, I believe it would help to convert such metaphors
to a formulation regarding the immanent field as a space for the organization of subject-object relations. One could argue that, at the very least,
the tracking shot attempts to represent thought as a function of the subject's differentiation from or relationality to the visual content: "the possessing of space by an organ of viewing."[35] In a way, then, it is an extension of the transcendental subject, implicating the camera as a mobile
viewing subject, passing through a world of objects. Prédal takes this
further to suggest that the forward tracking shot of *Last Year at Marienbad*
is, in fact, a type of violation of the object, or what he calls "cinematic rape
by forward-tracking."[36] Yet there is never any specific clarity in Resnais's
films to whom the image belongs, for whom it is an extension. The

tracking shot adds an element of ambiguity to the position of enunciation: the frame is stable yet fluid, consistently proportionate yet always moving.

Moreover, the moving camera posits the impression of omniscience, but this is nullified by a form of editing that decenters any single system of reference. Though his editing techniques have often been categorized as primarily concerned with memory, Resnais has argued against this, making a decisive division between the notion of memory and one that he finds more fitting: the notion of the *imaginary*.[37] While "the imaginary" has served as the grounds for many psychoanalytic studies of film, I prefer to consider it more as a mechanism that permits us to consider not the Lacanian process of human subject-formation but the construction of filmic subject-functions. As we saw with Mitry's categories of subjective imagery, there is no representation more fully subjective than the mental image. The mental image is no longer, like the point-of-view shot, an objective image seen from the standpoint of a character. The mental image is an entirely different regime of representation. An experiment at the center of Resnais's films during this period, the mental image sequence is frequently intertemporal, either a flashback or flashforward—a structure of the imaginary in which the referential system of a diegetic subject-position allows for a shift in diegetic time. "Is this not the foundation of a unified subject?" one might ask. But—as with the tracking shot—what would otherwise be a conventionally coded adjustment of temporal context becomes, for Resnais, a realm of incertitude, doubt, and ambiguity.[38] The sequences do not isolate a subject-function from the surrounding world, as with traditional forms of the code of subjectivity, but, instead, illustrate how the individual attempts to build a bridge between the inside and the outside.

What is shown in these sequences cannot necessarily be considered "memory" or "foreshadowing," since its denotative certainty is often nullified. The classical construction of the mental image—that is, implying that what we are seeing is, in fact, the character's representation of an experience—necessitates, as I demonstrated in the last chapter, certain configurations of speech and image, certain organizations of subject-object relations. With the voice-over flashback, such as in the opening sequences of *Hiroshima, mon amour*, speech often rests momentarily objective, in the present, thus permitting the visual image to deviate. The representation of memory as a structure of the immanent field, therefore, rests on a division between elements that can become highly problematic. In such subversive forms, Monaco argues, "Resnais is doing nothing less than asking us to give up preconceptions of causality and the flow of time"[39]—causality and time, I would argue, as forms of denotation, the structure of which is justified by a specific system of reference. Resnais is asking us, ultimately, to abandon our conventional understanding of causality and time as they are organized through subject-object relations. Deconstructing the monistic unity of the subject of memory, Resnais connotes that history and memory are not purely internalized phenomena, are not phenomena impervious to intertemporal and intersubjective influences.

In a particularly unique twist, Resnais also extends the intertemporality of the diegetic subject through the use of the flash-forward, which seems to have gone neglected in the majority of analyses of his oeuvre.[40] Whereas the flashback offers a character's representation of what has happened, the flash-forward presents us with a character's projection of future possibilities, a person's anticipation of the exterior realization of feelings or judgments that are, as yet, only interior, thus further decentering the present as a stable praxis for denotation. This second-take effect—be it in flashback or in flash-forward—provides a sort of repetition and transfiguration on repetition that is central to Resnais's deconstruction of the code of subjectivity. I would be inclined to disagree here with Wilson's suggestion that Resnais's films "move in repeating circles"[41]—after all, even the constant return to the past in *Muriel*, the familiar hypnotic wanderings of *Last Year at Marienbad*, and the multiple recurrences of the same memory in *I Love You, I Love You* spiral out of their own bases of repetition. There is always a slight difference, a slight alteration added to the organization of subject-object relations.

Other permutations of this experiment with repetition and difference include the representation of a character's imagination. In *The War Is Over*, for example, Resnais presents us with Diego's (the hero, played by Yves Montand) mental image of a young woman he does not know. Diego's imaginary unfolds in the form of a visual sequence that begins with a young woman, walking down the sidewalk in front of the moving camera, which follows her (fig. 4.1); this cuts to another shot, constructed with the same scale, composition, and camera movement, in the same setting and blocking, but of another woman (fig. 4.2); in subsequent shots she is replaced by another young woman, multiple times, the collective group of which follow through with the motion of walking down the sidewalk and entering a bar.

FIGURES 4.1–4.2
The War Is Over (1966): the imaginary appearances of Nadine.

These different women are manifestations of Diego's imaginary version of Nadine Sallanches (who turns out to be played by Geneviève Bujold). In this case the rapid succession of images represents how the unknown object, in its multiplicity of possibilities, can nonetheless be conjectured in the imaginary, even mastered to a degree by the coherence provided through continuities within the images' organization of subject-object relations. As Bordwell points out, "Similarity balances difference: graphically matched compositions and figure/camera movements play against the fact that each young woman is unique."[42] The formal continuity manages to contain the shifts in content, a continuity that extends further than just the visual design.

Bordwell also points out that we understand this to be Diego's subjective imaginary and not some objective image because of the continuity of the soundtrack. The soundtrack continues with the conversation that led into this insert sequence. Much as in *Hiroshima, mon amour*, the fracture between two formal elements provides for an overlapping between the objective (Diego's ongoing conversation, Nevers's verbal recollection) and the subjective (Diego's mental images of women, Nevers's mental images of France). And so we are lured into the illusion of a codified subject-function, prompting Youssef Ishaghpour to write: "Resnais conceives of the cinema not as an instrument of representation of reality, but as the best means for approaching the psychic function."[43] But are such constructions of subject-object relations connoting the "thought" process of an enclosed and unified subject, or the open collectivity of memory as a cinematic convention—that is to say, is Resnais attempting to simulate thought as we have conventionalized it, rationalized it, or is he using film form to conduct experiments in cinematic thinking?

Another example of an operation based on repetition and difference is the repetition of verbal descriptions, but accompanied by different images, such as we saw in *Last Year at Marienbad*. This represents the exchange of a thought or mental image from one mind to another, or perhaps more precisely the mutual construction of representation, much like Bakhtin's notion of the dialogic, but extended further than in Pasolini's example of free indirect discourse. With Resnais we have something akin to Kurosawa's *Rashomon* or Welles's *Citizen Kane*, which offer constant variations on the same referential content, in which the subjective and objective lose their conventional boundaries.

By fracturing the system of reference beyond the alignment of the objective and subjective, such films pull into the spotlight the very mode by which the artificial unity of an enunciating subject-function is required for narrative clarity. Like these other films, Resnais's work unravels the coded unity of a single subject-function in order to represent memory as something shared, collective, built from multiple perspectives. To expand a citation from Deleuze noted in the previous chapter's analysis of *Last Year at Marienbad*: "He discovers the paradox of memory as shared by two, by several . . . characters as completely different non-communicant sites that compose one global memory."[44] This "global memory"—which is articulated in a different cinematic way in Godard's *Contempt*—does not belong to a character only but binds characters through an immanent field constructed to include multiple subject-functions. This is the very premise of the mental image. Jean-Marie Schaeffer writes: "The manner in which beings relate themselves to reality: we gather knowledge about reality through 'mental representations,' induced by perceptual experiences but also by the internalization of innumerable social understandings already elaborated in the form of symbolic representations that are accessible to the public."[45] Schaeffer makes a crucial link here between perception, the mental image, and how each of these is conditioned by sociocultural codes of representation. The cinematic code of subjectivity is itself a "publicly accessible form of representation," a code that has been forged through a century of cinema's presence in our imaginary.

The subject, as Schwab points out, may very well be a cosmic normality, a natural condition of organizing the world, and it is inevitably signified through any process of representation. But the cinematic production of this differentiation, this book holds, is a codification based on certain organizations of the immanent field of formal relations, which operate to provide a rigidity that anchors this differentiation within a larger order of meaning that can, if desired, be unhinged, overturned. Resnais's films illustrate this argument through a constant subversion of conventional subjective forms, caused by slight alterations to the alignment of elements that make up these codes. I hope now to illustrate this further through an analysis of an often underappreciated jewel of Resnais's early period, *The War Is Over*.

THE WAR IS OVER AND THE CINEMATIC (DE)CONSTRUCTION OF THE CARTESIAN SUBJECT

Released in 1966, *The War Is Over* looks at a topic particularly tied to a person's being in the world: political action. Here, Resnais's dominant themes—uncertainty, temporal instability, history and the individual—resurface in a specific context: leftist activism in Western Europe in the 1960s. Of all of Resnais's films during this period, *The War Is Over* contains the most expansive variety of formal experimentations with filmic subjectivity, anchoring these experiments to a specific sociopolitical problem that was being debated widely among French intellectuals and artists of the 1960s, who had become firmly entrenched in the workers' and student movement. As such, the film was seen as a major step for Resnais, integrating his experimental formalism into a concrete and topical story that, for all intents and purposes, actually has a legible plot—prompting *Cahiers du cinéma* reviewer Michel Caen to write in his review: "Things have changed with Alain Resnais."[46]

Widely considered upon its release to be Resnais's most well-rounded film,[47] *The War Is Over* has, perhaps for this very reason, escaped the type of in-depth analysis afforded to many of his films from this era. Despite a number of intertemporal fluctuations, Ronald Bogue points out that with this film "one might suppose (as many critics do) that Resnais creates a present tense narrative."[48] Like *Last Year at Marienbad*, however, this film takes place in the present only inasmuch as the present is a meeting point for past and future trajectories of representation, a universal present. In this analysis I will focus on the unfolding of these temporal trajectories in conjunction with the construction and deconstruction of cinematic subject-functions. In *Narration in the Fiction Film* Bordwell offers a thorough analysis of the film's narrative devices in a section titled "The Game of Form."[49] Bordwell points out continuously that this film, a prototype for what he calls "art-cinema narration," produces ambiguous image-types while at the same time "defining the range of permissible constructions."[50] Though Bordwell claims in the same passage that this film "appeals to conventional structures and cues while at the same time introducing significant innovations," he goes on to situate these innovations as a function of denotative encoding. For Bordwell, that the narrative devices and formal experiments are justified through an alternate code of subjectivity makes the film explicable along classical narrative lines. I will argue, however, that this take on the film ignores the connotative significance of how the narration is built in relation to the organization of subject-object relations.

The War Is Over revolves around the character of Diego, a Spanish exile orchestrating Spain's communist movement from Paris. Having fought in the civil war during the 1930s, he fled and continued the fight in France, where he is now reaching a moment of existential crisis: he has dedicated his life to a cause that seems to be mired in the past and, at the same time, to have outgrown him. After decades of devotion to the cause, he finds that his comrades no longer view him as ideologically sound, while the new generation of activists is too radical for him. The setting is one of political party operations, but this is not a film about politics; it is about one individual's attempt to reconcile his internal perspective with his external context. In Wilson's words: "Rather than offer lessons on militancy, Resnais offers insight into the doubts, hesitation and commitment of an individual."[51]

As a collection of image-types, *The War Is Over* revolves around Diego's attempt to transform his own beliefs into an external reality. It is thus apt that Prédal titles his *Positif* review of *The War Is Over* "From Reflection to Action,"[52] for the film is just that: a ninety-minute movement from reflection to action, a text through which the barrier between interior and exterior is torn down. As such, this film is about much more than one man's struggle within the communist movement: it is about every person's quotidian struggle to exist in society, hovering between thoughts and beliefs on the inside and actions and events on the outside. In many ways I am tempted to call this film *Two or Three Things I Know About Diego*! Just as in the Godard film from the same year, Diego's plight is removed from the epic grandiosity of history books and modes of heroism and is grounded in the banality of everyday life. And, with it, so is the mental image grounded in a less fantastical context. "Imagination is not always fantastical," said Resnais in an interview just after the film's release: "most often, mental representations are rigorously banal, quotidian."[53]

It is thus emblematic of Resnais's films from this period, which bypass narrative action and historical explication, setting these mainstays of conventional cinema in the background of ordinary existence. This filmmaker's most "radical" deviation from classical mainstream fiction cinema may actually be his desire to treat what he called "the imaginary side of the quotidian, the banal part of the imagination."[54] The banal aspect of subjectivity permits Resnais to redirect the film's focus away from denotative content and toward the form itself. The film's construction of subjectivity seems simple on the surface, but I will explore here how *The War Is Over* allows a vast web of intertemporal and intersubjective fractures in order to assert the main character's dialogic relationship with the world around him.

The conventional code of subjectivity is utilized in this film on numerous levels. First, identification with Diego is signified by the film's narra-

FIGURE 4.3
Diego's visual prominence in the composition of *The War Is Over*.

tive logic. The film's action revolves around him, and his physical and mental representation occupies the majority of screen time. More important, though, the film's formal devices are composed according to his motion and perspective, thus positing his agency not only on a narrative level but also through the suturing of formal codes. The use of framing and camera movement in this film is conventional, classical, respectful of the code of subjectivity. Diego is always placed either in the prominence of the frame (foreground and/or center) or filmed from behind. This latter detail constantly places the camera both facing in Diego's spatial direction and, also, "behind him," as if in a position of support, encoding the image with both identification and empathy (fig. 4.3).[55]

The dynamic between shot and montage is integral to this identification as well. In conversations, for example, the use of crosscutting juxtaposes close-up images of him with medium shots of the people he talks to, implying them as objects of his gaze, at a further distance both from him and from the viewer. Similarly, camera movement in this film is relatively moderate for Resnais's oeuvre and, as Armes aptly notes, the moving camera is nearly always shot from Diego's perspective.[56] Even when it is not from his perspective, the camera's movement is guided by Diego's motion. This tracking shot, or following shot as I discussed earlier, is a conventional part of the code of subjectivity, a sign indexically (to use Silverman's term) signifying the apparatus's alignment with Diego's character, often going so far as to then assume his point of view. This occurs numerous times when Diego is walking, for example: the camera will move with him, following, as if the apparatus itself were linked to his physical agency. It is then extended through an eye-line match: he looks in a certain direction, and the camera cuts to the object of his gaze. This is complemented by the direct address of other characters' gaze into the camera, as if the camera, and through it the image itself, were organized from Diego's perspective. Unlike in *Two or Three Things I Know About Her*, direct address is meant in this film to align the camera with a diegetic character, with Diego, not to reveal the transcendental subject as a construction.

Ultimately, there is nothing particularly radical about the mise-en-scène of this film; it lacks the ornate luster and mocking mirrors of most of Resnais's visual extravaganzas. But the conventional illusion of narrative totality and the unilateral production of meaning are central to the film's philosophical experiment. Diego's is the subjective position signified by the text, yet his agency does not exist unilaterally. Quite the contrary, Resnais subverts the isolation and autonomous totality of the classical subject through the contextualization of Diego's mental images, which capture particular moments and project possible others, breaking down temporal barriers and conflating the real and imaginary. They are *his* subjective representations, but his interior does not exist in a vacuum. The immanent field opens his subjectivity up to a range of other voices, other subjects and possibilities. As Prédal notes concerning this film: "imagination is not vagabond but attaches itself to concrete problems."[57] Even when Diego's brain triggers fantasies, his skull resides in the physical world.

This tension between interior and exterior manifests itself in different ways. The opening scene of the film, for example, unfolds according to a dialectic flow between two voice-overs: one is Diego's voice, and another belongs to an anonymous narrator who turns out to be the man sitting next to Diego during this scene. The images show the world from Diego's perspective, introduced to us through what Bordwell calls visual "cues of subjectivity," which include aforementioned codes such as the juxtaposition of a viewing subject with the object of his vision and the direct address of an interlocutor.[58] The visual point of view established is connected through framing and editing to Diego's perspective. This implies, through the basic assumption of sensory harmonization, that the voice-over is his as well; however, the voice-over addresses a particular "you" as it ruminates on Diego's story. As Diego watches the scenery pass by, for example, the voice-over says: "You watch the scenery pass by." This is a marked contrast to the more conventional, sensory-total subjective enunciation of "I watch the scenery pass by," playing with language and agency much the way *Last Year at Marienbad* does and in direct conflict with the conventional "I saw" subjective enunciation in the opening scene of *Hiroshima, mon amour.* The sound-image is composed of two subject-functions, coexistent within the immanent field: Diego as visual and viewing subject, and someone else as aural subject.

Subjective twice over (not even counting the implicated subjectivities of the filmmakers, apparatus, and spectator), the film can still immediately become objective: the voice-over is revealed to be part of a dialogue between Diego and his driver. The voice-over becomes a diegetic conversation, which then leads into Diego's own voice-over, maintained in the second person. For Wilson this use of "you" suggests a distance between Diego and his experience, a "self-consciousness" or "objectivity" as she calls it.[59] In a way this speech-image composition renders him once-removed from his own experience. Narration becomes dialogue, and dialogue becomes a sort of internal exchange that connects the character to his past and future selves, thus entangling the system of reference within the polyvalent fracture of an intertemporalized "I." In this momentary experiment in cinematic thinking, provided by Resnais's dislodging of conventional sound-image codes and assaulting the very foundation of classical Cartesian subjectivity, we are led to the revelation that a Bergsonian world is also a Bakhtinian one. Roman Jakobson refers to this as the "intrapersonal" aspect of inner speech: "Inner speech . . . is a cardinal factor in the network of language and serves as one's connection with the self's past and future."[60]

Even this is not fully the case, however, because this voice-over itself is never stable. That is to say, since each image consists of a struggle between objective and subjective poles, no one element can be considered fully "internal." Bordwell rewords this as "the 'subjectively objective' voice in Diego's own mind, a kind of internalized Other that ponders his actions in an impersonal way."[61] Indeed, this adds an aspect of reflexivity, in which Diego—or the viewing subject-function—is set apart from the aural source of signification. With this simple pronoun the code of subjectivity is reformulated. Moreover, as Bordwell points out, the voice-over is not wholly subjective, for it is often not even in Diego's voice. "Is it then the voice of some 'authorial' narrator?" Bordwell demands. Or, in words that conjure both Münsterberg and Bakhtin, "is it a 'subjective other,' an impersonal objectification of his thoughts?"[62] Bordwell remarks on the ambiguity of the spoken discourse, which constantly wavers between the narration of events and the uncertainty of whether those events took place, and concludes with seeming discomfort: "Self-conscious narrator, or unselfconscious character? The uncertainty is never dispelled."[63]

Bordwell's interrogation illuminates the Diego-as-subject construct on numerous levels. Not only is there an external world for him, full of people and causes and actions, but there is also a lack of unity to his interior experience, which includes both an intertemporal fragmentation and a polyphony of voices. This deconstruction of the division between subject and object is not limited to experiments in sound-image codification and narration but is part of the greater network by which the film uses, reveals, and transforms the code of subjectivity. This network consists mainly of different types of insert sequences that constantly alter the system of reference. These sequences vary from the psychologically abstract (an objective image altered to connote the psychology of the character) to the intertemporally subjective (a future image projected by the character). An example of the syntagmatic progression from the first type to the second is provided in duplicate: two scenes of lovemaking, one between Diego and Nadine (the daughter of one of his collaborators, and herself a member of the radical student group) and the other between Diego and his longtime partner, Marianne (Ingrid Thulin). These two scenes are stylistically coded to connote the effect of each respective experience on Diego—these are subjective in the way that expressionism and neorealism can be seen as subjective, extensions of the characters' psyche to the totality of plastic representation.

The first scene is a surreal, ethereal fantasy: Nadine's body parts are filmed in close-up against a white backdrop, like a naked angel floating in a beam of light (fig. 4.4). These images are strongly similar to the images of isolated female body parts found in numerous of Godard's films (notably A Married Woman), though not in a self-conscious manner such as we find in Godard. While his films often grant agency to female characters, Resnais is not concerned with sexual politics. Much to the contrary, we see in these images a differentiation between the subject-function touching (Diego) and the object-function being touched (Nadine). In his review of the film Michel Caen evokes the stylistic sensuality of this scene, im-

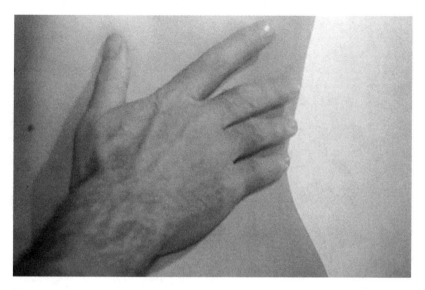

FIGURE 4.4
Nadine as lover: an ethereal object.

plicitly glorifying its classical objectification of the woman's body: "Nadine offers herself to him. Nude, the light radiating from her sides, forcing us to rediscover black-and-white cinema . . . her thighs open and the screen quite simply delivers the image of physical love to us."[64]

While the structuring of sexual difference in this sequence (and its analysis) merits criticism, it is of interest to this study for what Bordwell describes as a dichotomy of code, in which the representation "is both 'reality' (the couple did make love) and 'fantasy' (connotations of impossibly pure pleasure)," what I would argue to be overlapping objective and subjective image-types.[65] Despite Nadine's spatial dominance of the screen, there is a clear differentiation between subject and object. While they may share pleasure, their experience is not intersubjective; there is a differentiation constructed between them.

This scene is followed by a shot that is at first incomprehensible: a banister in an unidentified apartment building. We find soon thereafter, upon Diego's arrival in this building, that this is the railing leading to Marianne's apartment. But before discussing this editing technique, let me compare the previous scene (with Nadine) to the second such scene (with Marianne). The latter scene is different; the immanent field of formal relations manifests a different organization: intersubjective and

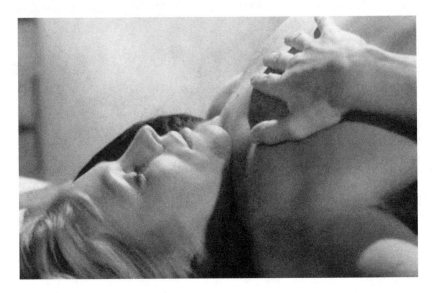

FIGURE 4.5
Marianne as lover: a real co-subject.

carnal, framed in ways so that there is no sense of differentiation between the people involved. This no longer seems fully like Diego's subjective expression but something more mutual, intersubjective. Whereas the scene with Nadine is an "essentially loveless, cerebral affair," Armes notes, the one with Marianne is infused with "warmth and passion" of two "sensual bodies seeking each other."[66] Following the scene with Marianne is also a flash-forward, this one to the political meeting that Diego will attend the next day (fig. 4.5).

Each of these erotic insert sequences ends with a flash-forward, a new weapon in Resnais's mental-image arsenal. As Bordwell points out, *The War Is Over* "creates a unique intrinsic norm" for the representation of diegetic subjectivity: instead of memory or fantasy, we are "to share the character's *anticipation* of events."[67] The intertemporal instability of the mental image grows more extreme as the film goes on, as the forms of representation enfold more possible times, more possible agencies, more possible subject-object compositions into the dialogic structure of the immanent field. As the film progresses, Diego finds himself stuck between his duty and his conscience: he must alert his colleague, Juan, of an ambush waiting in Madrid, without compromising the larger cause.

This mission becomes all the more complicated as other colleagues are arrested and even, possibly, killed; as his veteran peers denounce him for not having enough perspective on the greater cause of the movement; and, as the younger radicals rebuke him for the inefficiency of the traditional, strike-oriented and systematic—as opposed to violent—left.

Let me consider the multiple inserts involving Juan, who is allegedly being detained and tortured by the Spanish police. These inserts recur numerous times: once before the torture theoretically could have been going to happen, once as it is being considered a possibility because of the realization of a breach of confidence, and once when it has been determined as actual fact. It was once premonition, then speculation, and then what Bordwell calls "speculative flashback."[68] Another recurring insert-sequence is of the meeting with Diego's peers in the Communist Party, at which Diego is suspended from activity for having a "subjective view of the situation." This scene is represented multiple times as well: once while the anonymous voice-over prepares Diego for the near future, once after he has made love to Marianne, once as it actually happens in real time, and once while Diego is trying to decide what to do afterward. In both recurring insert-sequences the same scene is viewed as numerous types of mental image, each one accompanying a different mode of Diego's internalization of events and each one possible to situate along a temporal plane. There is the hypothetical past, the certain virtual past, the hypothetical present, and the hypothetical future. The same basic sequence is interchangeable as fear, regret, concern, and anticipation.

Each of these could be understood essentially as a structure of subject-object relations. As Deleuze notes concerning these dynamic editing patterns, "the function with Resnais is not the simple usage of the object, it is the mental function or the level of thought that corresponds to it."[69] Deleuze offers here a variation on the typical analysis of Resnais's films as representing the thought process: instead, as I have argued, we could see the film as a series of experiments in cinematic thinking, modes of relating the self to the world, organizations between subject and object. Resnais's image-type is not necessarily an expression of thought, which would be impossible to qualify or to corroborate; it is, however, a particular construction of subject-object relations, and thus the condition for the representation of thought—what Deleuze might refer to as the "enunciable." And, as these representations are laid out before the spectator, we are made privy to Diego's attempt to digest the world external to him and to transform this digestion into a decision and, then, action. Bordwell claims that the result of such a "highly restricted and deeply subjective narration" is that, "as we learn the narration's devices, we are inclined to trust Diego's judgment."[70] It seems to me quite the opposite, however: as the forms of representation dissolve what we know as conventional narration, subjectivity as a concept is itself deconstructed, revealed as incomplete, fragmented, and prone to error. We are relieved of the implications of having to trust or believe a particular filmic subject, and our focus is directed, instead, toward the immanent field through which this subject is constructed, through which this "judgment" is manifested.

I would thus posit a causal relationship between the structure of the image, as an organization of subject-object relations, and the denotative stability of narration. This becomes all the more clear in the final scene of the film: the lack of closure with which the film concludes offers a finale to this rejection of narrative logic and the conventional divisions between subject and object on which it is predicated. Instead of proposing an image as an illusory act of natural perception, the film is structured to illustrate the nonlinear and a-chronological process by which the character posits himself as a subject in relation to the external world. It is not a unilateral act of perception but is instead the dialogical interaction with the world around him, offered to us as a function of the relations organized within the immanent field. Such a dialogical interaction is often highlighted through the use of dissolves between images of Diego and other characters, what could be viewed as a merging of two separate subject-functions. This is perhaps best illustrated by the final images of the film, which consist of a dissolve from a shot of Diego, who has left for Spain, to one of Marianne, who rushes through the airport on a mission to save him (figs. 4.6–4.8).

This formal overlapping of images accentuates the permeability of the individuals and reveals the illusionary premise on which the purely isolated subject-function is constructed. As Bordwell points out: "The very last shots identify Marianne and Diego, making her our new (and limited) protagonist; she now obtains, perhaps, a depth of subjectivity commensurate with that earlier assigned to Diego."[71] Here is a perfect example of how Resnais refuses to use the code of subjectivity to isolate a particu-

FIGURES 4.6–4.8
The War Is Over ends by dissolving from Diego to Marianne, blending the two.

lar character. What is both unique and radical about Resnais is that the code of subjectivity is always used, instead, to subvert the notion of a fully independent subject, to show the subject as only one of many overlapping and interacting agents that meet within the immanent field.

I now must venture to say, along with Merleau-Ponty and Deleuze but in filmic terms, that the isolated, unified, Cartesian subject is a myth. Resnais helps us to look at how this myth is constructed, what its cinematic formal units are, how it is signified through film connotation. Just as in Godard's *Two or Three Things I Know About Her*, Resnais presents a connotative system that can help us to clarify the reconcilability between phenomenology and a semiotics of cinema, for it illuminates the fundamental organizing process used in the secretion of film codes and deconstructs them in order to reveal a subject-position's implication *in* the world. Such challenges to conventional film expression reveal to us the immanent field, providing us with a reflection on the filmic construction of the dualism between subject and object. This reflexivity has a particular aim, which many have understandably used to link filmmakers such as Resnais and Godard to the theater of Brecht. Discussing the rather unconventional montage of this film, Resnais himself stated: "This is cinema. We present you with real elements, sure, but we do not try to tempt you to believe that it is anything other than cinema. This is a type of honesty."[72] This "honesty" is the definitive value of a formalist approach to film-philosophy, for it permits us to understand how our larger systems of belief are formulated through the composition of subject-object relations laid bare in these texts. In the past two chapters I have progressively attempted to show this relationship as a function of the diegetic subject-function. But what if we take away this position? What of objective representation in cinema? To answer this question, I will return to the works of Jean-Luc Godard, whose deconstruction of the code of objectivity functions according to a reflexive principle summarized so well here by Resnais: "this is cinema."

FIVE

JEAN-LUC GODARD AND THE CODE OF OBJECTIVITY

> Nothing is more subjective than an *objectif* (lens).
> —Béla Balázs, *L'esprit du film*

IN THE PREVIOUS TWO CHAPTERS I HAVE EXAMINED THE construction of subject-functions *within* the text. Alain Resnais experiments extensively with this construction in order to challenge conventional assumptions concerning the division between individual and collective, interior and exterior, real and imaginary, as a function of the human characters of his films and also as a function of film as a medium. By altering and subverting the code of subjectivity, Resnais focuses film signification on the immanent field in which the form itself engenders a dialogic interaction between subject-functions, producing experiments in cinematic thinking that break down conventional subject-object dualisms to pose a philosophical inquiry into the nature of time, mental imagery, and communication. But what of perspective bereft of subject, or what I would call the objective pole of representation? In posing this question, I return to some of the primary problems of this study. Having devoted the previous two chapters to the ways in which film codifies different subject-functions, let me now consider the attempt to remove subjectivity from the text, to present the image as nonsubjective or, to put it simply, as *objective*.

The claim of cinematic objectivity has a long tradition rooted in the scientific origins of film. Edgar Morin argues that cinema was born "to study the phenomena of nature,"[1] and Siegfried Kracauer makes a similar argument about the scientific basis for cinema. In *Theory of Film* Kracauer details the camera's historical connection to the development of "scientific potentialities," tying the evolution of camera technology to the industrial pursuit of a mechanized reproduction of the objective world.[2] André Bazin, however, argues quite vehemently against this historiography,[3] and I would agree with his conclusion that, regardless of its historical roots in the sciences, cinema quickly went askew from this purpose, becoming a commercial industry primarily used for the production of fiction films. In other words the quest to study natural phenomena had many fractured interests at the same time: a desire for knowledge, technological innovation, and commercial gain. It is thus that Jean-Louis Comolli finds it necessary to challenge the distinction between cinema's scientific inheritance and its ideological inheritance, concluding, nonetheless, that this scientific origin can be seen as a definitive factor in the mythology of a neutral cinematic image.[4] I situate this book largely alongside theorists such as Comolli, though again I will avoid going so far as to advocate any necessary connection between film form and a particular ideological position or political regime. Nonetheless, I will conclude inevitably that a study of film codes, connotation, and the immanent field logically must lead toward an implication of wider sociocultural values.

Critics such as Comolli and many of his contemporaries (Baudry, Mac-Cabe, et al.) worked to dispel the myth of cinematic objectivity, a project in film theory that I have argued to be concurrent with more widespread intellectual attempts to deconstruct any epistemological model in which the viewer and viewed are irrevocably divided—in other words, the Cartesian or classical myth of the detached subject, the subject that is not itself in the world but exists on the inside of a binary separating the interior from the exterior. Godard's oeuvre, like that of Resnais, chronicles the disillusionment of this very myth of the detached subject. Godard's films raise questions about how the camera *sees* and how its meanings are structured to a high degree on the differentiation signified in the act of *looking*; the lens, as Balázs points out, is extremely subjective, and Godard finds numerous ways to turn that lens on itself, to explore this very subjectivity at the heart of cinema's objectivity. This reflexivity is not limited to the level of content or denotation; as Deleuze writes, with Godard "reflection rests not only in the content but also in the form of the image."[5]

Much in the way that scholars theorize (erroneously, I have argued) Resnais to have cultivated psychological realism into a new code of subjectivity, many critics claim that Godard's formal enterprise offers a new type of objectivity. Godard's constant antinarrative engagement with nonactors, in unscripted situations and through anti-illusionist forms, has led many to champion Godard for an ethnographic mode of representation that claims to describe rather than to explain, to witness rather than to judge, returning to certain methodological premises fundamental to phenomenology. Discussing Godard's connection to other aspects of 1960s culture such as the New Novel, Guido Aristanco describes modern literature and cinema as being definable according to the paradigm of "voir" rather than "expliquer," *to see* rather than *to explain*.[6] But doesn't this raise a familiar paradox? Is this not replacing one myth with another? Did we not see a similar problem inherent in the debate between Bazin and Eisenstein, as if one image-type were more or less signifying than another? As I have argued, there is no denotation without connotation.

We have seen that with *Vivre sa vie* Godard inherited a firm belief in the objective capacity of film, its ability to reproduce the sensory world *as it is*. I will argue here that Godard demonstrates an equal if not overriding awareness of film being built from certain codes, an awareness especially of the connotative basis for purporting to represent the world *tel quel*. Indeed, his work during this period could be described as a constant struggle between, on one hand, a desire to use the camera to reveal some truth in appearances and, on the other hand, a certain duty to reveal the constructed base of cinema, to turn our attention toward the operations of the immanent field itself. In his oeuvre I hope to reveal the complexities of an ongoing reflection on the code of objectivity and what is ultimately not a new form of objectivity but, instead, a destruction of the classical philosophical binary upon which the notion of objectivity is based.

THE CODE OF OBJECTIVITY

As we saw in chapter 1, the objective essence of film's reproductive act is implied through the illusion of natural perception created primarily by the camera mechanism. This process has, of course, led to many theories of film, such as those of Bazin and Metz, which take phenomenology for their basis and assume the camera to be a type of perceptual reduction. In a similar manner Morin claims that the history of photography imposes objectivity on the cinema. In other words the camera itself is objective. From this principle Morin postulates an equivalence between "the impression of reality" and "the objective truth."[7] But is this objective characteristic of film representation built into the apparatus, or is it a denial of its presence? The preservation of cinematic objectivity relies, after all, on the ability to hide this apparatus, to guard the impression of reality through codes of denotation that are meant, in complete circularity, to demonstrate the medium's essential objectivity. This argument returns us to the myth, perpetuated by Bazin and Kracauer, of the camera—the cold, precise machine, expertly constructed and performing its function without the sentimentality of human intervention.

Grounded in the notion of its being a mechanical capture of the visible world, this ontological characteristic of photographic representation led to the reification of the machine as a form that could bring humanity closer to the objective world. Stanley Cavell's claim that photography "satisfied a wish . . . to escape subjectivity and metaphysical isolation" is unmistakably relevant here.[8] This machine supposedly provides us with a special, direct connection to nature itself: the immanent field replaces the subjective human intermediary with the nonsubjective camera. As Bazin writes: "For the first time, nothing but another object imposes itself between the initial object and its representation."[9] But this notion of film representation carries with it a fundamental belief in how the immanent field *should* be organized, and such a reification of the camera-subject makes use of a connotative system built according to a specific differentiation between the looking subject and the object being looked at.

This fundamental division between viewing machine and viewed object has intertwined the connotation of objective representation with stylistic aspects of cinematic realism.[10] Bazin, that most ardent supporter of cinematic realism, was perhaps the greatest champion of objectivity in the history of film theory. While acknowledging that cinema is entirely staged, Bazin holds that, because of film form's essential roots in the photographic camera, cinema is both obligated and destined to serve an objective function, to reveal, as a result of its own detached structure of subject-object relations, something pure in appearances. As Dudley Andrew writes about Bazin: "He was the most important and intelligent voice to have pleaded for a film theory and a film tradition based on a belief in the naked power of the mechanically recorded image."[11] I outlined in chapter 1 how, in "Ontology of the Photographic Image," Bazin traces the history of the film image as being genealogically related to cultural-anthropological tools of reproduction. However, the pure mechanistic nature of the camera separates photography and cinema from other methods of representation. In the mechanical apparatus of the camera, Bazin ventures, we have finally found a truly objective means of reproduction. He consequently incorporates into this objectivist argument a very high praise for certain formal dynamics—such as depth-of-field and the absence of montage—that would codify film aesthetics according to the ontological debt that, Bazin claims, the photographic image owes to reality.

A major factor in the claim to film's objectivity is the camera's preservation of depth-of-field in the form of perspective, a perfect example of how the formal structure of representation becomes the legitimization of some metaphysical ontological relation to reality. An integral part of my analysis of the phenomenological subject and the frame in chapter 1, depth-of-field preserves what is arguably the fundamental connotative purpose of perspective: the centering of the frame as a viewing subject-position to which the image refers and, yet, which it also effaces. Seeking a historical genealogy for this practice in cinema, theorists from Bazin to Baudry trace the codification of visual depth back to the introduction of perspective in Renaissance painting. Bazin accords depth-of-field a special place in his arguments for cinematic realism, claiming that it allows for spatial complexity and thus provides the representation with a certain ambiguity inherent in natural perception.

More ideologically skeptical theorists, such as Baudry or Comolli, argue that perspective essentially frames the image as reducible to one central locus of meaning: the camera-subject as ocular reproduction of the world.[12] Baudry's analysis, and later that of Heath and many other critics, owes much to the conclusions of Erwin Panofsky's seminal work, *Perspective as Symbolic Form*, in which Panofsky describes perspective as the connotation that a picture or image is like a window on the world, and "we are meant to believe we are looking through that window."[13] In other words this formal construction effaces the fact that it is a formal construction, suggesting that the reproduced image is a particular type of image, pure re-presentation built with scientific precision: "perspective," Panofsky writes, "transforms psychophysical space into mathematical space."[14] This transformation is a code, which Panofsky ultimately postulates as an organization of the immanent field according to a certain composition of subject-object relations.

Although Panofsky is writing about painting, not cinema, one can draw distinct connections between his approach and the theory of film proposed by Rudolf Arnheim. Arnheim, a gestaltist much like Merleau-Ponty (Arnheim would, in fact, publish an article titled "Gestalt in Art" in 1943, two years before Merleau-Ponty's *Phenomenology of Perception*), argues that film form is not an imitation or duplication of its source, but is "a translation of observed characteristics into the forms of a given medium."[15] Perspective is one of the elements of this translation. Taking this in more of an overt ideological direction that echoes Barthes's theory of mythologies, Baudry claims that the construction of this "window" is based on the effacement of the technical base that produces the images being seen.[16] This effacement is necessary to place the spectator in the position of the camera: to offer the image as something that has not yet been exposed to philosophical judgment and thus to render the illusion that any critical capacity for what is being seen is held by the spectator. I recognize this illusion, which I have called denotation, as the target of Resnais's deconstruction of the code of subjectivity, and it is similarly revealed and deconstructed in Godard's oeuvre. After all, as Resnais claimed, and we must always acknowledge, this is cinema.

The effacement of the connotative structuring of film representation has been central to the tradition of documentary cinema. For the modes of film representation both extolled and, subsequently, deconstructed by Godard, one need only look at the films of Robert Flaherty, John Grierson, and Jean Rouch, in which the documentary forms of ethnography and social realism forged particular modes of representing the world *objectively*. In this tradition representation is divided strictly between the apparatus-subject (including the filmmaker) and the viewed object, a division meant to imply a certain authenticity to the representation and an innocence or neutrality in the rhetoric of the message. It is indeed this claim to objective detachment—detachment both from the referential content and from any rhetorical stance—that has, from Dziga Vertov to Michael Moore, rendered the documentary genre the most fertile ground for propaganda.

The early documentary was part travel guide, part newsreel. "The cinema launches itself in the world and becomes a tourist," Morin writes in summarizing early theories.[17] Cinema was to be a way of coming to know distant lands, of bringing the foreign closer: accumulating knowledge of the representational content structured as visual object. The first development of this code, for both stylistic and economical reasons, championed the stationary camera, the long take, and, later, depth-of-field, formal elements for which Bazin would praise the realism of Renoir's and Welles's fiction films.[18] Such a historical perspective reveals that formal characteristics of the documentary genre often cross over into fiction film's attempt to give the impression of authenticity, the claim to truth. Thus, a code of denotation is developed for "documenting" the real and is then adopted for giving the illusion of reality in a variety of genres. Remarkable cinematographic similarities can be found, for example, between English kitchen-sink documentaries of the 1930s and the connotative codes of Italian neorealism in the 1940s, a historical echo confirmed by Bazin's observation that "since the war, cinema has assisted in the obvious return to documentary authenticity."[19] With the evolution of cheaper and more mobile equipment, documentary practices later reversed their technical attributes, adopting a more flattened image produced in naturally lit situations by a handheld camera to mimic the aesthetic of nonprofessional home movies being made on the streets with cheaper and more mobile technology. Heavily influenced by such documentary filmmakers as Jean Rouch and the aesthetic known as *cinéma vérité*, the directors of the New Wave co-opted many of these technologies and techniques, including high-speed film stock, the handheld camera, and the discursive mode of the direct-address interview. Indeed, these devices remain stylistic connotations of objectivity today, in such different contemporary movements as reality television and the Dogme 95 manifesto, as well as in mainstream fiction films that require the illusion of reality for optimal spectatorial affect, such as the thrillers *The Blair Witch Project* (Daniel Myrick and Eduardo Sánchez, 1999) and *Cloverfield* (Matt Reeves, 2008).[20]

But cinematic objectivity is not easy to define: it is a certain implication that emanates through the immanent field—a connotation. As Cavell notes, cinematic objectivity is a "mood in which reality becomes reified for you, a mood of nothing but eyes, dissociated from feeling."[21] This idea of a "mood" is not far from what I have discussed more specifically as connotation, in which the structure of representation connotes the image as being a certain *type of representation*. This structure is the result of a particular organization of subject-object relations, in this case a differentiation between the viewing subject-function ("nothing but eyes") and the reified object of representation. Once again I return to one

of my preliminary debates: this aspect of the apparatus's being "dissociated" generates, in Bazin for example, a hostility toward montage.
Eisenstein's entire notion of montage involves the contrary: a process of
association that stirs a feeling in the spectator. It would be erroneous, however, to think that the evocation of an objective gaze is not rhetorical in
practice. This issue of the connotative foundation of cinematic objectivity
forces me here to confront a larger cinematic and extracinematic question
that has loomed like a shadow across this entire study, a question concerning the social, political, and ethical ramifications of these practices.
In addressing this issue, I will gradually begin to point this study toward
the horizon of a larger application of my conceptualization of film-philosophy, one that *does* implicate more widespread systems of thought and
extends to the cinemas of different directors, nations, and eras.

The notion of objectivity in cinema—being tied to ontological assumptions about the photographic camera, the early scientific pretense of cinema's birth, and various documentary traditions—belies problems in
film theory that have been most clearly raised concerning the identity
politics of representation.[22] Postcolonial theories of film and media, for
example, enact a connotative analysis of the appropriation of the exotic or
foreign as a visual other, signified as an object in relation to the viewing
subject. This returns me to the Althusserian critique of epistemology
mentioned in chapter 1, a critique that will resurface in this chapter's
analysis of Godard and the objectification of women in film. MacCabe
and Mulvey tie the objectification of women to cinema through the
"problem of sexual difference and of the alienation endemic to capitalist
society,"[23] a problem that is central to Godard's investigations during this
period. Looking at Godard's structures of representation, I will argue
that this "difference" and "alienation" are inseparable from the "mood"
of objective representation and that postcolonial, feminist, and other such
approaches can be articulated according to the theory of film connotation
and subject-object relations established in these pages. This alienation is
the separation between viewing subject and viewed object, between origin of meaning and article of information, which serves as the basis for
Vivre sa vie and is in various ways overturned via the dialogism of the
immanent field in *Two or Three Things I Know About Her*.

Based on the notions of epistemology and the scientific and documentary roots of cinema sketched out so far in this chapter, one could say

that the goals of cinematic objectivity can be traced to a desire to understand the essence of something by perceiving it. Conjuring aspects of Bazin's ocularcentric interpretation of phenomenology, Godard expresses this goal when he talks about *Vivre sa vie*: "How to show the inside? Well, by resting wisely outside."[24] However, the object in this case isn't just the natural world, but a person. And not just a person, but a type of person with a socially, culturally, and economically defined identity. A 1960s working-class Parisian woman. In *Vivre sa vie* Godard applies a classical notion of cinematic objectivity to the fictional inquiry into a woman's existence, permitting her a certain narrative agency but not a full interaction with the camera, turning her a sympathetic ear and yet a cold gaze. In a historical sense one could deduce from this an alignment between Godard and other filmmakers who have applied a similarly detached form of representation to the filming of female protagonists, including Dreyer, Bergman, and Bresson—all of whom, as can be gleaned from his writings and films, influenced Godard heavily. This positioning of the visual other as the gaze's object, this structure of differentiation between the perspective of the image and what it is an image of, is fundamental to the code of objectivity, a code whose formal elements connote an empirical relationship, a distance, between the apparatus and the world it represents.

This distance is something that Godard eventually abandons in *Two or Three Things I Know About Her*. In fact, one can detect a major shift as early as the film immediately following *Vivre sa vie*: *Contempt*. Though he is deeply implicated at times in its preservation, Godard arrives at a reformulation of the code of objectivity that ultimately deconstructs its central premise of differentiation. I will discuss this in my analysis of *Contempt*, which Wheeler Winston Dixon describes as "a turning point in Godard's career," demonstrating "a new depth and tragic maturity not present in the director's earlier efforts."[25] Just as we have seen with Resnais and the code of subjectivity, Godard manages to embrace and to expose the code of objectivity as a myth, to reveal the formal conventions beneath it and—as does Resnais—then to offer an alternative to it, built around the recognized implications of the form's presence, a focus on the connotative level of meaning: an experiment in cinematic thinking that opens the viewer to new possibilities concerning our interaction with the image, the world, and ourselves.

JEAN-LUC GODARD AND THE CODE OF OBJECTIVITY

The code of objectivity can be understood as the systematic connotation of a detached subject-position, an organization of the immanent field in such a way as to imply that the image is the product of an apparatus that rests outside the immanent field, giving the impression that what is being seen is not even a representation but is a direct observation of the ostensive photographic referent. Just as we saw in the last chapter's analysis of Resnais, Godard challenges every aspect of this code, from its individual formal characteristics, to its formulation of a linear narrative structure, to its process of removing all signs of its own production, to the philosophical vertebrae of its order of meaning. In *Breathless* (1960), *A Woman Is a Woman* (1961), and *Alphaville* (1965) Godard directly confronts cinematic genre and cliché, exposing the underlying determinations of the cinematic illusion. Then, with films such as *Pierrot le fou* (1965) and *Week-end* (1967), he wages an all-out war on illusionary film representation and narrative artificiality. Last, in films such as *Two or Three Things I Know About Her* and *Masculin féminin* (1966) one finds the complete transition from a deconstructive, antinarrative mode to a fully reflexive form that both reveals the structure of representation and grants a subjective voice to its object.

During this period Godard increasingly conflates the separation between subject and object and opens up the immanent field to a dialogic interaction between elements and agencies. The visual depth of the image is minimized, and characters look directly into the eye of the camera. In films such as *Two or Three Things I Know About Her* and *Contempt* the differentiation between diegetic subjects is diminished just as is that between subject and object of the image. Such effects blur the division between viewer and viewed, speaking and spoken. As Peter Wollen puts it, Godard's films "can no longer be seen as a discourse with a single subject,"[26] can no longer be traced to one unilateral source of representation. Despite previous maxims to the contrary, Godard ultimately rejects the myth of camera objectivity, viewing this objectivity rather as a characteristic produced by certain subject-object relations. Godard sets about to reveal this connotative foundation of cinematic objectivity through a number of formal practices.

One of these formal practices is the flattened image, as in *Two or Three Things I Know About Her*. Depth-of-field, Mitry points out, functions according to the illusion of total or full spatial perception, an image-type self-referentially connoting itself to be "observational perception."[27] In the flattened image, however, the distance between viewing subject and viewed object is spatially reduced, drawn closer. This conflation of visual space shocks the viewer out of the comfort provided by the conventional differentiated relationship between viewing and viewed. I need not resume here my entire discourse on depth-of-field; suffice it to remind the reader that the flattened image issues a rejection of the connotations that emanate from depth-of-field's organization of subject-object relations. Brian Henderson suggests that this subversion is typical of Godardian politics: an attack on, and demystification of, bourgeois modes of representation.[28] Regardless of whether it is antibourgeois or not (Godard himself could hardly be labeled proletarian and his films' political messages, at least during this period, are ambivalent), it is certainly a subversion of mainstream conventions. Indeed, the flatness of the image reveals and, in revealing, destroys the very illusion of natural perception offered in classical cinema, while at the same time secreting a new code for objectivity: the flattened image as ethnographic truth, in which the immanent field brings the source of representation and its content together in one shared dialogic space.

Indeed, many of the ways in which Godard deconstructs the code of objectivity are, themselves, new connotations of cinematic objectivity, much the same as Resnais deconstructs the enclosed diegetic subject-function in order to construct a new mode of psychological or subjective realism. I must reiterate, though, that through the frequent transformations of the immanent field in their films these directors refuse to validate either old or new code as anything absolute. For Godard this invalidation comes about in numerous other ways, including camera movements such as the enclosed shift I introduced in my analysis of *Vivre sa vie*, involving just a slight movement (either a pan or lateral tracking) of the camera from side to side. This manages to exclude one person from the image, always implying an incompletion to the dimensions offered by the camera mechanism, while connoting a sense of detachment from narrative meaning. It is an objectivity that acknowledges that the limitations of its images are defined by its formal base—an objectivity that nullifies its objectivism.

The connotations of this effect are further exaggerated by the lateral tracking shot. Taking on absurdly epic proportions in *Week-end*, Godard's tracking shot opposes itself to the tracking shot used by Resnais. Whereas Resnais's tracking shot escapes the X-axis of movement, opting for the vertical thrust of a forward-moving point of view, Godard's lateral tracking shot refuses the Z-axis of space instead, further flattening the arena of visual representation to two dimensions. However, like Resnais's tracking shot, and as with what I will call the spiral tracking shot of *Contempt*, Godard's tracking shot is not motivated by any one character, nor does it move as if linked to any particular narrative action. This refusal to align the camera with any diegetic element leads Henderson to remark that Godard's lateral tracking shot "serves no individual and prefers none to another."[29] This effect provides a certain openness or liberty to the image's movement, denying any narrative catalyst for the displacement of the camera. Henderson claims that the tracking shot and flattened depth provide an image that "cannot be elaborated but only surveyed,"[30] though I will argue that Godard subverts this very claim to observational sterility. I will also argue, however, in agreement with Henderson, that Godard *does* deny the connection between these forms and any single subject-function. We can begin to trace a theme in these formal tendencies: Godard refuses the totality or continuity that would signify one particular subject-function, foregrounding what Comolli calls Godard's "refusal to privilege one sign over others";[31] or, in Deleuze's Bergsonian terms, Godard refuses to select a system of reference. Like Resnais, Godard organizes the immanent field to produce a semiotic ambiguity resisting conventional hierarchies or structures of subject-object differentiation. This ambiguity is extended to the relationship between formal elements, such as camera movement and depth, speech and image, or the moving camera and the cut.

David Bordwell points out that another effect of the tracking shot, or long take in general, is to emphasize "the interruptive function of the cut."[32] This brings to light Godard's focus on the relationship between shot and montage as a way of foregrounding the arbitrariness of the form in relation to the actual object being represented. That is to say, Godard uses editing to dispel the implication that what the spectator is given is anything more essential than the selection of the filmmaker, a necessary but arbitrary organization of the immanent field based on the limitations of the form. This can be seen in Godard's signature editing technique: the jump cut. The jump cut is probably Godard's most well-known formal experiment and is produced simply by dropping frames within a continuous shot. The result is a shocking break in the continuity of the moving image: the image seems literally to jump, like a skipping record, revealing the constructed nature of film representation and implying that even the camera itself cannot offer a transcendental, unified subject-position. As Heath puts it, with Godard there is "no longer the single and central vision but a certain freedom of contradictions."[33]

Whereas the jump cut provides a disturbance in the relationship between two images, a second example would be a disturbance caused primarily through the internal montage of speech and image. As we saw with *Two or Three Things I Know About Her*, Godard experiments with various forms of speech-image codification, especially the use of off-screen voices and direct address. In each of these cases the harmony between the image and a speech act is broken in a way that the image is divided between two sources of enunciation, between subject-functions. One such sequence from *Contempt* (which I will analyze in depth later in this chapter) consists of a visual montage that includes shots of a lakeside path and the central female character (played by Brigitte Bardot) lying naked on a white-feather carpet. The woman is visually objectified while at the same time being given an alternative, voice-over subject-function. Her voice-over is, however, counteracted by that of her husband, and both voices are stripped of any agency as a result of the fact that they are repeated with no effect on the flow of visual expression, which is itself also looped with no necessary relation to the soundtrack (much as with the voice-over and organ in the opening sequence of *Last Year at Marienbad*).

The other kind of insert sequence used frequently by Godard is direct address, in what is usually an overt political message. Films such as *Pierrot le fou*, *Masculin féminin*, and *Week-end* use these inserts to freeze the narrative and to overturn the conventions of transparency maintained by fictional cinema. This leads Bordwell to write, "The central aspect of Godard's narrational process is self-conscious address to the audience."[34] But this self-consciousness is not only between the image and spectator; it implies all dimensions of the immanent field, including the content of representation and the larger, outlying structure of sociocultural values, beliefs, and conventions.

Moreover, this "self-conscious address" does not only come through the effect of direct address, or through references to film genre and history. Like Resnais, Godard makes the structure of film representation the very referent of his films by altering the level of signification set in the foreground. In both types of insert sequence mentioned here, for example, Godard subverts the formulation of a coherent denotation in order to produce a reflection on the connotative level of film. This is why he and Resnais complement each other so well, why they are such apt choices to illustrate the arguments of this book, and why they are so central to Deleuze's analysis, which I have argued is fundamentally an analysis of film connotation. This reflexivity is the driving force in the string of films Godard made between 1960 and 1968, beginning with *Breathless* and ending with *Week-end*. Always deeply engaged with contemporary social politics and cultural practices, Godard systematically directs this reflexive project of deconstruction toward the coded objectification of women in cinema. As Dixon points out: "The commodification of the human body (particularly the female body) becomes . . . the center of many of his key films."[35] I have argued in passing that this type of "commodification" is attached to the cinematic code of objectivity, and I will soon make it the centerpiece of a more specific example of film connotation, just as Godard makes it the centerpiece of his critique of film conventions.

This critique requires a revelation of the connotative base, a revelation that is particularly well achieved in *Contempt*, a film more explicitly about cinema than any other of Godard's films from this period. Arguing on Godard's behalf during a later period, when his films were more explicitly avant-garde, Wollen notes: "In his earlier films Godard introduced the cinema as a topic of his narrative"; yet, Wollen argues, not until his post-1968 Maoist period does Godard "show the camera on screen."[36] I will argue that this is not true, not in a metaphorical sense and not in a literal sense: Godard turns the camera on itself as early as 1963. Indeed, no film better illustrates the complexities enumerated thus far concerning Godard's work than *Contempt*, which takes place (both as a story and a production) amid two major cultural currents prominent in the 1950s and 1960s: the fall of the Hollywood studio system and the rise of mass-media pop culture, two institutions that are marked by the hypersexualized representation of women as objects. The cinematic dream, Godard shows us, is not just a collection of myths in the ephemeral stream of projected light but is based on the virtual play of desire and the visual consumption of skin and flesh—in a word, voyeurism, and I will argue here that voyeurism is based on a similar duality between viewing subject and viewed object as that which is used to connote cinematic objectivity.

As Cavell notes, the formal themes of *Contempt* provide "a deep statement of the camera's presence." But, he continues, this carries with it "a statement from the camera about its subjects, about their simultaneous distance and connection, about the sweeping desert of weary familiarity."[37] In other words, much as in *The War Is Over* and the formalization of political action, there is a certain harmony here in the immanent field between the representation's process of organization and the diegetic world it is organizing. As such, this film offers the perfect opportunity to bring together the many strands of this book and to incorporate them at last into a specifically cinematic investigation of cinema.

KINO-EYE IN THE MIRROR: *CONTEMPT* AND THE OBJECTIVE SUBJECT

As a result of its complicated production and almost instant status as an important event in the film world, *Contempt* has inspired a unique critical history. Most analyses have chosen to focus somewhat redundantly on the film's detailed process of production, including its relation to the Alberto Moravia novel on which it is based, as well as enumerating its numerous intertextual references. The bulk of this work has come from what could be called the *Censier* group of film critics (due to the name given to University of Paris III, Censier, where they have all taught), including Jacques Aumont, Michel Marie, and Alain Bergala.[38] Such critics focus on detailed analysis of the text and have produced somewhat similar discourses on the importance of Moravia's book, of the deterioration of Godard's marriage to Anna Karina during this time, and of the significance of cast member Brigitte Bardot's extratextual star persona. This film is surprisingly absent from the wealth of formal or ideological analysis of Godard's oeuvre, however, including MacCabe's early criticism, the many essays Henderson devotes to Godard's deconstructive tendencies, and Wollen's attention to his countercinematic practices. I hope, therefore, to contribute something original here to the study of Godard's work, exploring the systematic and philosophical ramifications of the film's configurations of the immanent field.

Summarizing the extreme juxtapositions at the heart of *Contempt*, Godard writes: "Truth opposes itself to lies, wisdom to the clouded mind, a certain Greek smile made of intelligence and irony to the uncertain modern smile built from illusion and contempt."[39] With Godard this final juxtaposition has a double meaning: not only does he situate this film between Greek classicism and Occidental modernity, but also between classical Hollywood and modern cinema. Made in 1963, *Contempt* arrives at the very moment when the Hollywood studio system—"the vertically integrated monolith that Godard celebrated (after a fashion) in his earlier writings"[40]—was collapsing, and new means of production and representation were beginning to emerge. Having long been fascinated with Hollywood as an object of both admiration and critique, Godard provides in *Contempt* his final tribute to—and condemnation of—the classical film industry.

Godard achieves this by turning the camera on itself, producing a generative circle of signification that makes film representation both signifier and signified of the film and, thus, provides cinema with its own mirror phase, in which it identifies with itself as both producer of meaning and, also, sociocultural object that reflects popular ideology. This duplicity, I will argue, is central to the film's organizations, which can be formulated as a certain doubling of the immanent field. *Contempt* sets up a reflexive mode of representation in which the codes being used are themselves put under the scrutiny of the camera even while they are being used. The *mise-en-abyme* presented in the narrative is crucial to this, less so for its content—as it may be, for example, in Fellini's *8 1/2* (1963) or Truffaut's *Day for Night* (1973)—than for the semiotic structure used to reflect on its own forms or representation. *Contempt* conjures a signifying chain wherein wider social desires and modes of perception are both factors in, and products of, the structures of the film's images.

The basic premise of the film takes Godard's fascination with prostitution as a metaphor and transposes it onto the world of filmmaking. Paul (Michel Piccoli) is a screenwriter, working on a film version of Homer's *The Odyssey* to be directed by Fritz Lang (who plays himself). Paul's wife, Camille (played by Bardot, icon of the pop-culture world that Godard would later term the "civilization of the ass"),[41] becomes the sacrifice on Paul's altar of commercial success. To contract Paul to write the film, the producer, a quintessentially brutish American named Jeremy Prokosch (Jack Palance), demands that Paul offer him Camille in exchange. As Dixon writes, it is Paul's willingness to prostitute himself, and her as well, that leads to Camille's eponymous *contempt*.[42] This association between cinema and prostitution is the premise for the self-reflexive nature of the text, which brings to the surface a constant battle with the subtle nuance of cliché, implying its own inability to escape the very forms of representation that it hopes to dismantle—the most striking example being the objectification of women. The contrast between the centripetal and centrifugal forces at play in this system of signification, between the attempt to pull away from classical codes and the limitations of the form itself, is echoed by the film's reliance on the pattern of the spiral.

Much as we saw with *The War Is Over*, *Contempt* allows the fulfillment of codes and then denies them by revealing them as constructed organizations of subject-object relations. An aesthetic model for the constantly receding intimacy between Paul and Camille, the film unfolds in a series of what I will call spiral tracking shots. Also, there is a sort of vertigo established through the juxtaposition of long takes with the flattened image, bringing two paradigms of cinematic objectivity—the duration of the shot and the depth of the image—into direct conflict. Finally, Godard uses insert sequences to experiment with sound and image in order to fracture any single subject-function, sensory elements moving separately and each one revealing the fabricated nature of the other. All of these elements contribute to the doubled or self-contradicting structure of the immanent field, which permits the overlapping of subjective and objective poles and is grounded at all times in a reflexive revelation of its own connotative foundations.

Contempt opens with a very unconventional, and equally famous, credit sequence: a woman (who turns out to be the character Francesca, played by Giorgia Moll), reading from a movie script, walks slowly toward the camera. Beside her, Raoul Coutard (Godard's cinematographer) tracks alongside her as Godard's voice reads the credits on the voice-over. Coutard follows her with the camera until he arrives in the forefront of the image. Coutard begins turning toward the spectator as Godard says, citing Bazin: "cinema substitutes for our gaze a world in accord with our desires."[43] Then, as the camera faces the spectator (fig. 5.1), he concludes: "*Contempt* is the story of this world."

This shot has been thoroughly dissected by the *Censier* group, and I will only touch on it as an introduction to the film's connotative self-reflexivity, initiated here through the image of the lens itself. The shot of Coutard, being filmed while filming someone else, reveals the text as a fabrication. The apparatus is revealed: from the very beginning of the film, any claim to objectivity, neutrality, or detachment is destroyed.

FIGURE 5.1
Raoul Coutard turns the camera of *Contempt* (1963) on the audience.

Moreover, it provides us with a paradigm for the film's doubled connotative structure: the differentiation provided between Coutard and the
woman is doubled in the differentiation between the shot and Coutard.
He is being posited as the object through the same process of differentiation in which he himself is engaged. This shot breaks the closed state of
cinematic signification by turning the camera on the spectator, subverting
conventional codes of suture and reversing the organization of subject-
object relations that made Coutard the object of the representation. We
find the immanent field to be contorted, doubled over on itself, in the
process of which the world outside the film is implicated in the text's
process.

A testament to how we look at and through the cinematic image, this
organization of the immanent field aligns the desires of the public with
the values to be connoted through the structure of representation. It offers, as Marc Cerisuelo puts it, "a veritable commentary at once on 'the
state of things' and on the history of cinema."[44] In other words *Contempt*
is a study of the signifying practices of the cinematic age, as well as a
signification itself of a certain symbiosis between such codes and sociocultural modes of perception and representation. When Godard says that
Contempt is "the story of this world," I would argue that he is referring to
the story of cinema's attempt to accommodate and to codify—to represent and to affirm—the connotative roots of objectivity, the cinematic
desire to learn the inside by showing the outside. The organization of
subject-object relations that formulates this desire is a voyeuristic one,

secreted into the illusion of empirical observation that is manifested in the immanent field according to the signification of a unilateral viewing subject—a fully formed philosophy sewn silently into the formal conventions of classical cinema. Moreover, the forward-thrusting extension of the empirical eye is a most phallic tool: the camera. As such, it is entirely fitting that the following scene consists of one long shot of Camille, naked and gleaming sensuously beneath the glare of multicolored lights, which shift from red to yellow to blue.

Lying in bed with her husband, Camille does a verbal inventory of her body, asking his approval as the shot tracks slowly across her outstretched form. "You like my breasts?" "Yes." This scene, which Kaja Silverman tellingly refers to as a "territorializing" process,[45] again doubles the immanent field on itself: the form of representation presents the contradiction of two inclusive signifying systems, incorporating codes of popular culture but also anticodes of experimental cinema. This conflict of signifying systems produces an unsettling effect of alienation, what Cerisuelo refers to as "a great violence . . . an 'unveiling' of the cinematographic rule."[46] This unveiling consists of a contradiction between different structures of representation. While the image of her body conjures an erotic impression, the effect of the lighting and the conversation contort this eroticism. Moreover, the coexistence within the immanent field of two discourses—the verbal taxonomy and the near-pornographic image—renders the erotic representation totally banal and cold, a result of the quotidian nature of this taxonomic verbal procedure, a verbal de-eroticization used in other of Godard's films during this period.[47] Moreover, as she names her body parts there is no specific correspondence between the parts named and what fills the frame; this frustration of what I have called the cinematic nominative process produces a sort of lackadaisical effect, a "weary familiarity" as Cavell puts it, a boredom with clichéd eroticism that is implied by the denial of a singular subject-function that would be deriving pleasure from it.

This scene introduces the premise of the entire film (and, one might go so far to say, of Godard's oeuvre in general): a reflexive, highly stylistic investigation of "the mechanics of feminine/masculine power relationships" as they are manifested through cinematic codes.[48] In other words it presents the structure of representation as an extension of sexual difference. The mechanical eye of cinema is revealed as the extension of the viewing desire of a particular type of human: the *objectif* (the French term for "lens") has a very subjective, gender-based foundation. It has been argued by many feminist theorists (with whom I agree fully, though whose primarily psychoanalytic models I will not use), that the desire signified through classical film conventions connotes a heterosexual male desire to possess. Mulvey and others observe that the means of production in cinema have always been in male hands; as such, the eye of cinema has always been attached to a male libido.[49] This places the history of film form in a position of particular relevance to the phenomenological notion that "all knowledge involves objectification and in a certain sense the violation of the object,"[50] reminiscent of the Althusserian notion of empiricism noted in chapter1. I hope to frame this as a problem of subject-object relations, in which the acquisition of knowledge through unilateral possession is a connotative foundation of the code of objectivity. In *The System of Objects* Jean Baudrillard assesses this very scene in *Contempt* to illustrate his argument that objectification is generally central to the passion for, and possession of, both things and sexual beings. This description of what Baudrillard calls fetishism concludes it as being reliant on differentiation and domination: "not to be able to grasp the object of desire in its singular totality as a person, but only in its discontinuity."[51] A woman is not a woman, Baudrillard continues, but is—as has been codified through media conventions—a sum of fragmented parts, just as Camille describes herself. She has no subjectivity, having been reduced to an assemblage of objects.

At its foundation I believe that this voyeuristic tendency can be extended to the connotative conventions of the code of objectivity. Leo Bersani and Ulysse Dutoit clarify Baudrillard's argument by pointing out that the act of looking turns the object of desire (sexual interest) into an object of fetish (erotic fascination).[52] Thus, the differentiation provided by the unilateral structure of the image itself exonerates the impulses of the viewing subject, mythologizing sexual objectification as objective representation. Godard manages to deconstruct this formal determination by fracturing the immanent field among numerous formal elements, numerous subject-functions—by, as Rancière might say, redistributing the sensible.

In the film as a whole Godard draws the connotative structure or organization of subject-object relations into the spotlight by juxtaposing two very different discursive paradigms, the classical and the modern, as we can see in the conflict posed between Fritz Lang's *The Odyssey* and *Con-*

tempt itself. This duality, I argue, is integrated into the juxtaposition between two forms of representation, which define their significations through their relative organization of subject-object relations. By way of introduction Cerisuelo helps to demarcate a certain aspect of modern cinema in the film's aesthetics and syntax: "The film demonstrates its modernity, at once both radical and mastered, in its combination of sequence-shots (or long shots), lateral tracking shots, and its connections of movement."[53] In other words we can look for the film's underlying significance in the interrelationships of its formal elements, in the structure of its immanent field. Godard, for example, constantly undermines the fly-on-the-wall implications of the long take, directing our attention toward the fact that the immanent field is, in fact, a construction of relations.

This acknowledgment of the limitations of the formal base is part of a larger network through which Godard appropriates technical aspects of the code of objectivity, only to reveal the apparatus as nonobjective, selective, motivated by connotative structures. This network includes the spiral tracking shot, the flattened image, and the insert sequence. The first of these, the spiral tracking shot, which composes nearly every outdoor scene in the film, begins in front of moving characters, moves slowly with the characters, allows them to pass, and follows momentarily. Then it cuts to reestablish itself once again in front. Through its motion and organization of space this shot connotes a particular relationship between the camera and the objects it films. Giving the impression that it is curling around, thus containing the objects, in the end it always jumps to slightly outside of this curve, breaking the impression of containment. It follows no particular character, allowing them each to ebb and flow in and out of the image. The shot then cuts to a different position, however, following the action; through such cuts we are made aware of the form's determinations of the immanent field.

This thematic shot is the quintessence of the notion of the *"ballade"* that Deleuze uses to describe Godard's films: a tendency of his characters to walk without direction, rambling lack of narrative focus, and a resistance to conventional film aesthetics, each of which is manifested through perpetual and seemingly aimless movement.[54] This lack of narrative focus is founded on a refusal of conventional subject-object relations. Much like the shifts in the speech-image code analyzed in chapter 3, the tracking shot—with Godard as with Resnais—refuses to grant a dominant agency to either the camera or the characters. They move together, then disperse. The camera watches, then participates, then watches again. The image is neutral, then engaged, then neutral: the immanent field, as a structure of subject-object relations, is constantly in a state of fluctuation between subjective and objective poles of representation.

The spiral tracking shot has a less mobile, miniature version in the enclosed shift. This device, in which the camera moves only slightly from one character to another, separates people who are otherwise positioned closely to each other, producing an alienation between visible objects such as we saw in *Vivre sa vie*. This visual device is perhaps most prevalent in a scene that takes place between Paul and Camille in their apartment, a twenty-minute conversation consisting mainly of two long takes, and in the course of which the camera is constantly revealed as an inefficient witness. At one particular moment Paul and Camille speak to each other from across a table. The camera slowly tracks from one to the other, in no way following the dialogue or any other causal logic, in no way provoked or provoking. It is a mood, as Cavell puts it, a dissociation of feeling. In this scene Camille finally tells Paul that she no longer loves him, a sentiment symbolized by the cold space that exists between the two characters. As opposed to Bazin's objective camera, this is one that cannot restore the unity of the reality in front of it. Moreover, the structure of representation is infused with a formal detachment from its objects, a detachment that prefigures—as opposed to being determined by—what is actually happening in the story.

As mentioned above, these connotative significations are all the more accentuated by being juxtaposed against the form of Lang's *The Odyssey*, which includes many shots of statues. Lang's film is composed primarily of rapid semicircular rotating shots, in which the camera performs a quick 180-degree turn around immobile granite characters. Whereas the characters of *Contempt* seem to move constantly, the characters of *The Odyssey* are sedentary. Instead, the *camera* moves quickly around *them*, giving the impression that the statues are moving: objects brought to life by the mobility of the camera subject (fig. 5.2).

The classical camera of mythical gods is distinctly rhetorical and relies functionally on the clear-cut division between viewing subject and viewed object. The difference between this and the camera of *Contempt* becomes particularly relevant in the doubling of the immanent field, such as occurs in brief cuts to Lang's images at crucial stages of Paul's

FIGURE 5.2
Statues are the characters of *Contempt*'s film-within-a-film, Fritz Lang's *The Odyssey*.

neglect for—and loss of—Camille. This juxtaposition of image-types helps to organize the immanent field as the meeting place, as Godard might put it, between the classical and the modern, a fluctuation between subject-object dynamics that aligns Godard with a modern shift in philosophical history.

Godard uses these two styles of filming to construct two different worlds—one that is stable and coherently based on a precise differentiation between subject and object, and another that is unstable and dialogic. In illustrating these two worlds, this film presents the juxtaposition between two different connotative systems. This thematic doubling of the immanent field is affirmed by the rejection of depth-of-field in the long take. The best example of this is when Paul, having seen Camille kiss Prokosch and having realized he has lost her, follows her down the steps to the sea in Capri. They are constantly moving toward the camera, but the flattened image means that they hardly displace themselves—they literally *go nowhere*—as they descend. In this mutation of aesthetic codes, the flattened image corrupts the objective realism of the long take for which Bazin praises the works of Renoir. The denoted space between them is condensed, as if to draw attention to it as a product of connotation. The "mood" of this shot is further accentuated moments later: Camille, swimming in the background, appears very close to Paul, as the background and foreground are not divided through depth. This juxtaposition of formal elements produces an immanent field both shared and empty, as Paul and Camille share an ambiguous space, which—

much like the enclosed pan—accentuates all the more the tragic divide between them.

The flattened image will, in Godard's films after *Contempt*, become a main fixture in his formal repertoire. This effect subverts the connotative structure that depth-of-field offers and resists the formation of a visual configuration that would offer the viewer the illusion of natural perception. Arnheim discusses the difference between the two-dimensional form and the three-dimensional illusion of the image as being one that accentuates the "unreality of the film picture."[55] This unreality is anathema to the code of objectivity. Moreover, Arnheim argues that the flattened image makes it so that the "purely formal qualities of the picture come into prominence," thus producing an "anti-functional effect."[56] In other words the connotative foundation is brought into focus, and the immanent field is liberated from any pretense toward denotation. The form draws attention to its own constructed nature and thus draws our attention to the very fact that it is awkward, unconventional. The flattened image ironically makes us aware of the space that separates us from the object of vision, as opposed to this space being naturalized and, thus, going unnoticed. *Contempt* is a constant meditation on ways of looking, how the space traversed between subject and object is organized to articulate larger relational problems. As such, conjuring principles of Merleau-Ponty's phenomenology discussed in chapter 1, Sylvie Ayme argues that this film "presents before us . . . the world as a common site even of vision."[57]

This communal site for vision is one that is dominated, according to Godard and many others, by the gaze as an extension of certain structures of power. *Contempt* could thus be analyzed as a film about the spectator—and the spectatorial position—during the age of cinema, embodied in the film by the character of Jeremy Prokosch. Prokosch *is* Hollywood, an industry geared to suit the desires of customers like him and fully certain in the philosophy that emanates from the connotations of the images he enjoys, the worldview he values. Moreover, he embodies the unilateral notion of subjectivity used to construct classical forms of narrative linearity. "Although he is repellent," Dixon asserts, "Prokosch is in control of his life,"[58] and thus his gaze is different from that of Paul, a castrated modern antihero whose subjective agency is bereft of the apparatus's support. These two gazes, two different image-philosophies, are constantly at odds, evidence once again of a doubling of the immanent field.

There is only one occasion on which *Contempt* implies a fully subjective representation: when Paul and Camille go to Prokosch's villa for the first time, and Prokosch makes clear his intentions. In this scene there is a moment when Bardot turns and looks at the camera; this is followed by a shot of Prokosch, staring at her. For this moment we are looking through his gaze, and Camille is the object of that gaze. But, as in the rest of the film, there is a doubling here between the classical and the subversive: while the eye-line match functions to suture us into Prokosch's subject-position, this suturing is demystified by Camille's staring directly into the camera (as opposed to her looking just to the side of the camera, as would occur according to classical convention). This cut presents a clash of image-types, one of which is based on the denotation of a looking subject and the other of which is based on revealing the connotation of this suture. Charged thus with opposing agencies, the immanent field becomes the site of struggle for dominance of this film's orders of meaning: a struggle of the experimental with the clichés of classical cinema, with the image of woman at stake.

This struggle also underpins an insert sequence in which Paul and Camille separately express their remorse in voice-over tracks. In each case the images shift between the erotic (Camille naked and outstretched) and the sentimental (a lakeside path) (figs. 5.3–5.5). The voice-overs alternate without clear logical connection to the images, as if transposing the connotative structure of the enclosed shift onto the speech-image code—they never quite seem in the same place at the same time. Silverman analyzes this scene, understandably, as an indication of what both Paul and Camille have lost: Camille's body.[59] I will view it, however, as a nondenotative reference. It is, instead, the decomposition of formal structures of differentiation and the crisscrossing of subject-functions: a revelation of film as an arena for the construction of subjectivity, an immanent field that is opened up all the wider as Camille, naked and outstretched on her stomach, lifts her head and stares into the camera.

Concerning this sequence, Bordwell writes: "we cannot be sure whether the voice-over phrases directly express the characters or are simply the narrator's mimicry."[60] Following the thread of his general analysis of art cinema, Bordwell insists that the guiding effect of Godard's work is the self-conscious articulation of the artist's narratorial voice. However, while the collation of spoken discourse and visual image remains ambiguous,

FIGURES 5.3–5.5
With sound and image derailed, a naked Camille (Brigitte Bardot) looks directly at the camera.

there is no reason to conjecture any voice other than the voices of the characters, who struggle—as throughout the film, as in *Last Year at Marienbad*—over the production of meaning both within the diegesis and in the organization of subject-object relations.

That is to say, the sources of the voices are identifiable, familiar. Bordwell does help, however, to point out a certain interaction here, within the immanent field, between the signifying agents of different sources, different sensory elements and formal sets of relations. This question of enunciation returns us to the earlier problem of language and meaning in cinema, or the problem of the aural subject, a problem that functions in this film not only as a question of the unfolding of images but also as a diegetic question concerning the production of representation. The problem of struggling speech acts and the origin of meaning is central to *Contempt* as a production, a story, and a set of images—in other words, as an immanent field, a philosophical experiment with film form. Shot and recorded in four languages, the film alternates primarily between English and French, though both Italian and German are used regularly. The only character who speaks all of these languages is Francesca, Prokosch's secretary. As such, she is solely responsible for the possibility of communication among the different characters. Thus, in a way she is the ultimate bearer of meaning, but this subject-function is denied by her naturalized sociocultural status as a woman, which relegates her to a particular function in the world of cinema. This is similar for Camille: even when her voice-over controls the aural track, her body is visually laid out before us as an erotic object. Yet she looks into the camera, making us realize that this objectification is self-conscious, intentional, and thus connotative of something beyond the titillating image of nudity that Prokosch will giggle at when watching the rushes for his own film.

This image of Bardot's Camille, naked, looking into the lens, goes further and comes closer than any other film discussed here to implicating the spectator and the external sociocultural world in the dynamic organization of the immanent field. Reiterating a problem I pointed to earlier in this chapter, this exemplifies Godard's struggle to find a form that at once defies and also reflects critically on the conventional objectification of women. Geneviève Sellier describes this struggle: "an oscillation between the will to rupture with the dominant schema which constructs the female character as an object of desire for the masculine gaze, and an exhibition of this schema, as much on the level of dialogue and situations as in the mise-en-scène and procedures of enunciation."[61]

The doubling of the immanent field in *Contempt* is exemplary of Godard's films during this period, revealing each image's "mark of cinema-ness" as Christian Metz puts it.[62] Yet this cannot be accomplished without appropriating in some way the cliché that one is trying to destroy. That is to say, conventional and subversive cinemas are constructed from the same immanent field, and a film text exists in a constant flux that has the potential to transform and to become something new, something different or polyvalent, to whatever degree it is allowed to escape the conventions established in classical paradigms. We can see in this image of Bardot where the denotation seems to imply a conventional use of cinematic objectivity; yet, on the connotative level, the detached and neutral subject of this objective gaze has already been revealed as a fabrication, thus doubling the immanent field as a self-deconstructive site for the interaction of different codes and discourses.

I would argue, then, that we consider Godard's mode of ethnography less as a means for describing what is being looked at than a means for revealing our society's ways of looking at things and, more fundamental to my problem here, the organizing process through which film structures this gaze as a composition of subject-object relations. This experiment in cinematic thinking extends the philosophical weight of cinema's subject-object mutations to a specific sociopolitical problem, offering us a looking glass through which this study can both conclude and open a door to wider and more specific vistas.

CONCLUSION

Where Film and Philosophy May Lead

There are more things in heaven and earth, Horatio, than are dreamt of in your philosophy.

—William Shakespeare, *Hamlet*

THE ANALYSIS OF JEAN-LUC GODARD'S *CONTEMPT* BRINGS MY book full circle and has permitted me to revisit some of the original questions posed in my opening pages, in the light of all that has been discussed in between. With this conclusion I intend to clarify how the methodology developed in this book might be utilized by more specific theoretical approaches and expanded to accommodate other film practices and modes of expression. No film is without an order of meaning, and no film manifests this otherwise than through its systems of reference, but neither is any film made outside of an industrial context or a material praxis completely detached from social values and political influences. The conclusions of this study, though enmeshed in the highly politicized rhetoric of French critical theory and the modernist texts of Jean-Luc Godard and Alain Resnais, are aimed at a much wider understanding of where film and philosophy meet, but how might this be applied? There are more things in cinema than are dreamt of in this book, so where do other films meet with philosophy, or what might their philosophy be?

I have elsewhere argued for the seductive nature of the moving image, seductive in the Baudrillardian sense and applying to all types of cinema.[1]

On the opening page of *Seduction*, Baudrillard defines his titular term as "the artifice of the world," claiming that "all things wish to lose themselves in appearance."[2] Although I have not examined here the industrial implications of such concepts—the dream factory, the star system, etc.— it is worth noting the degree to which all cinema is first and foremost a transparent surface appearance and resonance, a medium of light and sound. In other words all films—from *Marienbad* to *Top Gun* (Tony Scott, 1986) to *WALL-E* (Andrew Stanton, 2008)—are processes of becoming within the immanent field, processes of play that can and sometimes do refuse the monoliths of power and desire and, instead, seduce. As Baudrillard argues in terms that resonate strongly with the central theses of this book: "There is no active or passive mode in seduction, no subject or object, no interior or exterior: seduction plays on both sides, and there is no frontier separating them."[3] The immanent field is a site rich with the potential for seduction, and film connotation teeters on how this seductive capacity is tethered or liberated, resolved or left in question. I have explored this process in terms of a corpus of films from the 1960s that, to varying degrees, resist resolution and liberate the image to a multitude of possible meanings—but how might this theory of the immanent field and subject-object relations be applied to other types of cinema?

Deleuze himself does not rest with only the art-house canon of Resnais, Welles, and Antonioni but devotes quite a lot of time—especially in *Cinema 1: The Movement-Image*—to several mainstream Hollywood directors, including Howard Hawks, Vincente Minnelli, and Alfred Hitchcock. And there have been many noteworthy forays into the study of philosophy and mainstream cinema, including the books of Stanley Cavell, Stephen Mulhall's *On Film*, and a number of "X and Philosophy" titles, where X equals anything from The Coen Brothers to *Seinfeld*.[4] Garrett Stewart's *Framed Time* and Scott Bukatman's *Terminal Identity* do a great job of applying specifically Deleuzean analysis to, respectively, contemporary film and the popular genre of science fiction. The premise of my book, however, maintains that it is necessary not only to apply Deleuze's terms but to systematize them, as I have done in my theory of film connotation and the immanent field, and to consider Deleuzean film-philosophy as only part of a larger philosophical world that includes and even overlaps with other methodologies such as phenomenology. To encourage further inclusion and symbiosis, I hope here to acknowledge how the work proposed in these pages might constructively intersect with other critical methods and types of cinema.

THE VIEWING SUBJECT IN THE SUSPENSE GENRE

Genre theory offers an important alternative methodology for film study, one that is not utilized in my work but that is widely useful given that genre strongly informs a large number of films because of its role in industrial practices and film reception. One genre in particular—the suspense thriller—reflects back on the attraction of cinema as a medium by centralizing voyeurism in both its form and content and, in doing so, has consistently challenged the normative principles of illusion and subjectivity. This can be seen in the films of Fritz Lang (from the German *M* [1931] to his Hollywood remake of Renoir's *La chienne* [1931] *Scarlet Street* [1945]), Claude Chabrol (*Les bonnes femmes* [1960] and *Les biches* [1968] are perfect examples), and Brian De Palma (exemplary titles include *Sisters* [1973] and *Blow Out* [1981]). Nowhere is the role of voyeurism more central to the larger worldview of a director than with the master of suspense himself, Hitchcock, and the politics—both social and individual—of looking is central to his films' stories, as well as to his unfolding of individual images and image sequences. With the speed of their transformations between subjective and objective representation and their all-encompassing moral ambiguity and skepticism for modernity, Hitchcock's films provoke a profound reaction from viewers, threatening our sense of right and wrong and forcing us to wonder on what side of that binary we ourselves fall.

Hitchcock's work has received no lack of critical focus, from the *Cahiers du cinéma* crew's cinephilic obsession[5] to important feminist texts such as Laura Mulvey's aforementioned "Visual Pleasure and Narrative Cinema" and Tania Modleski's *The Women Who Knew Too Much*, to more overtly philosophical or psychoanalytical works such as Slavoj Žižek's *Everything You Wanted to Know About Lacan (But Were Afraid to Ask Hitchcock)*. But what might Hitchcock's films offer us in terms of the intersection between phenomenology and semiotics and the problem of film connotation? In their embrace and inversion of the role of voyeurism, Hitchcock's films provide a contrary experience: we are sutured into the position of the viewing subject through the form but positioned in front of a world that makes us uncomfortable with our desires. This discomfort is particularly strong in what is arguably Hitchcock's most innovative period during the 1950s, when he was making films such as *Rear Window* (1954), *Vertigo* (1958), and *Psycho* (1960), all of which revolve around the nexus between viewing subjectivity, desire of the viewed object, and psychopathic projections or manifestations of this desire.

From the standpoint of Merleau-Ponty's phenomenology I would argue that Hitchcock reveals the absolute viewing subject—conceptualized in classical philosophy and reified through the traditional codes of perspective and classical film editing—to be a mode of mania: a self-induced disconnection of the subject from the objective world brought about through the incapacity to be-in-the-world, to coexist as an object among others and to permit the subjectivity of the other. Moreover, as Deleuze reminds us, the image exists in tangent to other images, and, as such, the subject-object dynamic of the immanent field is constantly in flux, a process of ebb and flow. Thus, the complex precision in what seems to be such a simple connotation, the male gaze, is an alignment of at least three subjects: the character, the apparatus, and the spectator. And, as Modleski has pointed out regarding Hitchcock's films, the positioning of cinematic subjectivity—be it the source of viewing or the focal point of action—is in constant flux.[6] While many of Hitchcock's early films allow for a breakdown of the philosophical logic of classical subjectivity only to restore this order at the end, at least guaranteeing transcendental subjective clarity for the spectator, in his darker films this restoration is not made, and instead of suturing the viewing subject, the form (think of *Vertigo*'s many spirals) ultimately negates the power of the subject—both diegetic and viewing—to apply control or anchor meaning.

SOUND WAVES IN THE IMMANENT FIELD

As becomes more evident in Hitchcock's later films, such as *Psycho*, vision is not the only bearer of subjectivity in cinema (consider the mentally subjective sound accompanying objective images of Marion Crane driving down the highway); instead, the immanent field is made up of both sound and image, sometimes in harmony and sometimes in various stages of contradiction. Following the impact of films such as *Psycho*, the breakdown of sensory monism provided an important tool for the film-school generation that became New Hollywood's spokespersons for the counterculture during the Vietnam War era. Indeed, Deleuze notes that the Vietnam War and the disillusionment and social splintering with which it coincided marked a definitive breaking point in the history of both cinematic and ideological classicism, "a crisis at once of both the action-image and the American dream."[7] This is well demonstrated in the films of De Palma and finds an apotheosis of sound-image conflict in Francis Ford Coppola's *The Conversation* (1974), which manifests the paranoid conspiracy fascination of the post-Watergate era in a total collapse of the delineation between subjective experience and objective world.

Coppola's film articulates a very specific ideological skepticism born from the historical revelations of Watergate, Vietnam, and the political assassinations of the 1960s, positioning the problem of interior and exterior, real and imaginary, within the world of espionage and political intrigue, a sort of Hollywood admission that, for the concerns of a film like Resnais's *The War Is Over* to work in American studio cinema, they have to be removed from the quotidian and set against a generic context of murder, money, and guns. This is similar in the ongoing narrative experiments of Coppola's contemporary Martin Scorsese, whose *Casino* (1995) pushes the director's frequent narrative play to include multiple voice-over narrators and innovative sound-bridges; however, this stylistic innovation is always applied according to very clearly distributed systems of reference and is aligned to guarantee a stable order of meaning that, while engaging with edgy content such as sex, violence, and crime, returns to the reliance on a monistic and absolute notion of subjectivity. De Palma's *Blow Out*, in a similar spirit, offers a mind-boggling array of sound experiments, but even its most deconstructive moments are sutured within the director's patented pastiche of intertextuality and self-reflexivity, setting his filmic play within the narrative context of a Foley artist working in the film industry.

We might also apply this approach, though, to cinemas that have entirely different cultures of everyday sound or different normative practices, such as Bollywood films, for which the role of music and song is very different from that in Hollywood. Bollywood has a strong tradition of direct address and spectacle that does not subscribe to Hollywood's illusionist rules; does this mean that Indian audiovisual culture manifests a different philosophical framework? I would argue not, as mainstream Indian cinema is strongly escapist and tends to formulate similar closed orders of meaning within the immanent field, determining a specific engagement—albeit different from that in Hollywood—by which the spectator might access its meanings and messages. But I must admit that I am not an expert on Indian cinema or Indian philosophical traditions and thus invite others to assist me in this endeavor; similarly, I must acknowledge that Hollywood itself presents a number of exceptional moments and constantly pushes toward the conventionalization of new forms of representation.

The Code of Subjectivity in Millennial Hollywood

Much interest in Deleuze and cinema has involved a recent attempt to utilize Deleuze in the resurrection of Hollywood film analysis, a move in Deleuzean studies that has the joint aim and effect of extending Deleuze's influence beyond art or experimental cinema and also reviving critical validation of mainstream American movies. Two exemplary and oft-cited texts that challenge (albeit superficially, in my opinion) monistic or absolute subjectivity in a supposedly Deleuzean fashion are David Fincher's *Fight Club* (1999) and Christopher Nolan's *Memento* (2000), instant cult classics by two of Hollywood's most critically and commercially successful directors who retain, nonetheless, the cachet of being edgy auteurs. Despite clever misdirection, each of these films provides carefully sewn narrative structures to produce an ambiguous textuality wherein the ambiguity is derived from the psychological impairment—schizophrenia and amnesia, respectively—of the film's protagonist; nonetheless, they are two of the most commonly selected films to analyze in Deleuzean terms because of their ability to throw the status of the image into question.[8]

What separates these films from the texts selected in my study is the double negation of their anomalous representations: unlike the average characters caught in experimental modes of thinking in films such as *Last Year at Marienbad* and *Two or Three Things I Know About Her*, *Fight Club* and *Memento* justify their film experiments as expressions of their diegetic subjects' mental instability: these sick images are the product of sick minds within the text. As such, to whatever extent the films' formal experimentation may offer new ways of unraveling plot information, or visual tricks to confuse the audience, these are inherently stigmatized as the products not of a philosophical alternative but, quite the contrary, a deranged subject. This holds true for Nolan's subsequent action blockbuster *Inception* (2010) and the Wachowski brothers' special-effects-driven *Matrix* trilogy.

Mainstream action films have, however, developed a number of editing tendencies that merit consideration, balancing Deleuze's focus on montage with a newly revived notion of Tom Gunning's cinema of attractions. Gunning's theory of modern subjectivity, derived from the work of Walter Benjamin and Siegfried Kracauer,[9] posits the modern subject as being deprived of attention span; this condition was accommodated by the advent of film, according to Benjamin, in which "perception in the form of shock was established as a formal principle."[10] This is perhaps best manifested in the frantic, MTV-inspired rapid editing of action films by filmmakers such as Michael Mann and reaches a somewhat grotesque apotheosis in the chaotic camera jolts and jump cuts of Paul Greengrass's *The Bourne Ultimatum* (2007). Such editing and camera movement is difficult to place within an aesthetic genealogy connected to that of Resnais's early films, but might the connotation be similar? The identity question at the narrative center of the Bourne trilogy aside, is Greengrass's film depicting the fractured subjectivity of the postmodern world, connoting a splintered experience through miniscule shot durations and hundreds of tons of twisted metal? Could this perhaps be considered not even a question of subjectivity anymore but, in Merleau-Pontian terms, the extension of the objective world into our perceptual apparatus, a sort of hyperrealism?

The Code of Objectivity and the Poetry of Documentary Cinema

While these other genres, world cinemas, and directors demonstrate a range of practices in fiction filmmaking, there are many more horizons of moving-image culture than the feature-length fiction film. The code of objectivity, so central to the establishment of cinematic realism in fiction film, is also the basis for—and guiding connotative principle of—nonfiction or documentary cinema. As I discussed in chapter 5, the truth-codes of nonfiction film have historically been tied to advents in fiction cinema, and the cinematic code of objectivity has had a crucial influence on new information technology and media, from television to the Internet. In the last thirty years, however, there has been a gradual shift in the clear differentiation between fiction and nonfiction codes enacted by the "mockumentary" genre. Originating with films such as Rob Reiner's *This Is Spinal Tap* (1984) and Christopher Guest's *Waiting for Guffman* (1996) and extending across genres, with the digital aesthetic of *The Blair Witch Project* (1999) and *Cloverfield* (2008), this popular trend has gone so far as to become the new standard premise for sitcom television (see NBC's *The Office* and *Parks and Recreation*). The use of documentary codes to heighten the irony of comedy and to deepen the shock of horror merits an extensive study that cannot be provided here, but I think it important to note this development in order to complement a similar breakdown in the clear status of documentary film.

With the rejuvenation of the film essay and the commercial and critical success of Michael Moore's films (*Fahrenheit 9/11*, in particular, which in 2004 became the highest grossing documentary film in U.S. history and won the Cannes Film Festival's top honor, the *Palme d'Or*), the documentary genre has become as highly valid a commercial venture as it has a rhetorical tool for topical ideological warfare. Major documentary film events such as *Fahrenheit 9/11* or Morgan Spurlock's *Supersize Me* (2004) reinvent the documentary film as part information, part rant; however, they are *all* spectacle, and the intersection between fact and spectacle poses a fascinating philosophical nexus. Jacques Rancière points out that documentary cinema is not the opposite of fiction film but is, instead, just another way of distributing the sensible.[11] This basis for dismissing the border between real and imaginary—after all, even fictions are part of our real world, and our ways of arranging them speak deeply about our philosophical and ideological values and practices—is crucial in overturning our hierarchies of meaning, hopefully leading not to a nihilistic theater of the absurd but, instead, to a more dialogic embrace of uncertainty and the possibility of change.

As the lines between documentary and fiction film blur further, we must become more and more aware of the importance of the moving image as a philosophical tool—not only regarding the content of its actors' speech but regarding new organizations of the immanent field. Cultural literacy has made it the norm to use prefabricated images as the raw material for more complex signifying systems, and as our image-based modes of expression become more complicated, we need more than ever a theory of connotation for the moving image. As our use of the image grows more sophisticated, we must not lose sight of how important it is to understand our uses of it on a basic level. I have attempted in these pages to illustrate how the form of film—including the frame of the image, the juxtaposition of image-types, and the combination of sound and visuality—can be understood as the essential source of its significations, a precognitive breeding ground for philosophical methods churning in the dynamic relationships built through formal relationships. I have tried here to build a model of film semiotics from a more metaphysical structure, the basis of which is the phenomenological concept of subject-object relations. In order to illustrate this concept's relevance to film, I have looked at how the deconstruction of cinematic codes reveals film as a dialogic site of interaction between various sets of relations and structures of discourse, how film's capacity to redistribute the sensible allows it to foster great experiments in thinking, radical subversions of classical philosophical principles.

By analyzing the works of Jean-Luc Godard and Alain Resnais, I have looked at how the cinematic organization of subject-object relations provides for a fundamental structuring of film connotation, arguing—through the example of these filmmakers—on behalf of a cinema that, in the tradition of Merleau-Ponty and Deleuze, challenges the classical division between interior and exterior, real and imaginary, subject and object. By using specific examples of film signification to illustrate my theory of subject-object relations, I hope to have made clear how phenomenology and semiotics can find mutual ground in the study of film. The reconciliation of these two critical positions holds much promise for the future of film theory, and this book is offered as a step in that direction.

NOTES

Introduction: Where Film Meets Philosophy

1. Cavell's *The World Viewed* is a seminal text of film philosophy, problematiz-
    ing the conceptual relationship between ontology and the moving image, and
    Pursuits of Happiness extended his inquiry into American genre cinema.
    Jameson's work has almost always involved philosophical analyses of socio-
    political structures, but with *The Geopolitical Aesthetic* and *Signatures of the
    Visible* he published books devoted completely to film. For an introduction to
    the cognitivist approach to film analysis see, in particular, David Bordwell,
    Making Meaning; Nöel Carroll, *Mystifying Movies*; and Bordwell's and Car-
    roll's coedited *Post-Theory*. On filmosophy see Daniel Frampton's *Filmosophy*;
    a critique of neologism in contemporary postfeminist writing can be found
    later in this chapter.
2. Deleuze's writing, long concerned with art and literature, produced perhaps
    the quintessential film-philosophy work with the extensive two-part project,
    Cinéma 1: L'image-mouvement (1983) and *Cinéma 2: L'image-temps* (1985). While
    Hugh Tomlinson's and Barbara Habberjam's English translation, *Cinema 1:
    The Movement-Image* (1986), and Tomlinson and Robert Galeta's *Cinema 2: The
    Time-Image* (1989) are very strong English versions, I have chosen in this book
    to work directly from the original French texts. Unless otherwise noted, I will
    rely on my own translations.

3. See Carroll, *The Philosophy of Motion Pictures*; and Gaut, *A Philosophy of Cinematic Art*.

4. See Mullarkey, *Refractions of Reality*.

5. Del Rio, "Alchemies of Thought in Godard's Cinema," 62.

6. Rodowick, *Gilles Deleuze's Time Machine*, 215n10.

7. Deleuze, *Cinéma 1: L'image-mouvement*, 86–87. See Tomlinson's and Habberjam's translation in *Cinema 1: The Movement-Image*, 58–59.

8. Bogue, *Deleuze on Cinema*, 34.

9. Mitchell, *What Do Pictures Want?* 28.

10. Deleuze, *Cinéma 1: L'image-mouvement*, 93.

11. In Merleau-Ponty's words cinema "shows how something sets itself to signify . . . by the arrangement of temporal and spatial elements" ("Le cinéma et la nouvelle psychologie," in *Sens et non-sens*, 61–74, 73).

12. See, most notably, David Bordwell's *Narration in the Fiction Film*.

13. Rancière, *Aesthetics and Its Discontents*, 25.

14. Panofsky, *Perspective as Symbolic Form*, 7.

15. Burch, *Theory of Film Practice*, 144.

16. Metz, *Essais sur la signification au cinéma*, 1:198.

17. At this time Resnais took a five-year hiatus from feature filmmaking, while Godard embarked on a period of highly politicized filmmaking defined by an ongoing collaboration with Maoist activist Jean-Pierre Gorin.

18. Neupert situates this shift within a larger breakdown of the hierarchies between high and low culture that prefigured the French New Wave cinema. See Neupert, *A History of the French New Wave Cinema*, 19–22.

19. Rodowick, *Reading the Figural*, 170–71.

20. See, among others, Michel Marie's *The French New Wave*; and Richard Neupert's *A History of the French New Wave*.

21. Sellier, *Masculine Singular*, 49.

22. "Resnais c'est un romancier, moi, je suis un journaliste" (Pilard, "Entretien avec Jean-Luc Godard," 56).

23. By "dialogic" I am intentionally evoking the theory of M. M. Bakhtin, whose *Problems of Dostoevsky's Poetics* constitutes a study of Dostoevsky's novel as being a circularity or interaction between authorial and diegetic voices as well as the anticipated voice of the reader, a theory of the circulation of voices and agencies that Bakhtin extends in *The Dialogic Imagination*. As will become apparent, this book sets out to perform in many ways the same analysis on Godard and Resnais that Bakhtin does on the works of Dostoevsky.

24. Heath, *Questions of Cinema*, 242.

25. Merleau-Ponty cites, for example, the effects of mescaline as an exemplary breakdown of the hierarchy of the senses, allowing us the synthesized perceptual experience of hearing color (*Phénoménologie de la perception*, 263).

26. Originally titled *Folie et déraison and Naissance de la clinique*, these studies of the genealogy of differentiating between the "sane" and "insane," and the subsequent construction of institutions to marginalize the latter from society, were integral to the late 1960s upheaval against social hierarchies and inequalities.

27. See, for example, the influence of DeMille's and Griffith's films in France from 1915 to 1921 as documented in numerous industry studies, such as Richard Abel's *The Ciné Goes to Town* and *The Red Rooster Scare*.

28. For specifically Hollywood practices see Belton's *American Cinema, American Culture*; in *Film Art* Bordwell and Thompson expand these practices to the mainstream aesthetics of a wider, but primarily Western studio, context.

29. Barthes, "Towards a Semiotics of Cinema," 277.

30. Ibid., 281.

31. Barthes, *Mythologies* (originally 1957), repr. in *Œuvres complètes*, 1:826.

32. Eco, "Articulations of the Cinematic Code," 595.

33. Lesage, "*S/Z* and *Rules of the Game*," 50.

34. This argument, spelled out point by point in "The Neglected Tradition of Phenomenology in Film Theory," is summed up by Andrew in *Concepts in Film Theory*: "Whereas phenomenology strives to unveil the reason in human activity by attending in a special way to its surface manifestations," Andrew writes, "its arch-rival, structuralism, translates the surface features of a phenomenon into abstract terms which are then shown to bear a hidden logical relation" (133). However, is phenomenology not interested in the internal logical relation of perception and thought, and do not surface features make up the very elements of structure analyzed in structuralist discourse?

35. Carroll, *Theorizing the Moving Image*, 7.

36. Cohen-Séat, *Essai sur les principes d'une philosophie du cinéma*, 54.

37. See Shaw, *Film Consciousness*.

38. Merleau-Ponty, *Signes*, 154 (translated in Descombes, *Modern French Philosophy*, 104).

39. See Descombes, *Modern French Philosophy*, 101.

40. Lawlor, *Thinking Through French Philosophy*, 3.

41. Merleau-Ponty, *Sens et non-sens*, 74.

42. Merleau-Ponty, *Phénoménologie de la perception*, xv.

43. Descombes, *Modern French Philosophy*, 56.

44. Merleau-Ponty, *Signes*, 155 (translated in Descombes, *Modern French Philosophy*, 73).

45. Descombes, *Modern French Philosophy*, 71.

46. Merleau-Ponty, *Phénoménologie de la perception*, 85.

47. Merleau-Ponty, *Sens et non-sens*, 74.

48. Andrew, "The Neglected Tradition of Phenomenology in Film Theory," 627–28.

49. See Bazin, *Qu'est-ce que le cinéma?* 13.
50. Ayfre, "Neo-Realism and Phenomenology," 185.
51. Metz, *Le signifiant imaginaire*, 74.
52. Sobchack, *The Address of the Eye*, 131–33.
53. Münsterberg, *Hugo Münsterberg on Film*, 129.
54. Arnheim, *Film as Art*, 2–3.
55. See Heath, *Questions of Cinema*, 17.
56. Andrew, *Concepts in Film Theory*, 149.
57. The construction or signification of this "transcendental subject" is, in fact, the overriding object of critique in Baudry's "Ideological Effects of the Basic Cinematographic Apparatus."
58. See Nowell-Smith, "A Note on Story/Discourse."
59. Altman, "Psychoanalysis and Cinema."
60. Carroll, *Theorizing the Moving Image*, 257–60.
61. See Deleuze and Guattari, *Anti-Oedipus*.
62. Rodowick, *Reading the Figural*, 173.
63. For Schefer see *L'homme ordinaire du cinéma* and *Du monde et du mouvement des images*; for Rancière see *La fable cinématographique* and *The Future of the Image*.
64. Deleuze, *Negotiations*, 60.
65. Rodowick, "Dr. Strange Media," 1404.
66. Martin-Jones, *Deleuze and World Cinemas*, 8–14.
67. Kennedy, *Deleuze and Cinema*, 3.
68. Ibid., 15, 21.
69. Ibid., 24.
70. Beugnet, *Cinema of Sensation*, 2.
71. Wilson, *Alain Resnais*, 59.
72. Deleuze, *Negotiations*, 47.
73. Rodowick, *Reading the Figural*, 173.
74. Kael once wrote that "Alain Resnais's films come out of an intolerable mixture of technique and culture" (quoted in Monaco, *Alain Resnais*, 5); see Bordwell, *Narration in the Fiction Film*, 312.
75. Bordwell, *Narration in the Fiction Film*, 283.
76. Andrew, *Concepts in Film Theory*, 47.

1. PHENOMENOLOGY AND THE VIEWING SUBJECT

1. Andrew, *Concepts in Film Theory*, 19.
2. Sobchack, *The Address of the Eye*, 9.
3. Metz, *Le signifiant imaginaire*, 69.
4. Arnheim, *Film as Art*, 15.

5. Andrew, *Concepts in Film Theory*, 58.
6. Bellour, *L'analyse du film*, 48.
7. Mitry, *La sémiologie en question*, 103.
8. Merleau-Ponty, *Phénoménologie de la perception*, 345.
9. Ibid., 309.
10. Ibid., 321–25.
11. MacCabe and Mulvey, *Godard*, 45.
12. Bogue, *Deleuze on Cinema*, 43.
13. Münsterberg, *Hugo Münsterberg on Film*, 86–88.
14. Heath, *Questions of Cinema*, 33–37.
15. Mitry, *Esthétique et psychologie du cinéma*, 117.
16. Bogue summarizes Deleuze's assessment of this in *Deleuze on Cinema*, 43.
17. Merleau-Ponty, *Phénoménologie de la perception*, 321.
18. Arnheim, *Film as Art*, 39.
19. MacCabe and Mulvey, *Godard*, 40.
20. Metz, *Le signifiant imaginaire*, 69.
21. Barthes, *Critique et vérité*, in *Œuvres complètes*, 2:762.
22. Baudry, "Ideological Effects of the Basic Cinematic Apparatus," 345.
23. Bellour, *L'analyse du film*, 45.
24. Bazin, *Qu'est-ce que le cinéma?* 55.
25. Eisenstein, *The Film Sense*, 26.
26. Eisenstein, *Film Form*, 38.
27. Lanigan, *Speaking and Semiology*, 30.
28. Jay, *Downcast Eyes*, 263.
29. Ibid., 168.
30. Merleau-Ponty, *Le visible et l'invisible*, 33.
31. Henderson, "Two Types of Film Theory," 34.
32. Eisenstein, *Film Form*, 38. In many essays that make up the beginning of his book (such as "Through Theater to the Cinema," "The Unexpected," and "The Cinematic Principle of the Ideogram"), Eisenstein justifies the centrality of montage through a comparison of film with other arts, based on the notion of conflict. For example, he claims "conflict" to be the essence of all arts, noting the similarities between film and music (however, that three notes, played together in a chord, use the same aesthetic principle as three images set side-by-side, is a comparison that negates the obvious difference between the paradigmatic nature of the chord and the syntagmatic structure of montage) and the poetic form of the haiku (a comparison that ignores the fact that a haiku is a metalanguage that works on a primary linguistic process for which there is no equivalent in cinema).
33. Bazin, *Qu'est-ce que le cinéma?* 9.
34. Henderson, "Two Types of Film Theory," 36, 39.

35. Eisenstein, *Film Form*, 16.

36. It is important to keep in mind here, as Mitry emphasizes, that Eisenstein's notion of montage is a transformative "product," similar to that of Vertov's, as opposed to Pudovkin's additive understanding of montage as a "sum" (see Mitry, *Esthétique et psychologie du cinéma*, 194).

37. Eisenstein, *Nonindifferent Nature*, 35.

38. Eisenstein, *The Film Sense*, 24–25.

39. Bazin, "Ontologie de l'image photographique," in *Qu'est-ce que le cinéma?* 9–17, 9.

40. Ibid., 11.

41. Wollen, *Signs and Meaning in the Cinema*, 87.

42. Bazin, *Qu'est-ce que le cinéma?* 17.

43. This argument is best laid out in "Montage interdit" (*Qu'est-ce que le cinéma?* 48–61) and "L'évolution du langage cinématographique" (*Qu'est-ce que le cinéma?* 63–80), but it can also be found in his reviews of individual films and filmmakers, such as Renoir and Welles.

44. Bazin, *Qu'est-ce que le cinéma?* 54.

45. This differentiation between the shot and montage provides the framework for "L'évolution du langage cinématographique."

46. Bazin, *Qu'est-ce que le cinéma?* 72–76.

47. Andrew, *The Major Film Theories*, 143.

48. Bazin, "Défense de Rossellini," in *Qu'est-ce que le cinéma?* 347–57.

49. Bazin, *Qu'est-ce que le cinéma?* 70.

50. Descombes, *Modern French Philosophy*, 71.

51. Henderson, "Two Types of Film Theory," 390.

52. Mitry, *Esthétique et psychologie du cinéma*, 486.

53. Ropars-Wuilleumier, "Form and Substance, or the Avatars of the Narrative" (cited in Bordwell, *Narration in the Fiction Film*, 321).

54. Beh, "*Vivre sa vie*," 180.

55. Godard, "On doit tout mettre dans un film," 296.

56. Dixon, *The Films of Jean-Luc Godard*, 30.

57. Godard, "Entretien" 227–28.

58. Beh, "*Vivre sa vie*," 185.

59. Ibid., 181.

60. Esquenazi, *Godard et la société française des années 1960*, 131.

61. Silverman and Farocki, *Speaking About Godard*, 7.

62. Morin, *Le cinéma ou l'homme imaginaire*, 126–27. This method of perception as a set of different perspectives seems intimately linked, though without acknowledgment, to a passage in which Merleau-Ponty discusses the object as being an object of viewing not from nowhere but from anywhere, from "toutes les perspectives possibles" (see *Phénoménologie de la perception*, 83–85).

63. Silverman and Farocki, *Speaking About Godard*, 2.

64. Beh, "*Vivre sa vie*," 182.

65. Perkins, "*Vivre sa vie*," 33.

66. Bordwell, *Narration in the Fiction Film*, 282.

67. It should be noted that Godard refers to Dreyer many times in his writing, and one finds a clear influence from Dreyer's representation of women in the oeuvre of Godard.

68. Beh, "*Vivre sa vie*," 181.

69. Silverman, for example, argues that prostitution is the end of all personal desire, "and so the demise of subjectivity as such" (*Speaking About Godard*, 21).

70. Rancière, *La fable cinématographique*, 9.

71. Sontag, "Godard's *Vivre sa vie*," in *Against Interpretation*, 204.

72. Beh, "*Vivre sa vie*," 184.

73. Godard: "Je me suis dit à la fin que, puisqu'après tout mes ambitions avouées étaient de faire un film de gangsters normal, je n'avais pas à contredire systématiquement le genre: le type devait mourir" ("Entretien," 218).

74. Althusser, *For Marx* (cited in Rodowick, *The Crisis of Political Modernism*, 74).

75. MacCabe and Mulvey, *Godard*, 40.

76. Ibid., 79–104, 93.

77. *Mythologies* (1957) and *Les Choses* (1965) are good examples of their authors' contribution to the general critique, at this time, of the homogenization of the role of material and popular cultural objects in the conventions of daily life.

78. MacCabe and Mulvey, *Godard*, 52.

79. Merleau-Ponty, *Le visible et l'invisible*, 29.

80. Merleau-Ponty, *Les aventures de la dialectique*, 72 (in Descombes, *Modern French Philosophy*, 269).

81. Godard, "Ma démarche en quatre mouvements," 296.

82. Ibid., 297.

83. For a summary of this opposition see Jay, *Downcast Eyes*, 308.

84. Mitry, *Esthétique et psychologie du cinéma*, 79.

85. Trias, "L'œil du cinéma," 92–93.

86. For Deleuze see *Cinéma 1: L'image-mouvement*, 86. For Rancière see *La fable cinématographique*, 148.

87. Godard, "Ma démarche en quatre mouvements," 297.

88. MacDougall, "Prospects of Ethnographic Film," 138.

89. Cited by Godard in "Ma démarche en quatre mouvements," 270.

90. MacCabe and Mulvey, *Godard*, 93.

91. Léger, "A Critical Essay on the Plastic Quality of Abel Gance's *The Wheel*," 20. Léger's analysis revolves around Abel Gance's *La Roue* (1923), which uses close-up images of a wheel to shatter traditional divisions between material object and the agency of motion. For Léger this shift in subject-object relations

was central to the aesthetic philosophy of modern arts in general, and Gance's use of the close-up, in fact, set cinema finally among the modern arts.

92. Münsterberg, *Hugo Münsterberg on Film*, 86.

93. Burch, "De *Mabuse* à *M*: Le travail de Fritz Lang," 229 (cited in Heath, *Questions of Cinema*, 40).

94. Rancière, *La fable cinématographique*, 189–90.

95. Rodowick, *Gilles Deleuze's Time Machine*, 22.

96. Ayfre, "Neo-Realism and Phenomenology," 187.

2. FILM CONNOTATION AND THE SIGNIFIED SUBJECT

1. Lesage, "*S/Z* and *Rules of the Game*," 45.

2. Barthes, *S/Z*, 7.

3. Mayne, "*S/Z* and Film Criticism," 43.

4. Heath, *Questions of Cinema*, 8.

5. In *The Crisis of Political Modernism*, D. N. Rodowick offers a useful analysis of the role of subjectivity in structural and poststructural French thought.

6. This analysis owes a great debt to Kaja Silverman's *The Subject of Semiotics*, from which I must distance myself through my hesitance to integrate a theory of psychoanalysis into my study of film subjectivity.

7. Benveniste's original division concerns pronouns, of which there is no equivalent in cinema except as a signification of the mode of representation itself. For Benveniste see "Les relations de temps dans le verbe français." A reference to Benveniste's notion of *discours* can be found in Metz's attempt to find a more suitable linguistic metaphor for cinema (see, e.g., his *Essais sur la signification au cinéma*, 1:92).

8. This *filmolinguistic project* is the subject of Metz's most celebrated—and contested—essay, "Cinéma: Langue ou langage?" (in *Essais sur la signification au cinéma*, 1:39–94).

9. Deleuze uses this term (*Cinéma 2: L'image-temps*, 44) to differentiate his model, in the Peircean tradition, as a system of images and signs independent of language. Since he uses this term on numerous occasions, I have decided here to preserve it. I will similarly guard Deleuze's quintessential terms, *image-mouvement* and *image-temps*.

10. Metz is, of course, not alone in this general intellectual and theoretical evolution. While most leading semioticians and critics working in semiotics were more primarily concerned with literature (Barthes, Kristeva, et al.), the general problems offered in semiotics, and the general methodological approach referred to as structuralism, grew from the phenomenological movement of the 1940s and 1950s. Building on a model of structural linguistics, this ap-

proach completely inundated film theory (and most other "theories") for the better part of the 1960s, until it was complemented and then surpassed by psychoanalytic and ideology-based approaches. We can view this trajectory in the work of Metz himself, whose *Essais sur la signification au cinéma* (1968–72) and *Langage et cinéma* (1971) differ greatly in scope and method from *Le signifiant imaginaire* (1977).

11. Metz, *Essais sur la signification au cinéma*, 1:25–26.
12. Metz, *Le signifiant imaginaire*, 64.
13. Metz, *Essais sur la signification au cinéma*, 1:209.
14. Ibid., 14–20.
15. See ibid., 53.
16. Aside from Deleuze's criticism of Metz, which I will look at later in this chapter, other useful analyses include Sandro, "Signification in the Cinema"; Wollen, "Cinema and Semiology"; and Harman, "Semiotics and the Cinema."
17. Andrew, *The Major Film Theories*, 223.
18. Metz, *Essais sur la signification au cinéma*, 1:67 (a footnote added in a much later edition).
19. See Bordwell, *Narration in the Fiction Film*, 30–40.
20. Metz, *Essais sur la signification au cinéma*, 1:34.
21. Ibid., 96.
22. Ibid., 96–97.
23. Ibid., 53. This claim aligns Metz with a long line of theorists, including Eisenstein, Bazin, and Mitry, who view montage as the defining aspect of cinematic signification; one could view this point as a way of illustrating why Eisenstein embraced montage whereas Bazin, who wanted to preserve the immanent meaning of the visual content, rejected it.
24. Metz develops la Grande Syntagmatique in "Problèmes de dénotation dans le film de fiction" (*Essais sur la signification au cinéma*, 1:111–50) and puts it into practice in his detailed syntagmatic analysis of Jacques Rozier's 1962 *Adieu Philippine* (*Essais sur la signification au cinéma*, 1:151–76).
25. Andrew, *Concepts of Film Theory*, 68.
26. Jay, *Downcast Eyes*, 468.
27. Ibid., 460.
28. Metz, *Essais sur la signification au cinéma*, 2:153–54.
29. See, most notably, Baudrillard, *Simulacres et simulation*.
30. Metz, *Langage et cinéma*, 202.
31. Metz, *Essais sur la signification au cinéma*, 1:84.
32. Nichols, "Style, Grammar, and the Movies," 36.
33. Lesage, "*S/Z* and *Rules of the Game*," 46.
34. Mayne, "*S/Z* and Film Criticism," 45.

35. For those unfamiliar with suture theory, the term *suture* is used to give the impression of a surgical operation in which the text is cut open, the spectator is placed within it as transcendental subject, and then it is closed shut so as to remove any signs of this very operation.

36. Heath, *Questions of Cinema*, 6.

37. The intellectual history of "suture" began under the guise of Jacques-Alain Miller's original article on Lacanian linguistics, "La suture: Eléments de la logique du signifiant." Jean-Pierre Oudart then adapted certain of Miller's ideas to the photographic image and film montage in his own "La suture." Miller's and Oudart's articles were translated by the psychoanalysis-heavy English film journal *Screen* 18, no. 4 (1977/78): 24–34, 35–47.

38. Dayan, "The Tutor-Code of Classical Cinema," 28.

39. As Kaja Silverman points out, signification and subjectivity *are always* interdependent (Silverman, *The Subject of Semiotics*, 194).

40. For these two primary arguments see, most convincingly, William Rothman's "Against 'The System of Suture.'"

41. See Sobchack, *The Address of the Eye*, 131–36.

42. Jay, *Downcast Eyes*, 474.

43. Heath, *Questions of Cinema*, 90.

44. Ibid., 109.

45. Altman, "Psychoanalysis and Cinema," 258.

46. Heath, *Questions of Cinema*, 93.

47. Nowell-Smith, "A Note on Story/Discourse," 552.

48. Pasolini, "The Cinema of Poetry," 544.

49. For Mitry cinematic symbolism is not in and of itself conventional, but it draws from the range of the symbolic in everyday life (*Esthétique et psychologie du cinéma*, 71). However, cinema's methods of forming symbolic relations are dependent, nonetheless, on particular uses of the formal specificities of film.

50. Pasolini, "The Cinema of Poetry," 548.

51. Bogue, *Deleuze on Cinema*, 72.

52. Deleuze, *Cinéma 1: L'image-mouvement*, 106.

53. Abramson, "Structure and Meaning in the Cinema," 561.

54. Introductory remarks for Eco, "Articulations of the Cinematic Code," 590.

55. Penley, "*Film Language*, by Christian Metz," 18.

56. Eco, "Articulations of the Cinematic Code," 600.

57. Nichols, "Style, Grammar, and the Movies," 36.

58. Eco, "Articulations of the Cinematic Code," 601.

59. Among the most efficient and lucid summaries of Deleuze's cinema work see Rodowick's *Reading the Figural* (172–76). In my opinion Bogue's *Deleuze on Cinema* and Paola Marrati's *Gilles Deleuze: Cinéma et philosophie* are the defini-

tive full-length studies of Deleuze's cinema writing, indispensible to any work on this subject.

60. Rodowick, *Reading the Figural*, 172.

61. Marrati, *Gilles Deleuze*, 55–56.

62. Ibid., 9.

63. The best example of how Deleuze's taxonomy of image-types is constructed in relation to the differentiation between subjective and objective poles of representation is in his analysis of Samuel Beckett's *Film* (*Cinéma 1: L'image-mouvement*, 97–101), though this distinction also resurfaces explicitly in his analyses of Fellini and Antonioni.

64. Trifonova, *The Image in French Philosophy*, 11. This description is marked by Trifonova as being central to the de-aestheticized imagistic philosophy that evolved across the twentieth century from Bergson to Deleuze.

65. Ibid., 226.

66. Deleuze, *Cinéma 1: L'image-mouvement*, 93.

67. In pages 9–12 of *Gilles Deleuze: Cinéma et philosophie*, Marrati provides perhaps a more clear and precise summary of this central book than does Deleuze himself.

68. Should the reader wish for an explanation of this "excessively complicated attempt to reconcile Bergsonian image-ontology with Peircean imagistic semiology," I offer the following. Peirce begins with the visual image, the phenomenon of what appears, dividing this signifying act into three groups according to the sign's mode of reference and relation to the world: firstness (the icon, in which something refers only to itself); secondness (or the indexical sign, in which something only refers to itself through something else); and, thirdness (the symbol, in which something only refers to itself through its relation to something else) (*Cinéma 2: L'image-temps*, 45–47). Using these divisions, Deleuze constructs his sémiotique according to Bergson's three levels of subjectivity, when it is related to a certain image, a "centre d'indétermination," or subject (ibid., 94). Firstness is a sort of classical, absolute subjectivity, adapted by Deleuze as the preliminary act of subjectivity, subtractive perception, in which a subject only perceives that which is important. Secondness is a form of objectivity in which the subject is defined through something around it, henceforth viewed as the incurvation or transformation of the external world, the measurement of things' ability to affect the subject and the subject's ability to affect things around it. And thirdness is intersubjectivity, in which something is defined only through its relational accord with something else, in which each exists as both subject and object, the transformation of the subject-object relation into a greater transcendental subjectivity.

69. This is best summarized by Deleuze's incorporation of the various types of the image-movement into the two forms of the image-action (*Cinéma 1: L'image-mouvement*, 196–231).

70. Flaxman, introduction to *The Brain Is the Screen*, 23.

71. Bogue, *Deleuze on Cinema*, 66.

72. See Deleuze's extended passage on Metz (*Cinéma 2: L'image-temps*, 38–41).

73. Deleuze, *Cinéma 1: L'image-mouvement*, 71.

74. Deleuze, *Cinéma 2: L'image-temps*, 40.

75. Ibid.

76. Bogue, *Deleuze on Cinema*, 66.

77. Deleuze, *Cinema 2: L'image-temps*, 45.

78. Ibid.

79. Martin-Jones, *Deleuze and World Cinemas*, 25.

80. Ibid., 43–65.

81. Bogue, *Deleuze on Cinema*, 49.

82. Deleuze, *Cinéma 2: L'image-temps*, 45.

83. Rodowick, *Reading the Figural*, 172.

84. "The only subjectivity is time, non-chronological time seized at its foundation, and we are interior to it and not the other way around" (Deleuze, *Cinéma 2: L'image-temps*, 110).

85. Merleau-Ponty, *Phénoménologie de la perception*, 469.

3. Sound, Image, and the Order of Meaning

1. Deleuze, *Cinéma 2: L'image-temps*, 105–10.

2. Jakobson, *Language in Literature*, 469.

3. Schwab, "Escaping from the Image," 109.

4. See Deleuze, *Cinéma 2: L'image-temps*, 292–341.

5. See, in particular, Pisters's chapter "(De)Territorializing Forces of the Sound Machine," in her *The Matrix of Visual Culture*; for Redner see *Deleuze and Film Music*.

6. Marcorelles, "Jean-Luc Godard's Half-Truths," 5.

7. Heath, *Questions of Cinema*, 177. For Hegel see *Aesthetics: Lectures on Fine Art*, vol. 1.

8. Chion, *The Voice in Cinema*, 125; Bordwell and Thompson, *Film Art*, 193.

9. In "Style and Medium in the Motion Pictures" (reprinted in *Three Essays on Style*), Panofsky decries speech as a technological advance that will anchor film in the reproduction of the real. Similarly, in *Film as Art* Arnheim devotes an entire chapter to this, viewing the inevitably realist use of speech as a tragic blow to the essential characteristics that make film an art (motion, duration, changes in perspective and size). These writers, it must be noted, were

writing just at the advent of speech in cinema; as we will find, speech and spoken language do not necessarily condemn film signification to a harmonious sensory connotation of realism.

10. Eisler, *Composing for the Films* (cited in Heath, *Questions of Cinema*, 201).

11. Chion, *The Voice in Cinema*, 49–50. This argument is particularly inconsistent as its support is derived from the fact that hearing is the first developed sense; thus, the fetal baby becomes familiar with the speech of its mother's voice before her appearance. However, the resonance and tone of a voice is in no way interchangeable with language speech.

12. Barthes, *Le système de la mode*, 23 (translated and cited in Willemen, "Cinematic Discourse," 161).

13. Willemen, "Cinematic Discourse," 161.

14. MacCabe and Mulvey, *Godard*, 18.

15. Scheinfeigel, "Quand le son détourne l'image," 82.

16. Jay, *Downcast Eyes*, 470.

17. For an analysis of this hierarchy see Doane, "Ideology and the Practice of Sound Editing and Mixing."

18. Chion, *The Voice in Cinema*, 3.

19. Ibid., 19.

20. Mitry, *Esthétique et psychologie du cinéma*, 194.

21. Many feminist theorists have considered the subversive or decodifying use of speech to be the most potent weapon in the cultural struggle against the myths supported by dominant practices, no doubt explaining why a startling majority of the analyses of speech and subjectivity are attributable to proponents of feminist criticism, perhaps the most systematic being performed in Mary Ann Doane in "The Voice in the Cinema: The Articulation of Body and Space"; and Christine Gledhill in "Recent Developments in Feminist Criticism." There are numerous reasons for this, including foremost the centrality of speech to the Lacanian framework adopted by many feminist theorists; on a fundamental level, though, speech is a marginalized sense in film practice and theory, an alternative space of signification as opposed to the phallocentric thrust of the voyeuristically gazing visual image. Through this argument such theorists transpose a sociocultural struggle onto an attempt to reverse— or even simply to appropriate and to deform—the hierarchy provided between sound and image.

22. Deleuze, *Cinéma 2: L'image-temps*, 339.

23. Chion, *The Voice in Cinema*, 23.

24. Ibid., 50–51. Chion's explicit analysis of the formal basis for a particular type of subject-function includes the absence of reverb, for example, to supply a dry voice; according to Chion, reverb situates speech in a particular space, thus alienating the spectator from the subjective position possibly created by the

voice. The lack of reverb means a lack of particular space to which the voice is attached, and thus the I-voice "can resonate in us as our own."

25. Doane, "The Voice in the Cinema," 36.

26. This is the central argument of his analysis in "Le rouge de *La chinoise*: Politique de Godard," in *La fable cinématographique*, 189.

27. Scheinfeigel, "Quand le son détourne l'image," 83–84.

28. Mitry, *Esthétique et psychologie du cinéma*, 291.

29. Mitry, *La sémiologie en question*, 176.

30. Münsterberg, *Hugo Münsterberg on Film*, 90–91.

31. Carroll, *Theorizing the Moving Image*, 302.

32. Ropars-Wuilleumier, "How History Begets Meaning," 173.

33. This notion of écriture is particularly prominent in Alain Fleischer's *L'art d'Alain Resnais*, and while it does evoke certain relevant problems of enunciation and discourse, it seems to diminish Resnais's specifically cinematic mode of expression.

34. Mitry, *La sémiologie en question*, 176.

35. Armes, *The Cinema of Alain Resnais*, 86.

36. It should be noted here, though it is not of direct relevance, that the entire film was conceived by scriptwriter Marguerite Duras as a representation of the impossibility of discussing or expressing the immensity of what happened in Japan in August 1945.

37. "Table ronde sur *Hiroshima, mon amour*," 40.

38. Mitry, *Esthétique et psychologie du cinéma*, 333.

39. Ibid., 334–35.

40. Luchting, "*Hiroshima, mon amour*, Time, and Proust," 310.

41. Ropars-Wuilleumier, "How History Begets Meaning," 179.

42. Wilson, *Alain Resnais*, 52–53.

43. The best example of the overwhelming romanticism with which critics have treated this film is the "Table ronde sur *Hiroshima, mon amour*," empaneled by the group at *Cahiers du cinéma* upon the film's release.

44. Armes, *The Cinema of Alain Resnais*, 74.

45. See the analyses of Luchting ("*Hiroshima, mon amour*, Time, and Proust") and of Haim Callev (*The Stream of Consciousness in the Films of Alain Resnais*), who prefer to see the film as being specifically about "seeing."

46. Leutrat, *Hiroshima, mon amour* (cited in Wilson, *Alain Resnais*, 48).

47. Metz, *Le signifiant imaginaire*, 105.

48. Burch, "Qu'est-ce que la Nouvelle Vague?" 24–25.

49. Charles F. Altman points out that, whereas Barthes's model of the Oedipal myth as the generator of narrative structures was dominant in psychoanalytic theory in the 1960s, it was replaced by Lacan's *stade du miroir* as the preferred

theoretical analogy, as is most evident in *Communications*, no. 23 (1975), which was dedicated to psychoanalysis and cinema (see Altman, "Psychoanalysis and Cinema," 518–19).

50. Deleuze, *Cinéma 2: L'image-temps*, 135.

51. Bogue, *Deleuze on Cinema*, 143.

52. Ibid., 145.

53. Robbe-Grillet, *L'année dernière à Marienbad*, 12. Even this degree of coherence, however, is shattered by the end of the film, when the female character begins to assert her own audiovisual agency in the discourse.

54. Alter, "Alain Robbe-Grillet and the 'Cinematographic Style,'" 365.

55. Wilson, *Alain Resnais.*, 71.

56. See Oxenhandler, "*Marienbad* Revisited."

57. Prédal enumerates at least sixteen possible scenarios explaining the text, though he does not pursue a single one (see *Alain Resnais: Études cinématographiques*, 86–87).

58. See André S. Labarthe and Jacques Rivette, "Entretien avec Resnais and Robbe-Grillet," 4–5.

59. See Brunius, "Every Year at Marienbad; or, The Discipline of Uncertainty"; and Callev, *The Stream of Consciousness in the Films of Alain Resnais*, 224.

60. Bordwell, *Narration in the Fiction Film*, 312.

61. Wilson, *Alain Resnais*, 69.

62. Leutrat, *Last Year at Marienbad*. Leutrat goes on to draw connections between this film, which bears witness "to the particular techniques of repetition which cinema employs," to the notions expounded in Deleuze's *Différence et répétition*.

63. Wilson, *Alain Resnais*, 70.

64. Metz, *Essais sur la signification au cinéma*, 1:62.

65. See Prédal, *Alain Resnais*, 48. This argument has also been vocalized by both Leutrat and Liandrat-Guigues in personal conversation, as well as in various seminars and lectures; see Leutrat's *Last Year at Marienbad*; and Leutrat and Liandrat-Guigues, *Alain Resnais: Liaisons secrètes, accords vagabonds*.

66. Deleuze, *Cinéma 2: L'image-temps*, 153.

67. Ibid., 154.

68. See Descombes, *Modern French Philosophy*, 157.

69. Deleuze, *Cinéma 2: L'image-temps*, 348.

70. Cited in Monaco, *Alain Resnais*, 130.

71. Deleuze, *Cinéma 2: L'image-temps*, 163.

72. Wilson, *Alain Resnais*, 72.

73. Ibid., 75.

4. ALAIN RESNAIS AND THE CODE OF SUBJECTIVITY

1. Schwab, "Escaping from the Image," 131.
2. Ibid.
3. Heath, *Questions of Cinema*, 127.
4. See Bellour, *L'analyse du film*, 46; and Wilson, *Alain Resnais*, 9.
5. Wilson, *Alain Resnais*, 2.
6. Neill, "Empathy and (Film) Fiction."
7. The details of this literary style are most systematically formulated in Alain Robbe-Grillet's *Pour un nouveau roman*.
8. Prédal, *Alain Resnais*, 168.
9. Bron, "Un cinéma au service de l'énergie narrative du spectateur," 73.
10. Quoted in Armes, *The Cinema of Alain Resnais*, 27.
11. Bordwell, "The Art Cinema as a Mode of Film Practice," 717.
12. Concerning the identification with filmic characters, I am particularly fond of the system developed by Murray Smith in his *Engaging Characters*. Smith assesses the various modes through which film expression creates a link between spectator and character; in this chapter I will be looking at what happens in a different type of fiction, one in which identification is turned inside out and the subject to be identified with is revealed as part of an intersubjective existence.
13. Silverman, *The Subject of Semiotics*, 23–24.
14. Mitry, *Esthétique et psychologie du cinéma*, 300.
15. Jost, "Narration(s): En deçà et au-delà." This translation comes from Stam, Burgoyne, and Flitterman-Lewis, *New Vocabularies in Film Semiotics*, 93.
16. Mitry, *Esthétique et psychologie du cinéma*, 300.
17. Heath, *Questions of Cinema*, 46.
18. See Rothman's argument in "Against 'The System of Suture.'"
19. See Branigan, "The Point-of-View Shot," repr. in Nichols, *Movies and Methods*, 2:672–90.
20. Heath, *Questions of Cinema*, 48.
21. Mitry, *La sémiologie en question*, 108.
22. See Browne, "The Spectator-in-the-Text."
23. For a detailed catalogue of incremental differences see Mitry, *Esthétique et psychologie du cinéma*, 300
24. Maillot, "Un face-à-face transatlantique: Resnais/Welles," 45.
25. Monaco, *Alain Resnais*, 13.
26. As Monaco writes: "it is the quintessential distillation of his obsession with time, memory, and the imagination" (*Alain Resnais*, 121).
27. Benayoun, *Alain Resnais*, 131.
28. Labarthe and Rivette, "Entretien avec Resnais and Robbe-Grillet," 6.

29. Deleuze makes a brief comparison between Resnais and Buñuel, concerning the narration and use of multiple actresses for one part in *Cet objet obscur du désir* (1977). It seems even more fitting, however, to compare Resnais to the Buñuel of *Tristana* (1970), which concludes with an implosion of past and present images.
30. "Table ronde sur *Hiroshima, mon amour*," 43.
31. Baudry, "Ideological Effects of the Basic Cinematographic Apparatus," 345.
32. Fleischer, *L'art d'Alain Resnais*, 33.
33. Ibid., 34.
34. Armes, *The Cinema of Alain Resnais*, 152.
35. Oms, *Alain Resnais*, 38.
36. Prédal, *Alain Resnais*, 66. While this seems to accord with Wilson's analysis of the film as one of rape fantasy, it poses an interesting take on the differentiation between subject and object provided by this formal device.
37. In their typically omniscient manner Jean-Louis Leutrat and Suzanne Liandrat-Guigues catalogue Resnais's stance on this difference over a series of quotes from interviews and films over a span of three decades. See Leutrat and Liandrat-Guigues, *Alain Resnais*, 265–66.
38. Deleuze uses this very phenomenon as a basis for his notion of the subjectivity of time in the time-image. As David Rodowick notes, referring to the underlying theme of uncertainty in Resnais: where the true is replaced by the conditional, time becomes a semiotic force. See Rodowick, *Gilles Deleuze's Time Machine*, 104.
39. Monaco, *Alain Resnais*, 140.
40. One need only look at a historiography of criticism on Resnais's work to discern the focus on memory in particular. An insightful exception to this is Benayoun's *Alain Resnais*.
41. Wilson, *Alain Resnais*, 15.
42. Bordwell, *Narration in the Fiction Film*, 220.
43. Ishaghpour, *D'une image à l'autre*, 182.
44. Deleuze, *Cinéma 2: L'image-temps*, 153
45. Schaeffer, *Pourquoi la fiction?* 104.
46. Caen, "Les temps changent," 75.
47. For a systematic summary of the film's reception see Marcel Mattey, "*La guerre est finie*."
48. Bogue, *Deleuze on Cinema*, 144–45.
49. Bordwell, *Narration in the Fiction Film*, 213.
50. Ibid., 222.
51. Wilson, *Alain Resnais*, 111.
52. Prédal, *Alain Resnais*, 160.
53. Caen, "Les temps changent," 75.

54. Benayoun, *Alain Resnais*, 180.

55. Although I will not expound on the difference between the two, it is useful at least to acknowledge; an illustration of this difference is offered in the dialogue presented between Neill's "Empathy and (Film) Fiction" and Berys Gaut's "Identification and Emotion in Narrative Film."

56. Armes, *The Cinema of Alain Resnais*, 145.

57. Prédal, *Alain Resnais*, 160.

58. Bordwell, *Narration in the Fiction Film*, 213.

59. Wilson, *Alain Resnais*, 112.

60. Jakobson, *Main Trends in the Science of Language*, 33.

61. Bordwell, *Narration in the Fiction Film*, 226.

62. Ibid., 219.

63. Ibid., 226.

64. Caen, "Les temps changent," 75.

65. Bordwell, *Narration in the Fiction Film*, 225.

66. Armes, *The Cinema of Alain Resnais*, 146.

67. Bordwell, *Narration in the Fiction Film*, 218–19.

68. Ibid., 225.

69. Deleuze, *Cinéma 2: L'image-temps*, 159.

70. Bordwell, *Narration in the Fiction Film*, 225.

71. Ibid., 220.

72. Quoted in Benayoun et al., "Ne pas faire un film sur l'Espagne (Entretien avec Alain Resnais)," 172.

5. JEAN-LUC GODARD AND THE CODE OF OBJECTIVITY

1. Morin, *Le cinéma ou l'homme imaginaire*, 14. Morin is quoting Demney's *Les origines du cinématographe* (1909) and no doubt making reference to the numerous texts written during the natal years of cinema on the scientific purpose of the apparatus, including, perhaps foremost, Etienne-Jules Marey's *La Chronophotographie*.

2. Kracauer, *Theory of Film*, 4.

3. See Bazin, "Le mythe du cinéma total," in *Qu'est-ce que le cinéma*, 19–24.

4. See Comolli, "Technique et idéologie."

5. Deleuze, *Cinéma 2: L'image-temps*, 18.

6. Aristanco, "Langage et idéologie dans quelques films de Godard," 5.

7. Morin, *Le cinéma ou l'homme imaginaire*, 134–39.

8. Cavell, *The World Viewed*, 21.

9. Bazin, "Ontologie de l'image photographique," in *Qu'est-ce que le cinéma*, 9–17, 13. This is, in fact, the crux of Bazin's quintessential essay on the evolution of visual arts and the characteristics of realism. Bazin, as Godard would

later do, goes so far as to posit the somewhat specious claim that the fact that the camera lens is called an *objectif* in French actually bestows on the machine some higher level of truth-recording. This logic is, philologically, clearly backwards.

10. Here I must make a certain distinction between cinematic realism and the code of objectivity. Realism, in the Barthesian model, is the compilation of a network of codes in order to offer a narrative according to a structure with which the reader or spectator would be familiarized through sociocultural conventions. This aspect of narration and content is the central focus of Kracauer's theory of camera objectivity and could be argued to be equally central to Bazin's arguments for neorealism. Nonetheless, as we saw in chapter 1, these same arguments make recourse to the formal connotation of this realism, which make up what I call the code of objectivity. The code of objectivity is, more specifically, a network of formal compositions placing the spectator in a position meant to mimic the detached perception attributed to mechanical empiricism. Realism is an aesthetic school and mode of representation; the code of objectivity is a particular dynamic of semiotic generation. Nonetheless, I agree with Noël Carroll's argument against the logical link between the two. Placing himself against Kracauer, Bazin, and Cavell, Carroll challenges the idea that the objective nature of the apparatus is a logical argument for the realism of the representation (see Carroll, *Theorizing the Moving Image*, 42–43).

11. Andrew, *The Major Film Theories*, 134.

12. Baudry, "Ideological Effects of the Basic Cinematographic Apparatus," 345.

13. Panofsky, *Perspective as Symbolic Form*, 27.

14. Ibid., 31.

15. Arnheim, *Film as Art*, 2–3.

16. Baudry, "Ideological Effects of the Basic Cinematographic Apparatus," 345–48. This can be differentiated from the aspects of the code of subjectivity by placing the spectator in the position of the camera-subject, as opposed to the character-subject.

17. Morin, *Le cinéma ou l'homme imaginaire*, 23.

18. In "Technological and Aesthetic Influences of Deep-Focus Cinematography in the United States," Patrick Ogle performs a historical analysis of deep focus. As he notes, deep focus came about primarily as a result of technological developments in film stock; in a strange twist of the realist notion of photographic ontology, one of Renoir's assistants during this period was Henri Cartier-Bresson, who gained international notoriety through photographs using a similar depth of field (61).

19. Bazin, *Qu'est-ce que le cinéma*, 27.

20. Such stylistic characteristics are fully visible today in the social realism of directors such as Lars von Trier, the Dardenne brothers, and Lukas Moodysson.

21. Cavell, *The World Viewed*, 129.

22. This argument has probably been best catalogued, on a uniform sociocultural level, by the works of Edward Said. In the realm of film studies see the works of Ella Shohat and Robert Stam, especially *Unthinking Eurocentrism*.

23. MacCabe and Mulvey, *Godard*, 40.

24. Godard, "Entretien," 229.

25. Dixon, *The Films of Jean-Luc Godard*, 52.

26. Wollen, "Godard and Counter-Cinema," 503.

27. Mitry, *Esthétique et psychologie du cinéma*, 270.

28. See Henderson, "Toward a Non-Bourgeois Camera Style."

29. Ibid., 2.

30. Ibid., 11.

31. Comolli, "A rebours?" 86.

32. Bordwell, *Narration in the Fiction Film*, 328.

33. Heath, *Questions of Cinema*, 38.

34. Bordwell, *Narration in the Fiction Film*, 332.

35. Dixon, *The Films of Jean-Luc Godard*, 30.

36. Wollen, "Godard and Counter-Cinema," 503.

37. Cavell, *The World Viewed*, 129

38. These professors of Université Paris III were dubbed by Jean Mitry as "the disciples of Christian Metz" (*La sémiologie en question*, 187), a reference that perhaps sheds light on the focus on denotation and psychoanalysis in their respective studies of this film and of Godard in general.

39. Godard, "Scenario du Mépris," 242–43.

40. Dixon, *The Films of Jean-Luc Godard*, 46.

41. In voice-over, *Pierrot Le fou* (1965).

42. Dixon, *The Films of Jean-Luc Godard*, 47.

43. It is, of course, fascinating that Godard not only chooses here to quote Bazin (godfather of the *Cahiers* group and champion of cinematic realism) but, furthermore, does not quote him accurately. This reference has been the object of much analysis that I do not find useful or necessary to catalogue here.

44. Cerisuelo, *Le mépris*, 10.

45. Silverman and Farocki, *Speaking About Godard*, 34.

46. Cerisuelo, *Le mépris*, 31.

47. In *Pierrot le fou*, for example, Marianne lists parts of Ferdinand's body and claims to touch them; he responds: "Me, too, Marianne." A similar example would be the recounting, without the support of images, of an orgiastic tale of sodomy in *Week-end*.

48. Dixon, *The Films of Jean-Luc Godard*, 45.

49. See Mulvey's seminal work, "Visual Pleasure and Narrative Cinema." This is of course a very complicated historical and economic proposition and has been convincingly argued both pro and con by feminist theorists.

50. Dermot Moran, summarizing the theories of Levinas, *Introduction to Phenomenology*, 341. Levinas's theory of the face as phenomenon would be a curious complement to feminist theory in general. Many critics of this film have defined it as a film about the gaze, an argument with which I agree; however, this gaze must be specified as a cultural vessel and also as a diegetic problem of organizing representation, as I intend here to do.

51. Baudrillard, *Le système des objets*, 141.

52. Bersani and Dutoit, *Forming Couples: Godard's "Contempt,"* 10.

53. Ceriscuelo, *Le mépris*, 61.

54. See Deleuze, *Cinéma 2: L'image-temps*, 18.

55. Arnheim, *Film as Art*, 15.

56. Ibid., 58–59. Arnheim strikingly makes reference in this argument to Dreyer's *La passion de Jeanne d'arc*, a filmmaker and particular text that I have found to be extremely important in Godard's formation as a critic and director.

57. Ayme, "'Répète un peu pour voir,'" 81.

58. Dixon, *The Films of Jean-Luc Godard*, 45.

59. Silverman and Farocki, *Speaking About Godard*, 45.

60. Bordwell, *Narration in the Fiction Film*, 322–23.

61. Sellier, "Représentations des rapports de sexe dans les premiers films de Jean-Luc Godard," 286.

62. Metz, *Langage et cinéma*, 202.

CONCLUSION: WHERE FILM AND PHILOSOPHY MAY LEAD

1. See Vaughan, "The Paradox of Film."

2. Baudrillard, *Seduction*, 1.

3. Ibid., 81.

4. The Blackwell Philosophy and Popular Culture Series (recent films addressed include *Inception*, *The Girl with the Dragon Tattoo*, and *Green Lantern*) specifically encourages its contributors not to maintain an academic formality in order to make its philosophical content as accessible as possible. Open Court also has an entire series of such books, edited by William Irwin, including *Seinfeld and Philosophy* and *The Simpsons and Philosophy*.

5. Notable examples include Claude Chabrol and Eric Rohmer's *Hitchcock* and François Truffaut's interview-format book, *Hitchcock*.

6. See, in particular, Modleski's reading of *Rear Window* in *The Women Who Knew Too Much*.

7. Deleuze, *Cinéma 1: L'image-mouvement*, 283.

8. See, for example, Temenuga Trifonova, *The Image in French Philosophy*, 265–89.

9. This notion of modernity as microcosmically embodied by the new cinema spectator, originally developed in Walter Benjamin's "The Work of Art in the Age of Reproduction" and the work of Siegfried Kracauer, is well summarized and developed further in Thomas Elsaesser, "Cinema—The Irresponsible Signifier or 'The Gamble with History': Film Theory or Cinema Theory."

10. Benjamin, "Some Motifs in Baudelaire," cited in Gunning, "An Aesthetic of Astonishment," 742.

11. See Rancière's extensive study of documentary practices in *La fable cinématographique*, 201–37.

BIBLIOGRAPHY

Abel, Richard. *The Ciné Goes to Town*. Berkeley: University of California Press, 1998.

——. *The Red Rooster Scare: Making Cinema American*. Berkeley: University of California Press, 1999.

Abramson, Ronald. "Structure and Meaning in the Cinema." In Nichols, *Movies and Methods*, 1:558–68.

Alter, Jean V. "Alain Robbe-Grillet and the 'Cinematographic Style.'" *Modern Language Journal* 48, no. 6 (Oct. 1964): 363–66.

Althusser, Louis. *For Marx*. Translated by Ben Brewster. London: Penguin, 1969.

Altman, Charles F. "Psychoanalysis and Cinema: The Imaginary Discourse." *Quarterly Review of Film Studies* 2, no. 3 (August 1977): 257–72. Reprinted in Nichols, *Movies and Methods*, 2:517–30.

Andrew, Dudley. *Concepts in Film Theory*. Oxford: Oxford University Press, 1984.

——. *The Major Film Theories*. Oxford: Oxford University Press, 1976.

——. "The Neglected Tradition of Phenomenology in Film Theory." In Nichols, *Movies and Methods*, 2:625–31.

Aristanco, Guido. "Langage et idéologie dans quelques films de Godard." *Études cinématographiques: Jean-Luc Godard: au-delà du récit*, no. 57/61 (1967): 5–16.

Armes, Roy. *The Cinema of Alain Resnais*. London: Zwemmer, 1968.

Arnheim, Rudolf. *Film as Art*. Berkeley: University of California Press, 1957.

———. "Gestalt and Art." *Journal of Aesthetics and Art Criticism* 2 (1943): 71–75.

Ayfre, Amédée. "Neo-Realism and Phenomenology." In *Cahiers du cinéma: The 1950s*, edited by Jim Hillier, 182–91. London: BFI, 1985.

Ayme, Sylvie. "'Répète un peu pour voir': Jean-Luc Godard et la catégorie de la répétition." *Études cinématographiques: Jean-Luc Godard: au-delà du récit*, no. 57/61 (1967): 63–134.

Bakhtin, Mikhail. *The Dialogic Imagination*. Edited by Michael Holquist. Translated by Caryl Emerson and Michael Holquist. Austin: University of Texas Press, 1981.

———. *Problems of Dostoevsky's Poetics*. Edited and translated by Caryl Emerson. Manchester: Manchester University, 1984.

Balázs, Béla. *Theory of the Film: Character and Growth of a New Art*. Translated by Edith Bone. London: Dobson, 1952.

Barthes, Roland. *Le système de la mode*. Paris: Seuil, 1967.

———. *Œuvres complètes*. Vols. 1 and 2. Paris: Seuil, 2002.

———. *The Responsibility of Forms*. Translated by Richard Howard. Oxford: Farrar, Straus and Giroux, 1986.

———. "Sémiologie et cinéma." In *Œuvres complètes*, 2:622–24.

———. *S/Z*. Translated by Richard Miller. New York: Hill and Wang, 1974.

———. "'Towards a Semiotics of Cinema': Barthes in Interview with Michel Delahaye, Jacques Rivette." In *Cahiers du cinéma: The 1960s*, edited by Jim Hillier, 275–85. Cambridge, MA: Harvard University Press, 1986.

Baudrillard, Jean. *Le système des objets*. Paris: Gallimard, 1968.

———. *Seduction*. Translated by Brian Singer. New York: St. Martin's, 1990.

———. *Simulacres et simulation*. Paris: Galilée, 1985.

Baudry, Jean-Louis. "Ideological Effects of the Basic Cinematographic Apparatus." In Braudy and Cohen, *Film Theory and Criticism*, 343–54.

Bazin. André. *Qu'est-ce que le cinéma?* Paris: CERF, 2002.

Beh, Siew Hwa. "*Vivre sa vie*." In Nichols, *Movies and Methods*, 1:180–85.

Bellour, Raymond. *L'analyse du film*. Paris: Callman-Lévy, 1995.

Belton, John. *American Cinema, American Culture*. 3rd ed. New York: McGraw-Hill, 1994.

Benayoun, Robert. *Alain Resnais: Arpenteur de l'imaginaire*. Paris: Stock, 1980.

———. "Resnais le permanent." In *"Positif" revue de cinéma: Alain Resnais*, 144–52. Paris: Gallimard, 2002.

Benayoun, Robert, et al. "Ne pas faire un film sur l'Espagne (Entretien avec Alain Resnais)." In Benayoun, *Alain Resnais*, 170–82.

Benveniste, Emile. "Les relations de temps dans le verbe français." In *Problèmes de linguistique générale*, 237–50. Paris: Gallimard, 1966.

Bersani, Leo, and Ulysse Dutoit. *Forming Couples: Godard's "Contempt."* Oxford: Legenda, 2003.

Beugnet, Martine. *Cinema of Sensation: French Film and the Art of Transgression*. Edinburgh: Edinburgh University Press, 2007.

Bogue, Ronald. *Deleuze on Cinema*. New York: Routledge, 2003.

Bordwell, David. "The Art Cinema as a Mode of Film Practice." In Braudy and Cohen, *Film Theory and Criticism*, 716–24.

———. "*Citizen Kane*." In Nichols, *Movies and Methods*, 1:273–90.

———. *Making Meaning*. Cambridge, MA: Harvard University Press, 1989.

———. *Narration in the Fiction Film*. Madison: University of Wisconsin Press, 1985.

Bordwell, David, and Noël Carroll, eds. *Post-Theory*. Madison: University of Wisconsin Press, 1996.

Bordwell, David, and Kristin Thompson. *Film Art: An Introduction*. 7th ed. New York: McGraw-Hill, 2004.

Branigan, Edward. "The Point-of-View Shot." In Nichols, *Movies and Methods*, 2:672–90.

Braudy, Leo, and Marshall Cohen, eds. *Film Theory and Criticism*. 5th ed. New York: Oxford University Press, 1999.

Bron, Jean-Albert. "Un cinéma au service de l'énergie narrative du spectateur." *Contre Bande: Alain Resnais*, no. 9 (2003): 51–75.

Browne, Nick. "The Spectator-in-the-Text: The Rhetoric of *Stagecoach*." *Film Quarterly* 34, no. 2 (winter 1975–76): 26–38.

Brunius, Jacques. "Every Year at Marienbad; or, The Discipline of Uncertainty." *Sight and Sound* 31, no. 3 (summer 1962): 122–27.

Bukatman, Scott. *Terminal Identity*. Durham, NC: Duke University Press, 1993.

Burch, Noël. "De *Mabuse* à *M*: Le travail de Fritz Lang." In "Cinéma théorie lectures," edited by D. Noguez, special issue, *Revue d'Esthétique* (1973): 227–48.

———. "Qu'est-ce que la Nouvelle Vague?" *Film Quarterly* 13, no. 2 (winter 1959): 16–30.

———. *Theory of Film Practice*. Translated by Helen R. Lane. Princeton, NJ: Princeton University Press, 1981.

Burch, Noël, and Jorge Dana. "Propositions." *Afterimage*, no. 5 (spring 1974): 45.

Caen, Michel. "Les temps changent." *Cahiers du cinéma*, no. 179 (June 1966): 75–76.

Callev, Haim. *The Stream of Consciousness in the Films of Alain Resnais*. New York: McGruer, 1997.

Carroll, Noël. "Jean-Louis Baudry and 'The Apparatus.'" In Braudy and Cohen, *Film Theory and Criticism*, 778–94.

———. *Mystifying Movies*. New York: Columbia University Press, 1988.

———. *The Philosophy of Motion Pictures*. Malden, MA: Blackwell, 2008.

———. *Theorizing the Moving Image*. Cambridge, UK: Cambridge University Press, 1996.

Carroll, Noël, and Jinhee Choi, eds. *Philosophy of Film and Motion Pictures*. Malden, MA: Blackwell, 2006.

Cavell, Stanley. *Pursuits of Happiness*. Cambridge, MA: Harvard University Press, 1981.

———. *The World Viewed*. Cambridge, MA: Harvard University Press, 1979.

Cerisuelo, Marc. *Jean-Luc Godard*. Paris: Editions des Quatre-Vents, 1989.

———. *Le mépris*. Chatou: Les Editions de la Transparence, 2006.

Chabrol, Claude, and Eric Rohmer. *Hitchcock*. Paris: Éditions universitaires, 1957.

Chion, Michel. *The Voice in Cinema*. Edited and translated by Claudia Gorbman. New York: Columbia University Press, 1985.

Cohen-Séat, Gilbert. *Essai sur les principes d'une philosophie du cinéma*. Paris: Presses universitaires de France, 1946.

Comolli, Jean-Louis. "A rebours?" *Cahiers du cinéma*, no. 168 (July 1965): 86–87.

———. "Technique et idéologie." *Cahiers du cinéma*, no. 229 (May-June 1971): 4–21.

Comolli, Jean-Louis, and Jean Narboni. "Cinéma/Idéologie/Criticism." *Cahiers du cinéma*, no. 216 (Oct. 1969): 11–15.

Dayan, Daniel. "The Tutor-Code of Classical Cinema." *Film Quarterly* 28, no.1 (fall 1974): 22–31.

De Lauretis, Teresa, and Stephen Heath, eds. *The Cinematic Apparatus*. London: Macmillan, 1980.

Delavaud, Gilles, Jean-Pierre Esquenazi, and Marie-Françoise Grange, eds. *Godard et le métier d'artiste*. Paris: L'Harmattan, 2001.

Deleuze, Gilles. *Cinéma 1: L'image-mouvement*. Paris: Minuit, 1983. Translated by Hugh Tomlinson and Barbara Habberjam as *Cinema 1: The Movement-Image* (Minneapolis: University of Minnesota Press, 1986).

———. *Cinéma 2: L'image-temps*. Paris: Minuit, 1985. Translated by Hugh Tomlinson and Robert Galeta as *Cinema 2: The Time-Image* (Minneapolis: University of Minnesota Press, 1989).

———. *Différence et répétition*. Paris: Presses universitaires de France, 2003.

———. *Negotiations*. Translated by Martin Joughin. New York: Columbia University Press, 1995.

Deleuze, Gilles, and Félix Guattari. *Anti-Oedipus*. Translated by Robert Hurley, Mark Seem, and Helen R. Lane. London: Continuum, 2004.

Del Rio, Elena. "Alchemies of Thought in Godard's Cinema: Deleuze and Merleau-Ponty." *SubStance* 34, no. 3 (2005): 62–78.

Demney, Georges. *Les origines du cinématographe*. Paris: H. Paulin, 1909.

Descombes, Vincent. *Modern French Philosophy*. Translated by L. Scott-Fox and J. M. Harding. Cambridge, UK: Cambridge University Press, 1981.

Dixon, Wheeler Winston. *The Films of Jean-Luc Godard*. Albany: State University of New York Press, 1997.

Doane, Mary Ann. "Ideology and the Practice of Sound Editing and Mixing." In De Lauretis and Heath, *The Cinematic Apparatus*, 47–56.

———. "The Voice in the Cinema: The Articulation of Body and Space." *Yale French Studies*, no. 60 (1980): 33–50.

Dyer, Richard. *Stars*. London: BFI, 1981.

Eco, Umberto. "Articulations of the Cinematic Code." In Nichols, *Movies and Methods*, 1:590–607.

Eisenstein, Sergei. *Film Form*. Edited and translated by Jay Leyda. New York: Harcourt, 1949.

———. *The Film Sense*. Edited and translated by Jay Leyda. London: Faber and Faber, 1943.

———. *Nonindifferent Nature*. Translated by Herbert Marshall. Cambridge, UK: Cambridge University Press, 1987.

Eisler, Hanns. *Composing for the Films*. London: Dennis Dobson, 1947.

Elsaesser, Thomas. "Cinema—The Irresponsible Signifier or 'The Gamble with History': Film Theory or Cinema Theory." *New German Critique* 40 (winter 1987): 65–89.

Esquenazi, Jean-Pierre. *Godard et la société française des années 1960*. Paris: Armand Colin, 2004.

Flaxman, Gregory, ed. *The Brain Is the Screen*. Minneapolis: University of Minnesota Press, 2000.

———. "Cinema Year Zero." In Flaxman, *The Brain Is the Screen*, 87–108.

———. "Introduction." In Flaxman, *The Brain Is the Screen*, 1–59.

Fleischer, Alain. *L'art d'Alain Resnais*. Paris: Centre Georges Pompidou, 1998.

Foucault, Michel. *Folie et déraison*. Paris: Plon, 1961.

———. *Naissance de la clinique*. Paris: Presses universitaires de France, 1963.

Frampton, Daniel. *Filmosophy*. London: Wallflower, 2006.

Gaut, Berys. "Identification and Emotion in Narrative Film." In Carroll and Choi, *Philosophy of Film and Motion Pictures*, 260–70.

———. *A Philosophy of Cinematic Art*. Cambridge, UK: Cambridge University Press, 2010.

Gledhill, Christine. "Recent Developments in Feminist Criticism." In Braudy and Cohen, *Film Theory and Criticism*, 251–72.

Godard, Jean-Luc. "Entretien." In *Jean-Luc Godard par Jean-Luc Godard*, 1:215–36.

———. *Jean-Luc Godard par Jean-Luc Godard*. Edited by Alain Bergala. 2 vols. Paris: Cahiers du cinéma, 1998.

———. "Ma démarche en quatre mouvements." In *Jean-Luc Godard par Jean-Luc Godard*, 1:296–98.

———. "On doit tout mettre dans un film." In *Jean-Luc Godard par Jean-Luc Godard*, 1:295–96.

———. "Scenario du Mépris." In *Jean-Luc Godard par Jean-Luc Godard*, 1:241–48.

Gunning, Tom. "An Aesthetic of Astonishment: Early Film and the (In)credulous Spectator." *Art and Text* 34 (spring 1989): 31–45.

Harman, Gilbert. "Semiotics and the Cinema: Metz and Wollen." In Braudy and Cohen, *Film Theory and Criticism*, 78–86.

Heath, Stephen. *Questions of Cinema*. Bloomington: Indiana University Press, 1981.

Heath, Stephen, and Patricia Mellencamp, eds. *Cinema and Language*. Los Angeles: American Film Institute, 1983.

Hegel, G. W. F. *Aesthetics: Lectures on Fine Art*. Vol. 1. Translated by T. M. Knox. Oxford: Clarendon Press, 1975.

Henderson, Brian. "The Long Take." In Nichols, *Movies and Methods*, 1:314–24.

———. "Toward a Non-Bourgeois Camera Style." *Film Quarterly* 24, no. 2 (winter 1970–71): 2–14.

———. "Two Types of Film Theory." *Film Quarterly* 24, no. 3 (spring 1971): 33–42.

Ishaghpour, Youssef. *D'une image à l'autre*. Paris: Denoël/Gonthier, 1982.

———. "Jean-Luc Godard: Cinéaste de la vie moderne—le poétique dans l'historique." In Delavaud, Esquenazi, and Grange, *Godard et le métier d'artiste*, 155–68.

Jakobson, Roman. *Language in Literature*. Cambridge, MA: Harvard University Press, 1987.

———. *Main Trends in the Science of Language*. London: Allen and Unwin, 1973.

Jameson, Fredric. *The Geopolitical Aesthetic*. Bloomington: Indiana University Press, 1992.

———. *Signatures of the Visible*. New York: Routledge, 1990.

Jay, Martin. *Downcast Eyes: The Denigration of Vision in Twentieth-Century French Thought*. Berkeley: University of California Press, 1994.

Jost, François. "Narration(s): En deçà et au-delà." *Communications* 38 (1983): 192–212.

Kennedy, Barbara. *Deleuze and Cinema: The Aesthetics of Sensation*. Edinburgh: Edinburgh University Press, 2000.

Kracauer, Siegfried. *Theory of Film*. New York: Oxford University Press, 1960.

Labarthe, André S., and Jacques Rivette. "Entretien avec Resnais and Robbe-Grillet." *Cahiers du cinéma*, no. 123 (Sept. 1961): 1–21.

Lanigan, Richard L. *Speaking and Semiology: Maurice Merleau-Ponty's Phenomenological Theory of Existential Communication*. The Hague: Mouton, 1972.

Lawlor, Leonard. *Thinking Through French Philosophy*. Bloomington: Indiana University Press, 2003.

Lawrence, D. H. *The Rainbow*. London: Penguin, 1995.

Léger, Fernand. "A Critical Essay on the Plastic Quality of Abel Gance's *The Wheel*." In *Functions of Painting*, translated by Alexandra Anderson, 20–23. London: Thames and Hudson, 1973.

Lesage, Julia. "*S/Z* and *Rules of the Game*." *Jump Cut*, nos. 12–13 (1976): 45–51.

Leutrat, Jean-Louis. *Hiroshima, mon amour*. Paris: Nathan, 1994.

———. *Last Year at Marienbad*. Translated by Paul Hammond. London: BFI, 2000.

Leutrat, Jean-Louis, and Suzanne Liandrat-Guigues. *Alain Resnais: Liaisons secrètes, accords vagabonds*. Paris: Cahiers du cinéma, 2006.

Luchting, Wolfgang A. "*Hiroshima, mon amour*, Time, and Proust." *Journal of Aesthetics and Art Criticism* 21, no. 3 (spring 1963): 299–313.

MacCabe, Colin, and Laura Mulvey. *Godard: Images, Sounds, Politics*. London: Macmillan, 1980.

MacDougall, David. "Prospects of Ethnographic Film." In Nichols, *Movies and Methods*, 1:135–49.

Maillot, Pierre. "Un face-à-face transatlantique: Resnais/Welles." *Contre Bande: Alain Resnais*, no. 9 (2003): 31–49.

Marcorelles, Louis. "Jean-Luc Godard's Half-Truths." Translated by Ernest Callenbach. *Film Quarterly* 17, no. 3 (spring 1964): 4–7.

Marey, Etienne-Jules. *La Chronophotographie*. Paris: Gauthier-Villars, 1899.

Marie, Michel. *The French New Wave*. Translated by Richard Neupert. London: Blackwell, 2003.

———. *Le mépris*. France: Cle International, 1998.

Marks, Laura. *The Skin of the Film*. Durham, NC: Duke University Press, 2000.

Marrati, Paola. *Gilles Deleuze: Cinéma et philosophie*. Paris: Presses universitaires de France, 2003.

Martin-Jones, David. *Deleuze and World Cinemas*. London: Continuum, 2011.

Mattey, Marcel. "*La guerre est finie*." *Image et son*, no. 244 (Nov. 1970): 49–72.

Mayne, Judith. "*S/Z* and Film Criticism." *Jump Cut*, no. 12/13 (1976): 41–44.

Merleau-Ponty, Maurice. *L'éloge de la philosophie*. Paris: Gallimard, 1953.

———. *Les aventures de la dialectique*. Paris: Gallimard, 1955.

———. *Le visible et l'invisible*. Paris: Gallimard, 1964.

———. *Phénoménologie de la perception*. Paris: Gallimard, 1945.

———. *Sens et non-sens*. Paris: Gallimard, 1996.

———. *Signes*. Paris: Gallimard, 1960.

Metz, Christian. *Essais sur la signification au cinéma*. 2 vols. Paris: Klincksieck, 2003.

———. *Langage et cinéma*. Paris: Libraire Larousse, 1971.

———. *Le signifiant imaginaire*. 1974. Paris: Christian Bourgois Editeur, 2002.

Miller, Jacques-Alain. "La suture: Eléments de la logique du signifiant." *Cahiers pour l'analyse*, no. 1 (1966): 39–51.

Mitchell, W. J. T. *What Do Pictures Want?* Chicago: University of Chicago Press, 2005.

Mitry, Jean. *Esthétique et psychologie du cinéma*. Paris: CERF, 2001.

———. *La sémiologie en question: Langage et cinéma*. Paris: CERF, 1987.

Modleski, Tania. *The Women Who Knew Too Much*. New York: Methuen, 1988.

Monaco, James. *Alain Resnais: The Role of the Imagination*. New York: Oxford University Press, 1978.

Moran, Dermot. *Introduction to Phenomenology*. Oxon: Routledge, 2000.

Morin, Edgar. *Le cinéma ou l'homme imaginaire*. Paris: Minuit, 1956.

Mulhall, Stephen. *On Film*. London: Routledge, 2002.

Mullarkey, John. Refractions of Reality: Philosophy and the Moving Image. London: Palgrave Macmillan, 2009.

Mulvey, Laura. "Visual Pleasure and Narrative Cinema." *Screen*, no. 3 (autumn 1975): 6–18.

Münsterberg, Hugo. *Hugo Münsterberg on Film: "The Photoplay: A Psychological Study" and Other Writings*. Edited by Allan Langdale. New York: Routledge, 2002.

Neill, Alex. "Empathy and (Film) Fiction." In Carroll and Choi, *Philosophy of Film and Motion Pictures*, 247–59.

Neupert, Richard. *A History of the French New Wave Cinema*. Madison: University of Wisconsin Press, 2002.

Nichols, Bill, ed. *Movies and Methods*. 2 vols. Berkeley: University of California Press, 1976, 1985.

———. "Style, Grammar, and the Movies." *Film Quarterly* 28, no. 3 (spring 1975): 33–49.

Nowell-Smith, Geoffrey. "A Note on Story/Discourse." In Nichols, *Movies and Methods*, 2:551–57.

Ogle, Patrick. "Technological and Aesthetic Influences of Deep-Focus Cinematography in the United States." In Nichols, *Movies and Methods*, 2:58–83.

Oms, Marcel. *Alain Resnais*. Paris: Rivages, 1988.

Oudart, Jean-Pierre. "La suture." *Cahiers du cinéma*, nos. 211 (1969): 36–39; and 212 (1969): 50–55.

Oxenhandler, Neal. "*Marienbad* Revisited." *Film Quarterly* 17, no. 1 (autumn 1963): 30–35.

Panofsky, Erwin. *Perspective as Symbolic Form*. Translated by Christopher S. Wood. New York: Zone, 1997.

———. *Three Essays on Style*. Edited by Irving Lavin. Cambridge, MA: MIT Press, 1997.

Pasolini, Pier Paolo. "The Cinema of Poetry." In Nichols, *Movies and Methods*, 1:542–58.

Penley, Constance. "*Film Language*, by Christian Metz: Semiology's Radical Possibilities." *Jump Cut*, no. 5 (1975): 18–19.

Perkins, V. F. "*Vivre sa vie*." In *The Films of Jean-Luc Godard*, edited by Ian Cameron. New York: Praeger, 1969.

Pilard, Philippe. "Entretien avec Jean-Luc Godard." *Image et son—le revue de cinéma: Jean-Luc Godard*, no. 211 (Dec. 1967): 51–58.

Pisters, Patricia. *The Matrix of Visual Culture*. Stanford: Stanford University Press, 2003.

Prédal, René. *Alain Resnais: Études cinématographiques.* Paris: Minard, 1968.

Rancière, Jacques. *Aesthetics and Its Discontents.* Translated by Steven Corcoran. Cambridge, UK: Polity, 2009.

———. *La fable cinématographique.* Paris: Seuil, 2001.

———. *The Future of the Image.* Translated by Gregory Elliott. London: Verso, 2007.

Redner, Gregg. *Deleuze and Film Music.* Bristol: Intellect, 2011.

Robbe-Grillet, Alain. *L'année dernière à Marienbad.* Paris: Minuit, 1961.

———. *Pour un nouveau roman.* Paris: Gallimard, 1963.

Rodowick, D. N. *The Crisis of Political Modernism.* Urbana: University of Illinois Press, 1988.

———. "Dr. Strange Media." *PMLA* 116, no. 5 (Oct. 2001): 1396–1404.

———. *Gilles Deleuze's Time Machine.* Durham, NC: Duke University Press, 1997.

———. *Reading the Figural.* Durham, NC: Duke University Press, 2001.

Ropars-Wuilleumier, Marie-Claire. "Form and Substance, or the Avatars of the Narrative." In *Focus on Godard,* edited by Royal S. Brown, 17–34. Englewood Cliffs, NJ: Prentice-Hall, 1972.

———. "How History Begets Meaning: Alain Resnais's *Hiroshima, mon amour.*" In *French Film: Texts and Contexts,* edited by Susan Hayward and Ginette Vincendeau, 173–85. New York: Routledge, 1990.

Rothman, William. "Against 'The System of Suture.'" *Film Quarterly* 29, no. 1 (autumn 1975): 45–50.

Sandro, Paul. "Signification in the Cinema." In Nichols, *Movies and Methods,* 2:391–406.

Schaeffer, Jean-Marie. *Pourquoi la fiction?* Paris: Seuil, 1999.

Schefer, Jean-Louis. *Du monde et du mouvement des images.* Paris: Cahiers du cinéma, 1997.

———. *L'homme ordinaire du cinéma.* Paris: Cahiers du cinéma, 1980.

Scheinfeigel, Maxime. "Quand le son détourne l'image." *Cinergon,* no. 17/18 (2004): 75–84.

Schwab, Martin. "Escaping from the Image: Deleuze's Image-Ontology." In Flaxman, *The Brain Is the Screen,* 109–40.

Sellier, Geneviève. *Masculine Singular.* Translated by Kristin Ross. Durham, NC: Duke University Press, 2008.

———. "Représentations des rapports de sexe dans les premiers films de Jean-Luc Godard." In Delavaud, Esquenazi, and Grange, *Godard et le métier d'artiste,* 277–89.

Shaw, Spencer. *Film Consciousness: From Phenomenology to Deleuze.* Jefferson, NC: McFarland, 2008.

Shohat, Ella, and Robert Stam. *Unthinking Eurocentrism.* London: Routledge, 1994.

Silverman, Kaja. *The Subject of Semiotics.* New York: Oxford University Press, 1983.

Silverman, Kaja, and Harun Farocki. *Speaking About Godard*. New York: New York University Press, 1998.

Smith, Murray. *Engaging Characters: Fiction, Emotion, and the Cinema*. New York: Oxford University Press, 1995.

Sobchack, Vivian. *The Address of the Eye*. Princeton, NJ: Princeton University Press, 1992.

Sontag, Susan. *Against Interpretation, and Other Essays*. New York: Picador, 2001.

Stam, Robert, Robert Burgoyne, and Sandy Flitterman-Lewis. *New Vocabularies in Film Semiotics*. London: Routledge, 1992.

Stewart, Garrett. *Framed Time*. Chicago: University of Chicago Press, 2007.

"Table ronde sur *Hiroshima, mon amour*." In *La nouvelle vague*, 36–62. Paris: Cahiers du cinéma, 1999.

Trias, Jean-Philippe. "L'œil du cinéma." *Cinergon*, no. 6/7 (1998/99): 87–97.

Trifonova, Temenuga. *The Image in French Philosophy*. Amsterdam: Rodopi, 2007.

Truffaut, François. *Hitchcock*. New York: Simon and Schuster, 1967.

Vaughan, Hunter. "The Paradox of Film: An Industry of Sex, a Form of Seduction." *Film-Philosophy* 14, no. 2 (2010): 41–61.

Willemen, Paul. "Cinematic Discourse: The Problem of Inner Speech." In Heath and Mellencamp, *Cinema and Language*, 141–67.

Wilson, Emma. *Alain Resnais*. Manchester: Manchester University Press, 2006.

Wollen, Peter. "Cinema and Semiology: Some Points of Contact." In Nichols, *Movies and Methods*, 1:481–92.

———. "Godard and Counter-Cinema: *Vent D'est*." In Nichols, *Movies and Methods*, 2:500–511.

———. *Signs and Meaning in the Cinema*. London: BFI, 1974.

Žižek, Slavoj, ed. *Everything You Always Wanted to Know About Lacan (But Were Afraid to Ask Hitchcock)*. New York: Verso, 1992.

INDEX

8½ (Fellini, 1963), 184
Abel, Richard: *The Ciné Goes to Town*,
    209n27; *The Red Rooster Scare*,
    209n27
Abramson, Ronald, 91
Albertazzi, Giorgio, 128
Alter, Jean V., 126
Althusser, Louis, 63, 177, 188
Altman, Charles F., 88
Andrew, Dudley, 15, 21, 28, 36, 50, 81,
    83, 172
Antonioni, Michelangelo, 175
Aristanco, Guido, 171
Armes, Roy, 115, 119, 151, 159, 164
Arnheim, Rudolf, 7, 20, 37, 105, 174,
    192, 218n9
Aumont, Jacques, 183
Ayme, Sylvie, 192

Bakhtin, Mikhail 78, 90, 155, 162; *The
    Dialogical Imagination*, 208n23;

Problems of Dostoevsky's Poetics,
    208n23
Balázs, Béla, 169, 170
Bardot, Brigitte, 183, 184, 195–96
Barthes, Roland, 9, 13, 43, 75–7, 81, 84,
    107, 143, 174; *Mythologies*, 64, 213n77
Baudrillard, Jean, 188, 197–98
Baudry, Jean-Louis, 20, 21, 43–44, 86,
    146–47, 151, 170, 173, 174; "Ideological
    Effects of the Basic Cinematographic
    Apparatus," 210n57
Bazin, André, 44, 46, 49–52, 77, 96,
    145, 170, 171–73, 175–77, 185, 190, 191,
    215n23, 225–26n9
Beh, Siew Hwa, 54, 55, 57, 59, 63
Bellour, Raymond, 39, 141
Belton, John, 11
Benayoun, Robert, 150
Benjamin, Walter, 203, 228n9
Benveniste, Emile, 78, 214n7
Bergala, Alain, 183

FILM AND CULTURE
A series of Columbia University Press
EDITED BY JOHN BELTON

What Made Pistachio Nuts? Early Sound Comedy and the Vaudeville Aesthetic
Henry Jenkins

Showstoppers: Busby Berkeley and the Tradition of Spectacle
Martin Rubin

Projections of War: Hollywood, American Culture, and World War II
Thomas Doherty

Laughing Screaming: Modern Hollywood Horror and Comedy
William Paul

Laughing Hysterically: American Screen Comedy of the 1950s
Ed Sikov

Primitive Passions: Visuality, Sexuality, Ethnography, and Contemporary Chinese Cinema
Rey Chow

The Cinema of Max Ophuls: Magisterial Vision and the Figure of Woman
Susan M. White

Black Women as Cultural Readers
Jacqueline Bobo

Picturing Japaneseness: Monumental Style, National Identity, Japanese Film
Darrell William Davis

Attack of the Leading Ladies: Gender, Sexuality, and Spectatorship in Classic Horror Cinema
Rhona J. Berenstein

This Mad Masquerade: Stardom and Masculinity in the Jazz Age
Gaylyn Studlar

Sexual Politics and Narrative Film: Hollywood and Beyond
Robin Wood

The Sounds of Commerce: Marketing Popular Film Music
Jeff Smith

Orson Welles, Shakespeare, and Popular Culture
Michael Anderegg

Pre-Code Hollywood: Sex, Immorality, and Insurrection in American Cinema, 1930–1934
Thomas Doherty

Sound Technology and the American Cinema: Perception, Representation, Modernity
James Lastra

Melodrama and Modernity: Early Sensational Cinema and Its Contexts
Ben Singer

Wondrous Difference: Cinema, Anthropology, and Turn-of-the-Century Visual Culture
Alison Griffiths

Hearst Over Hollywood: Power, Passion, and Propaganda in the Movies
Louis Pizzitola

Masculine Interests: Homoerotics in Hollywood Film
Robert Lang

Special Effects: Still in Search of Wonder
Michele Pierson

Designing Women: Cinema, Art Deco, and the Female Form
Lucy Fischer

Cold War, Cool Medium: Television, McCarthyism, and American Culture
Thomas Doherty

Katharine Hepburn: Star as Feminist
Andrew Britton

Silent Film Sound
Rick Altman

Home in Hollywood: The Imaginary Geography of Hollywood
Elisabeth Bronfen

Hollywood and the Culture Elite: How the Movies Became American
Peter Decherney

Taiwan Film Directors: A Treasure Island
Emilie Yueh-yu Yeh and Darrell William Davis

Shocking Representation: Historical Trauma, National Cinema, and the Modern Horror Film
Adam Lowenstein

China on Screen: Cinema and Nation
Chris Berry and Mary Farquhar

The New European Cinema: Redrawing the Map
Rosalind Galt

George Gallup in Hollywood
Susan Ohmer

Electric Sounds: Technological Change and the Rise of Corporate Mass Media
Steve J. Wurtzler

The Impossible David Lynch
Todd McGowan

Sentimental Fabulations, Contemporary Chinese Films: Attachment in the Age of Global Visibility
Rey Chow